"Ciocchini and Radics are absolutely clear: in our upside-down world we must re-examine set canons – including those related to crime and law – otherwise. This is particularly important when we think about, and with, the South. The South's ample and interconnected geography has, all too often, been considered exclusively as a site of troubles. *Criminal Legalities in the Global South* shows us that it is much more than that. This cutting-edge edited collection brings together an exciting group of South-oriented contributors to demonstrate that in our twisted present there is no better place to come up with new frameworks and ideas than in that place where 'most of the world' exists and struggles, continuing its search for new futures."

Luis Eslava, *Senior Lecturer, Kent Law School, University of Kent, UK*

"*Criminal Legalities in the Global South* places at the heart of its inquiry populations who have been traditionally neglected by the social sciences, drawing attention to their experiences and contestations with criminal laws that seek not only to control their actions but also to define who they are. The volume is an important and welcome addition to the growing body of socio-legal scholarship interested in the worldviews, perceptions, and decisions of those who live under subjugated social, legal, economic, and political conditions around the world."

Lynette J. Chua, *Associate Professor of Law, National University of Singapore, Singapore*

"This book draws together an impressive group of experts to offer new perspectives into the vexing topic of crime and justice in the Global South. Emerging from the pages of this book is the crippling legacy of colonial legality, tensions between tradition and modernity, and critical issues concerning political and economic rights and inequality that resonate across contexts. This volume issues a significant call to embrace the diversity, complexity, and plurality of Global South legalities."

Melissa Crouch, *Associate Professor, Law Faculty, University of New South Wales, Australia*

"A valuable exploration of the relationships between criminal justice, local culture, and politics in a variety of locations in the Global South, which described how law is used in post colonies and what can be learned from this."

David Nelken, *Professor, School of Law, King's College London, UK*

Criminal Legalities in the Global South

This edited volume presents the work of academics from the Global South and explores, from local and regional settings, how the legal order and people's perceptions of it translates into an understanding of what constitutes "criminal" behaviors or activities. This book aims to address the gap between criminal law in theory and practice in the Global South by assembling 11 chapters from established and emerging scholars from various underrepresented regions of the world.

Drawing on research from Singapore, the Philippines, Peru, Indonesia, India, the Dominican Republic, Burma, Brazil, Bangladesh, and Argentina, this book explores a range of issues that straddle the line between social deviance and legal crimes in such societies, including extramarital affairs, gender-based violence, gambling, LGBT issues, and corruption. Issues of inclusivity versus exclusivity, modernity versus tradition, globalization of capital versus cultural revivalism are explored. The contributions critically analyze the role politics and institutions play in shaping these issues. There is an urgent need for empirical studies and new theoretical approaches that can capture the complexity of crime phenomena that occur in the Global South. This book will provide essential material to facilitate the development of new approaches more suitable to understanding the social phenomena related to crime in these societies.

This book will make an important contribution in the development of Southern criminology. It will be of interest to students and researchers of criminology and sociology engaged in studies of sentencing and punishment, theories of crime, law and practice, and postcolonialism.

Pablo Ciocchini is a lecturer at the University of Liverpool in Singapore. He teaches Critical Criminology and Socio-legal Studies. He holds an LLM from the National University of La Plata (Argentina), an MA in the sociology of law from the Oñati International Institute for the Sociology of Law (Spain), and a PhD in sociology of law from University of the Basque Country. His articles have been published in *Crime, Law and Social Change*, *Critical Criminology*, the *International Journal of Law in Context*, the *Asian Journal of Social Science*, among others. He is interested in criminal courts, judicial reforms, police accountability, state violence, and critical socio-legal theory and methodology.

George Radics is a lecturer in the Department of Sociology at the National University of Singapore. He teaches Law and Society, Selected Topics on Law and Justice, Sociology of Emotions, and Classical Sociological Theory. After receiving his PhD in sociology from the National University of Singapore (NUS), he earned a juris doctor with a concentration in Asian law from the University of Washington and worked for the Supreme Court of Guam for two years. He is a member of the New York Bar. His articles have been published in the *Columbia Human Rights Law Review*, *Santa Clara Journal of International Law*, *Asian Journal of Social Science*, and the *Philippine Sociological Review*. His work involves the judicial system, notions of justice, human rights, minorities, and comparative legal studies.

Routledge Studies in Crime and Justice in Asia and the Global South

Edited by Wing Hong Chui
City University of Hong Kong

Russell Hogg
Queensland University of Technology

John Scott
Queensland University of Technology

Crime and justice studies, as with much social science, has concentrated mainly on problems in the metropolitan centers of the Global North, while Asia and the Global South have remained largely invisible in criminological thinking. This research series aims to redress this imbalance by showcasing exciting new ways of thinking and doing crime and justice research from the global periphery.

Bringing together scholarly work from a range of disciplines, from criminology, law, and sociology to psychology, cultural geography, and comparative social sciences, this series offers grounded empirical research and fresh theoretical approaches and cover a range of pressing topics, including international corruption, drug use, environmental issues, sex work, organized crime, innovative models of justice, and punishment and penology.

Punishment in Contemporary China
Its Evolution, Development and Change
Enshen Li

Criminal Legalities in the Global South
Cultural Dynamics, Political Tensions, and Institutional Practices
Edited by Pablo Ciocchini and George Baylon Radics

Organized Crime and Corruption Across Borders
Exploring the Belt and Road Initiative
Edited by T. Wing Lo, Dina Siegel, and Sharon I. Kwok

For more information about this series, please visit: www.routledge.com/criminology/series/RSCJAGS

Criminal Legalities in the Global South

Cultural Dynamics, Political Tensions, and Institutional Practices

Edited by Pablo Ciocchini and George Radics

Routledge
Taylor & Francis Group
LONDON AND NEW YORK

First published 2020
by Routledge
2 Park Square, Milton Park, Abingdon, Oxon OX14 4RN

and by Routledge
605 Third Avenue, New York, NY 10017

First issued in paperback 2021

Routledge is an imprint of the Taylor & Francis Group, an informa business

British Library Cataloguing-in-Publication Data
A catalogue record for this book is available from the British Library

Library of Congress Cataloging-in-Publication Data
Names: Ciocchini, Pablo Leandro, 1978– author. | Radics, George Baylon, 1979– author.
Title: Criminal legalities in the Global South : cultural dynamics, political tensions, and institutional practices / Pablo Ciocchini and George Baylon Radics.
Description: Abingdon, Oxon [UK] ; New York, NY : Routledge, 2019. | Series: Routledge studies in crime and justice in Asia and the Global South | Includes bibliographical references and index.
Identifiers: LCCN 2019019696 (print) | LCCN 2019020076 (ebook) | ISBN 9780429459764 (eBook) | ISBN 9781138625631 (hardback : alk. paper)
Subjects: LCSH: Criminal law—Developing countries. | Criminal procedure—Developing countries. | Crime—Developing countries. | Criminal law (Islamic law)—Developing countries. | Human rights—Developing countries.
Classification: LCC K5015.4 (ebook) | LCC K5015.4 .C4465 2019 (print) | DDC 345/.124—dc23
LC record available at https://lccn.loc.gov/2019019696

ISBN 13: 978-0-367-77747-0 (pbk)
ISBN 13: 978-1-138-62563-1 (hbk)

Typeset in Bembo
by Apex CoVantage, LLC

Contents

Illustrations

Figure

Tables

Contributors

Claudia Paiva Carvalho is a Professor at the Brazilian Institute of Public Law (IDP), Brazil. She received her doctorate in law from the University of Brasilia in 2013. Her research experience is mainly in the areas of history of law, constitutional law, state theory, and transitional justice. She was a former Researcher of the Latin American Transitional Justice Network (Rede Latino-Americana de Justiça de Transição – RLAJT) (2015–2016) and of the National Truth Commission (2014), working on the theme "Sexual Crimes: Justice and Archives."

Carolina Yoko Furusho is an Erasmus: Erasmus Mundus Doctoral Fellow in Cultural and Global Criminology (University of Kent, United Kingdom, and University of Hamburg, Germany). She is a Socio-legal Researcher (LLM, UCL, and BCL, University of São Paulo) and a member of the Brazilian Bar Association. Previously, she held visiting positions at Columbia Law School, McGill Faculty of Law, and the European and the Inter-American Courts of Human Rights. She has experience in the public and private law sectors in Brazil, as well as in human rights nonprofits in London and New York. Her research interests include feminist and postcolonial studies, international and comparative law, particularly human rights, equality, and social justice.

Wilson Hernández is an Adjunct Researcher at the Group for the Analysis of Development (GRADE) based in Lima, Peru. He holds a BA in economics from the University of Lima and a master's degree in comparative development studies from the *École des Hautes Études en Science Sociales*, France. His research topics cover gender-based violence, crime victimization, fear of crime, and geospatial analysis of crime, as well as public policy evaluations.

Jayson Lamchek is a Postdoctoral Fellow at the Faculty of Law, NUS. He is the author of *Human Rights-Compliant Counterterrorism: Myth-Making and Reality in the Philippines and Indonesia* (Cambridge University Press, 2019). He completed his PhD at the Australian National University as an Endeavor Scholar. As an associate at the Public Interest Law Center in Manila and then as a consultant lawyer for nongovernmental organizations, Jayson spent more than seven years working in the Philippines advocating for various political causes. These causes ranged from the compensation of victims of human rights violations under the Marcos regime to the promotion of indigenous and environmental rights.

Emilio Peluso Neder Meyer has been a tenured full-time Associate Professor of Constitutional Law at the Federal University of Minas Gerais (UFMG), Brazil, since 2013 where he teaches graduate (master's and PhD) and undergraduate courses. He has served as a Visiting Researcher at UFMG's Institute of Advanced Interdisciplinary Studies (2018–2019), a Research Fellow of the Brazilian National Council for Scientific and Technological Development, and Director of the Study Center on Transitional Justice of the Federal University of Minas Gerais (http://cjt.ufmg.br). Additionally, Meyer served as Former General Secretary of the Latin America Transitional Justice Network (2016–2017) and was Visiting Researcher at the King's College London Brazil Institute (2014–2015). He is an alumnus of the King's College Transnational Law Summer Institute (2016). Meyer was also a founding member of the Critical Transitional Justice Network and is a member of the International Law and Politics Collaborative Research Network. In 2013, he was awarded the prize for the best law thesis in Brazil by the Brazilian Ministry of Education's CAPES Foundation.

Julieta Mira is a Researcher at the Instituto de Investigaciones Gino Germani (Faculty of Social Sciences, University of Buenos Aires (UBA)) and at the Instituto de Investigaciones Jurídicas y Sociales Ambrosio Gioja (Faculty of Law, UBA). She has a PhD in social sciences, a master's in communication and culture, and a degree in sociology from the Faculty of Social Sciences, UBA. She was awarded an honorable mention for her doctoral dissertation by the UBA and the editorial EUDEBA. She received her master's degree in human rights and democratization from the European Inter-University Centre for Human Rights and Democratization (EIUC, Venice), and bachelor's degree in Law from the Faculty of Law, also from UBA. She has received a number of prestigious scholarships, including EIUC (Italy), National Agency of Scientific Researches and Technologies Promotion (Argentina), University of Buenos Aires – Secretary of Science and Techology (Argentina), and Erasmus Mundus Action 2 – ARTESS (Katholieke Universiteit Leuven, Belgium). Her research interests are mainly in the areas of transitional justice, human rights, justice reform, criminal justice, sociology of law, legal profession, and legal activism.

João Araújo Monteiro Neto graduated in Law from the University of Fortaleza (2001), received his specialization in criminal law from the University of Fortaleza (2004), master's in Constitutional Law from the University of

Fortaleza (2008), and PhD in law from the University of Kent in the United Kingdom. He is currently assistant Professor of Law at the Center of Legal Sciences at the University of Fortaleza, teaching and researching in the areas of information technology law, Internet governance and regulation, regulatory entrepreneurship, digital human rights, privacy and criminal law and procedure.

Elliott Prasse-Freeman received his PhD from the Department of Anthropology at Yale University. He has conducted long-term fieldwork in Myanmar and is working on a book project focusing on Burmese subaltern political thought as adduced from an extended ethnography of activism and contentious politics in the country's semi-authoritarian setting. He is also currently studying Rohingya political subjectivity amid dislocation and mass violence, with a particular focus on their maneuvers in the context of post-sovereign governmental regimes that incorporate human rights discourse, humanitarian care/exclusion, and biopolitical regulation.

Anisur Rahman is an Assistant Professor at the Asian University for Women in Chittagong, Bangladesh. As a historian of law, his primary research interests lie in the intellectual history of law and include the historical construction of Islamic law and modernity in South Asia, history of Islam in South and Southeast Asia, South Asian legal history, and world history approach. By reconstructing the history of how colonial and postcolonial legal processes began to redefine and reconfigure elements of a Muslim marriage and modernity in Islam, his PhD dissertation contributes to the broader conversation on Islamic law and modernity in South Asia.

Nestor Eduardo Araruna Santiago holds a postdoctorate in law from the University of Minho, Portugal (2016) and received his PhD in tax law (2005), master's degree (2000), and specialization (2000) in criminal sciences from the UFMG. Santiago has served as a full Professor of the Post-Graduation Program in Constitutional Law and the University of Fortaleza (UNIFOR) and an Adjunct Professor IV of the Law Course of the Federal University of Ceará. His research interests are criminal procedural law, criminal law, and democracy and the law. He has served as a leader of the research group "Criminal and Criminal Procedural Protection of Rights and Fundamental Guarantees" (UNIFOR), linked to the Laboratory of Criminal Sciences (LACRIM – UNIFOR).

Danish Sheikh is an Assistant Professor and Associate Director of the Centre for Health, Law Ethics and Technology at the Jindal Global Law School in New Delhi, India. His research largely focuses on the intersection of law and the humanities, and the legal regulation of gender and sexuality. He has law degrees from NALSAR University of Law, Hyderabad, and the University of Michigan, Ann Arbor, which he attended on a Grotius Fellowship. His writing has appeared in law reviews such as the *Yale Human Rights and Development*

Law Journal and the *Law and Society Trust Review*, while his commentary has appeared in publications, including the *Hindu*, the *Indian Express*, *Business Standard*, the *Wire, Mint, Deccan Chronicle, Daily News and Analysis, Scroll*, and *DailyO*. Beyond his academic work, Danish engages in fiction writing and theater. His works include the coauthored anthology *Invisible Libraries*, for which he won the TFA Award for Creative Writing in 2016.

Preface

Working on the Global South comes with both its rewards and challenges. On the one hand, it has the potential to unlock our imagination and inspire a new generation of scholarship – one no longer bound by teleological narratives of development or approaching the "end of history." The "Global South" re-envisions our world in a manner that recognizes and venerates the experience of those typically overlooked by mainstream academia. In an upside-down world, we can learn to see the parallel yet intertwined lived realities that much of the world experiences. Shattering the existing confines of modernist thinking, studying the Global South can invert the world order and introduce a kaleidoscope of new ideas and realities.

On the other hand, working on the Global South demands a dedication to the periphery and showcasing work from scholars and regions not typically explored. This requires overcoming the obstacles of language, disparate histories, tensions, conflicts, and the practical hurdles of time zones, funding issues, communication, and visa status. Many of the authors in this volume are young scholars embarking upon the treacherous journey of knowledge production, one fraught with both intellectual and political landmines, as well as the reality that academia is increasingly becoming a harsh industry that can be exploitative and precarious. For those on the margins, this troubling reality can be even more oppressive, making the project of exploring the South difficult when those dedicated to the project are many times struggling to cope with the crushing demands of our profession and life in general.

Luckily, the number of venues that allow us to share and exchange ideas on the Global South are growing. Many of the scholars in this edited volume are alumni of Kings College London's Transnational Law and Summer Institute and Harvard Law School's Institute for Global Law and Policy. Additionally, the editors have over the past several years used the Law and Society Association's (LSA) annual meeting as an opportunity to gather and showcase our work. From 2015 to the present, the editors served as coordinators of the "Judicial Reform in the Global South" International Research Collaborative for the LSA. In 2016, we changed the title of our network to "Global South Legalities" to be more inclusive of the multiplicity of work being done in the area of, and tangentially related to, the law. This edited volume is but one product of this incredibly fruitful network.

Over the past five years, out of this network, we have organized panels for the inaugural Asian Law and Society Association conference in Singapore in 2016 and the Asian Law Institute annual conference in Manila, Philippines, in 2017. With financial support from the LSA, we coordinated several panels at the LSA annual meetings in 2016 (New Orleans), 2017 (Mexico City), and 2019 (Washington, DC). In preparation for these major conferences, two international workshops were organized in Singapore: the first at the University of Liverpool campus in Singapore in 2016 and the second at the National University of Singapore in 2018. Out of all of these activities, we have produced numerous articles and two special issues, one in the *Asian Journal of Social Science* (Radics and Ciocchini, 2018) and the other in *Revista de Derecho y Ciencias Sociales* in Spanish (Ciocchini and Kostenwein, 2017).

None of this work would have been possible without the generous support from the University of Liverpool through its Research Development Fund and the Department of Sociology of the National University of Singapore. In preparation for this manuscript, many of the authors in this edited volume flew to Singapore in September 2018 to present their chapters and review the chapters of others. The workshop was instrumental in the sharing of theoretical frameworks and the search for commonalities between the nations of the Global South. This workshop would not have taken place without a Staff Support Research Scheme grant provided by the Faculty of Arts and Social Sciences at the National University of Singapore, and a Small Project and Networking grant from Kings College London's Transnational Law Institute. Additional thanks must be made to the LSA for its continued support of our project and for enabling many of our participants in this volume to attend the LSA annual meeting in Washington, DC, in June 2019 to present their chapters.

Finally, this manuscript would never have materialized without the dedication and hard work of all of the authors who stuck with us to the very end. This project has taken close to three years to complete, from conceptualization to production. Dr. Ciocchini and Dr. Radics would like to thank all of the authors who have joined us along the way for their commitment in spite of the numerous competing demands. We are also extremely grateful for the fantastic editorial assistance of Isaac Lam, who helped facilitate the workshop and saw each chapter from their infancy stages to completion, and Sharifah Nabilah Syed Omar, who joined us in the last few months to help push this project to completion. Lastly, we would like to thank Thomas Sutton, senior editor from Routledge, who believed in this project from the start, and editorial assistant Jake Rainbow for constantly checking in on us and providing us with essential production details.

Pablo Ciocchini
University of Liverpool
George Radics
National University of Singapore

Introduction

Reinterpreting chaos as diversity

An alternative legal approach from the Global South

Pablo Ciocchini

Studies on the Global South have blossomed in the last decade. This has been a welcomed development to overcome the long-time neglect from social sciences to the particularities of these societies. In the past, social sciences have either focused on central societies (with the exception of anthropology, which was born to study "primitive" societies) or, whenever they have moved their attention to the Global South, they have imposed a patronizing ethnocentric gaze on their analysis (Connell, 2007).

This edited volume joins this refreshing new wave of studies of the Global South offering a socio-legal perspective on the social tensions around the definition and enforcement of, and resistances to, criminal law. The analyses in this book focus on the tensions between criminal law and local cultural dynamics, political tensions, and institutional practices. They explore the tensions between the idealized construction of the criminal law, its selective enforcement, and how it is experienced by the people in societies from the Global South.

Book titles are meant to inform prospective readers about the content of them. This is particularly true of this edited volume. In the first place, by referring to criminal legalities, it already warns readers that law is not assumed as a static and easily identifiable phenomenon but, on the contrary, as dynamic and frequently indistinguishable from politics and other normative orders. In the second place, by referring to the Global South, it claims that societies can be grouped by using a spatial metaphor, South, but qualified with a reference to the interconnectedness in which we currently live.

In what follows, we will discuss the implications of these two claims. To facilitate the exposition, we will first explore the strengths and limitations of the concept of the Global South. Later, we will move to discuss how 'legality' de-essentializes the legal dimension of practices and conceptualizes it instead as a dynamic and ever-contested process. Following that discussion, we will explore the tensions between the criminal law and the local culture, politics, and institutional practices. We will conclude by reflecting on the transdisciplinary approach required to apprehend the complexity of these phenomena.

The emergence of the Global South

The term "Global South" has emerged in international relations, political science, and economic studies (Dados and Connell, 2012), and it has later spread to other social sciences, such as anthropology (Motta and Nilsen, 2011), sociology (Emerald et al., 2016), and criminology (Carrington et al. 2018). It has also been used by legal (Bonilla, 2013) and socio-legal (Santos and Rodríguez-Gavarito, 2005) scholars.

Global South replaces terms with heavily negative connotations such as "underdeveloped" or "developing" countries and "third world." Those terms defined societies in relation to the level of economic and social success they achieved, using Western societies as the standard. This reproduced the colonial mentality that presented European cultural values and socio-political arrangements as the common desirable goal for every society. The concept of the Global South is free from those assumptions. By classifying societies among the South-North division, it recognizes they are not in the same position. However, such classification refers to a fixed spatial reference, and as such, it preempts the aspirational implications of "progress" implicit in the other terms. Thus, the North is not presented as a goal for those in the South; societies are not conceived as unfulfilled projects, but instead they are embraced in their own diversity.

Although the Global South concept is widely used, there is little consensus on its extension. The classification of societies between North and South is closely related to the division among core, peripheral, and semi-peripheral societies in Wallerstein's "world-system" theory (Dados and Connell, 2012). While the core-periphery division heavily emphasizes the economic role of societies in the international division of labor, the reference to the South brings to the front the cultural and socio-political dimensions, both heavily influenced by the colonial past. Evidently, the location of a society in the Southern or Northern hemispheres does not necessary reflect its historical or present position in the world order, as the cases of Australia or Mexico illustrate. However, the reference to the South should be understood as metaphoric rather than geographical (Dados and Connell, 2012; Santos, 2016). In this sense, the South is a "metaphor for the human suffering caused by capitalism and colonialism on the global level, as well as for the resistance to overcoming or minimising such suffering" (Santos, 2016: 18). Therefore, societies cannot be classified in the South or North merely for their geographic position, nor for their role in the international division of labor. The Global South points to a section of the world that has suffered the colonial experience and that it still is suffering its enduring political, cultural, and social legacy. Countries such as Brazil or Singapore are included in this collection despite the former being ranked eighth in the world for its gross domestic product (GDP) and the latter ninth for its GDP per capita (IMF, 2018). However, as the chapters in this collection by Neto and Santiago and Meyer and Carvalho show, Brazil's legal system is still operating under a colonial mentality that criminalizes behaviors culturally accepted by the local population, such as *jogo do bicho*, while it fails to officially acknowledge and prosecute the crimes committed during the past authoritarian governments. In the case of Singapore, as Radics shows, the enduring effects of the colonial past are apparent in the criminalization of the LGTB community. Half a century after its independence, the legacy of the colonial legislation and the Victorian values that informed it are still present in the Singaporean society.

It is worth reflecting on the global adjective that accompanies the reference to the South. It highlights the interconnections between the southern countries, the results of colonial histories, and the current phenomenon of globalization (Dados and Connell, 2012). This is apparent in a series of common issues found in the chapters of this collection. Thus, in Lamchek's chapter on Indonesia and Mira's chapter on Argentina, the tensions among different actors (notably police and civil rights groups) of the process to reform criminal procedures are exposed. On the one hand, both the old procedures and the new ones have been imported or "transplanted" from the Global North (Mattei, 2003). Furthermore, the insistence on the legal reforms evidences the enduring effects of the colonial commitment to social engineering and the dogmatic belief that the law is a proper instrument for doing so. On the other hand, it also exposes the violence that Global South societies suffer, much of which is a product of abusive, corrupt, and inefficient police forces. As the chapters by Ciocchini on the Philippines and Prasse-Freeman on Myanmar describe, those police forces are reproducing practices developed during the authoritarian past regimes that most Global South societies have experienced.

To recognize that societies in the Global South shared some common experiences should not be confused with arguing that they are homogenous or that the problems they faced are all the same. On the contrary, this work proceeds from the assumption that there is no monolithic Global South, and this is evidenced in the diversity of the issues covered by the chapters included in this collection. Although they all share a focus on the role that the law plays in society, such a role is mediated by the indigenous culture, the institutional history, and local economic and political arrangements. Thus, as Furusho argues in this collection, the criminalization of Haitian immigrants in the Dominican Republic cannot be fully understood without their colonial and postcolonial history. Similarly, Rahman's and Sheikh's chapters show that the roots of the legislation that endorses the patriarchal regime in Bangladesh and India are to be found in the complex interactions between colonial and local religious values. These cases illustrate how urgently needed it is to address them, and we believe a proper understanding of the factors that shape them is a necessary first step. We have to acknowledge that the Global South has suffered an epistemological violence that has prioritized the narratives from the Global North, silencing the Global South's voices and experiences (Willems, 2014). This volume seeks to contribute to recover those silenced voices to pave the way for a South-South dialogue in which societies can learn from each other.

Legalities

The contributions of this collection can be located within the traditional line of inquiry of socio-legal studies that focuses on the ideas and values embedded in the law, the conflicting interests behind its interpretation, and the actual practices it legitimizes. They also share a critical approach to the official law and the state, in particular to its law enforcement institutions. Such a critical approach is founded in the recognition of the obscure role criminal law and the institutions that enforce it, i.e. the criminal justice system, play on our societies. On the one hand, the law and the criminal justice system justify, facilitate, and foster state violence against vulnerable sectors of the population. This role is evidenced in the criminalization of poor drug abusers in the Philippines (Ciocchini), Haitian immigrants in the Dominican Republic (Furusho), and minorities (e.g., LGBT community in Singapore (Radics) or India (Sheikh), women in Bangladesh (Rahman) or Brazil (Meyer and Carvalho), or opposition members in Myanmar (Prasse-Freeman)). On the other, the law and the criminal justice system protect those in power, as it is illustrated by the dismissal of corruption cases without further investigation in Peru (Hernández) or the resistance from police to reform the criminal law to maintain their power and to avoid facing more accountability or transparency (Lamchek).

Another key shared feature of the contributions of this book is the emphasis in their analysis on the tensions between the criminal law and local culture, the institutional practices, and the broader politics. These tensions are to be found in every society, but the borders between the different dimensions of social life, public and private, politics, religion, and the law are notoriously porous in the Global South. This porosity tends to be interpreted from a Northern perspective as chaotic (Gupta, 1995). However, it is important to recognize that (without idealizing or essentializing such social arrangement), on the one hand, such interpretation is based on at ethnocentric assumption on how societies should ideally operate, and on the other hand, such porosity is the result of tensions originated in the colonial past and continued by contemporaneous neocolonial politics, such as the ongoing efforts to import alien legal solutions from the Global North into the Global South.

In recognition that distance between the official state law and the legal practices may be significantly larger in societies of the Global South than in societies of the Global North, we have chosen to refer to legalities instead of law. So, as opposed to a focus on strictly formal institutions, the concept of "legality" is used here to overcome the limitations of official legal definitions of crime to encompass the plurality, and sometimes ambiguity, of the phenomena considered "criminal" in the explored societies. By using legalities, the emphasis is placed on the precariousness of the status of legal attributed to some social practices. Such precarity defies a key feature of the Western understanding of the law: its predictability. Western law is assumed to bring predictability to social interaction by codifying desirable social practices (Bourdieu, 1987: 845–847). However, the tensions between diverse informal and formal legal orders are more apparent in the Global South, as it is illustrated by the analysis included in this collection of the tension triggered by the criminalization of a socially accepted gambling game in Brazil (Neto and Santiago). Nevertheless, this should not be misread as a lack of predictability, which is an essential feature of any society to organize its daily life. Instead, as it has been claimed by legal pluralism studies (Merry, 1988) and is also illustrated in several chapters in this collection, there are multiple social orders competing, each with its own rules. Therefore, the strength of the officially sanctioned rules, and their predictability, varies widely in different social spaces.

That the official law is not necessarily dominant in every social space is true not only in relation with the people, as opposed to the state, but also within the state's institutions themselves. This is evident in several contributions in this collection, such as the analysis of the gray legal zone within which law enforcement agencies and judicial actors operate in the "War on Drugs" in the Philippines (Ciocchini), as well as the political function courts are expected to play in the government in Myanmar (Prasse-Freeman) or the public statement by senior officials in Singapore explaining that although they will not abolish the law that criminalizes sex between mutually consenting adult men, they will not enforce it either (Radics). In all these cases, criminal law plays a fundamental role, but it is not the commonly assumed role of differentiating socially acceptable from unacceptable behaviors but rather of establishing the state's authority to intervene in those social spaces. The mode of intervention may, as illustrated by the contributions, acquire nonlegal or extralegal forms while it is also grounded, although loosely in some cases, in the law. However, these tensions between the law and conflicting cultural values, institutional practices or political interests have different characteristics that will be explored in the following sections.

The cultural dynamics: global and traditional values

As we have mentioned earlier, societies in the Global South are still suffering the enduring effects of colonization. Although the experience of this process varies widely, colonization was justified as a civilizing enterprise. Civilizing was understood by Western powers as the replacement of the local values and practices with their own (Quijano and Ennis, 2000). The intensity and form of this process was dependent on the Western power involved (e.g., the United Kingdom, France, Netherlands, Portugal) and of characteristics of the local society suffering the colonization. With the political independence of the former colonies, that process did not end, but it transmuted into a process of neocolonialism presented as modernization (Comaroff and Comaroff, 2012). This process of modernization was driven by the goal of achieving socioeconomic and political development by importing legislation, institutions, and economic projects from the Global North. This process of importation was founded in the idea that societies of the Global North are superior, and so they are the model to be followed by the rest. But since these institutions and laws have been developed in a different context, their importation in the societies of the Global South created strains and contradictions, and the intended progress was not achieved (Nader and Grande, 2002). Thus, the failure of the modernization process, instead of raising awareness of the inadequacy of those laws and institutions, ended up reinforcing the colonial mentality that considered them backward societies and blamed local culture for such (Merry, 2003).

However, we should also acknowledged in the analysis the strategic use of the local cultural values and tradition by the local elites from the Global South. Thus, facing the cultural imperialism from the central societies, leaders from the Global South have appealed to traditional values to oppose criticisms coming from the Global North. This has been especially notable in regard to human rights complaints (Merry, 2003). But, as it is described in the chapter discussing the situation of LGTB in Singapore included in this collection (Radics), local values are also "constructs" that do not necessary represent the whole native population. This is so because they tend to represent local populations as monolithic and homogenous when, in fact, they are diverse. More importantly, in many cases, they are the "reinterpretation" of local values by the colonizers, as analyzed in the discussion of the British legislation and its ulterior interpretation by local courts that criminalize adultery in Bangladesh (Rahman) or sex between mutually consenting adult men in India (Sheikh).

Although in some chapters, the cultural tensions are more deeply discussed than in others, the ubiquitousness of this tension in the Global South is still apparent in every chapter of this collection. It is clearly evident in Brazil, as the tension between the social acceptance of "jogo do bicho" and the refusal by the state to legally recognize it shows (Neto and Santiago), as well as in the struggles of reformers in Argentina to replace a legislation associated with authoritarian values with one based on democratic standards (Mira).

The cultural tension underscores the peculiar status of law. While law it is a key component of the local culture and its provisions reflecting such cultural values, due to its authoritative power, it also has a strong influence on the local culture (Nelken, 1995). However, as the contributions in this collection illustrate, the compliance and acceptance of the official law is not as effective as the legal framework assumes it to be. Thus, some universalizing aspirations of law – i.e., it should be equal to everyone – clash with the heterogeneity of social life. Such clashes are more evident in societies of the Global South because, in many occasions, the law is inspired by alien values, but also because the state, the incarnation of the law itself, has little or a nonactive presence in some locations (e.g., shantytowns or remote rural areas).

Political tensions: the politics of law

The distinction between law and politics has always been a contested one. Traditionally, legal scholars and legal professionals have claimed the autonomy of the legal field from the rest of fields that organize social life (e.g., economic, political). They argued that the legal rationality significantly differed from the economic or the political rationality (Bourdieu, 1987). However, such clear boundaries have been questioned by critical scholars. Some Marxist scholars drawing from an economic determinism have denied any autonomy to the law, claiming it merely mirrors the organizational needs from the mode of production (Hunt, 1985). More sophisticated neo-Marxist perspectives, based on the Gramscian tradition, have recognized the relative autonomy of the state and, consequently, of law, while still recognizing primacy to the economic forces (Cutler, 2005). Lastly, scholars from the critical legal studies tradition have claimed that the judges' decisions are based on their own ideology (Kennedy, 1996). They have claimed that legal materials – i.e., legislation, legal precedents, and any other relevant legal sources – constrain the judge's alternatives, but, nevertheless, he/she will maneuver within the space he or she offers to justify a predetermined outcome (ibid.). Although they vary widely in the level of autonomy with the law, these three critical perspectives raise awareness about the need to interpret the law in relation to the other organizing dimensions of social life (politics, economics, culture).

The contributions in this collection are eminently critical. Despite the fact that they do not necessarily follow any of the schools of thoughts described earlier, they recognize that law is not fully independent from other normative values. As the analysis of Myanmar included in this collection shows, law can be instrumentally used for political purposes, either by governments and elites or by local organized opposition groups (Prasse-Freeman). But contributions also show that the law is not merely instrumental to politics but is itself the fruit of these political processes, as the analysis of the reform of the criminal procedure in Indonesia (Lamchek) and Argentina (Mira) demonstrates. Furthermore, the law heavily shapes the realm of politics. First, as we mentioned earlier, it is a key cultural source establishing and distinguishing what is acceptable in a given society. Thus, the law restrains our imagination of alternative social arrangements because it shapes our common sense. Therefore, any political decision that goes against it is required to accumulate a similar level of political capital to remove that legislation from the hegemonic imaginary and introduce the new one. According to Poulantzas (2014), the state is the material condensation of the relation of forces. Therefore, laws, the state's official expression of its normative order, could also be read as a material condensation of the relations of forces. From this definition it can be interpreted that laws merely translate politics; however, there are two elements in that definition that warn us that such a relationship is not unidirectional or direct. First, laws are not merely the result of political decisions but of a historical political process. That means that they reflect not only the current situation but also the historical forces. Thus, laws never share the same temporal dynamics as politics and economic forces. They are the fruit of numerous compromises, and as such, they tend to have certain inertia (Spitzer, 1983). Such inertia is fundamental to the maintenance of the status quo, providing predictability and ensuring continuity. Second, recognizing the materiality of the law also means to acknowledge its own power to maintain the relation of forces it has condensed. Thus, laws shape the political struggles favoring the conservation of the forces in power.

The tension between law and politics described earlier is more dramatic in the context of the Global South. Although this tension between politics and law crosses the vast majority, the authoritarian past in most countries of the Global South brings another layer of complexity. During these authoritarian regimes, the distinction between law and politics, understanding the latter as the power of the sovereign to exert legitimate violence, collapsed (Prasse-Freeman). It has taken many years of transitional policies to (re)build the civil society – i.e., the set of nongovernmental institutions that organizes social life – and state institutions in many countries are still heavily shaped by authoritarian practices developed in the past. Thus, the success reached by those transitional processes vary vastly among regions and societies. Despite some of the contributions focusing more on the consequences of the authoritarian government, particularly the ones analyzing Argentina (Mira), Myanmar (Prasse-Freeman), and Brazil (Meyer and Carvalho), these enduring effects are apparent in all the contributions. Thus, it can be attributed to the authoritarian past much of the role of the law enabling police violence in the Dominican Republic (Furusho), Indonesia (Lamchek), and the Philippines (Ciocchini), as well as enabling discriminatory practices against minorities in Singapore (Radics), Bangladesh (Rahman), and India (Sheikh).

The institutional practices: enforcing the law without complying with it

Besides the gap between the law in the books and the law in action, which in the Global South can be wider than in the Global North because of the cultural tensions mentioned earlier, and the legal distortions that the collapse with politics have created, another significant factor shaping the legal experience are the actual practices by state agencies, particularly law enforcement agencies. As Becker has put it decades ago, "Institutions are refractory. They do not perform as society would like them to." (Becker, 1967: 242). While such refractory nature is the result of numerous factors, there are some that are more intensively present in the Global South than others – namely, a huge disproportion between official goals and available means (i.e., material and human resources) to achieve them; a profound contradiction between the institutional culture, heavily shaped by the authoritarian history, and internal legal procedures defined by the law; a constant tension between the official institutional goals and the expectations set by politicians and the media; an endemic corruption affecting public institutions in many societies of the Global South; and, finally, as a result of the previous factors, a low level of confidence in the state institutions by local populations. Each of these factors contributes to widening the gap and fostering inefficient institutions that avoid public scrutiny and operate autonomously in a legal gray zone.

This is evident in way police, prosecutors and judges operate under the "War on Drugs" in the Philippines (Ciocchini), the role judges play in politically motivated trials in Myanmar (Prasse-Freeman), and judges' resistance to sentence the perpetrators of crimes against women during the military dictatorship in Brazil (Meyer and Carvalho). It is also clear in the systematic dismissal of corruption cases by Peruvian prosecutors (Hernández), or the resistances from the police, judges, and local politicians to legal changes in Indonesia (Lamchek) and Argentina (Mira). In all these cases, the institutional culture, which in a sense synthetizes the factors described earlier, reinterprets the law so it will not interfere with the informal power arrangements in place. This institutional resistance to change evidences the naivety of expecting significant social changes by merely modifying the law without accompanying it with more radical social, economic, political, and institutional changes.

The transdisciplinary approach

There is nowadays a recognition among social scholars of the need to overcome some of the artificially created disciplinary boundaries (Banakar and Travers, 2005). The contributions in this collection are truly transdisciplinary, and while they share a critical socio-legal perspective, they use a range of different conceptual frameworks and methods to explore the role law plays in societies of the Global South.

The diversity of their conceptual tools evidences the broadness of the legal phenomenon. Thus, Furusho applies Stumpf's (2006) crimmigration framework to explore the criminalization of Haitian immigrants in the Dominican Republic. Mira uses Douglas's (1986) cosmologies to capture ideas and values that reformers associate with legislative change. Prasse-Freeman resorts to Agamben's (2004) theory of the state of exception to interpret the role trials have played in Myanmar's past and present regimes. And Rahman follows Foucault's (1978) analysis of the disciplinarian function sexuality has played to reveal how the criminalization of adultery in Bangladesh served to maintain women in a position of subalternity. The conceptual richness of the contributions speaks of the complexity of the legal phenomenon and the need for sophisticated tools to be able to analyze the intricacies of the diverse relationship between law and other social dimensions.

The diversity in the conceptual framework is accompanied by the diversity in the methodology used to identify, gather, and analyze data. Lamchek, Ciocchini, Prasse-Freeman, and Mira prioritize interviews with local actors; Rahman focuses on the analysis of historical leading cases; Meyer and Carvalho, Sheikh, and Radics scrutinize recent legal cases in their legal, social, and political dimension; Neto and Santiago explore a particular social practice (*jogo do bicho*) that openly challenges the state's legal order, focusing their analysis on the internal tensions in the rationality that structures the legal order that the open challenge evidences; finally, Hernández takes a quantitative approach to reveal the prosecutors' shortcomings when dismissing corruption cases. Therefore, the contributions in this volume are each truly transdisciplinary and taken together offer the reader a better understanding of the multiple ways in which legalities are imposed, appealed, obeyed, or resisted in the Global South.

A mode of conclusion

This collection's main objective was to gather together contributions from around the Global South to contribute to the production of knowledge from societies that have been historically neglected by the social sciences. These contributions shared some common topics, such as the cultural tensions and a shared colonial history, but also the way such pasts shape current societies and how such societies take very different forms. In this sense, this volume celebrates the diversity and difference of each society. The criminal legalities are heavily influenced by the history of those societies. Nevertheless, they present tensions and the role law plays nowadays cannot be merely predicted by looking at their history. An understanding of the role criminal legalities play requires a thorough analysis of the political, cultural, and institutional tensions that are currently shaping the relevant actors' legal practices. The contributions in this volume show that such analysis is not simple, especially because the peculiarities of the social dynamics in those societies distance them from the assumed model of central societies. But despite those difficulties, or perhaps because of them, the results are not only useful to better understand those societies but also raise questions about our sociological and legal assumptions about the way broader societies operate.

References

Agamben, G. (2004) *State of Exception*, Chicago University Press, Chicago.

Banakar, R. and Travers, M. (2005) "Law, Sociology and Method" in R. Banakar and M. Travers (eds.) *Theory and Method in Socio-Legal Research*, Hart Press, Oxford. pp. 1–25.

Becker, H. (1967) "Whose Side Are We On?," *Social Problems*, vol. 14, no. 3, pp. 239–247.

Bonilla, D. (2013) *Constitutionalism of the Global South: The Activist Tribunals of India, South Africa, and Colombia*, Cambridge University Press, Cambridge.

Bourdieu, P. (1987) "The Force of Law: Toward a Sociology of the Juridical Field," *The Hastings Law Journal*, vol. 38, no. 5, pp. 805–853.

Carrington, K., Hogg, R., Scott, J. and Sozzo, M. (2018) *The Palgrave Handbook of Criminology and the Global South*, Palgrave Macmillan, New York.

Comaroff, J. and Comaroff, J. (2012) "Theory from the South: Or, How Euro-America Is Evolving toward Africa," *Anthropological Forum*, vol. 22, no. 2, pp. 113–131.

Connell, R. (2007) "The Northern Theory of Globalization," *Sociological Theory*, vol. 25, no. 4, pp. 368–385.

Cutler, C. (2005) "Gramsci, Law, and the Culture of Global Capitalism," *Critical Review of International Social and Political Philosophy*, vol. 8, no. 4, pp. 527–542.

Dados, N. and Connell, R. (2012) "The Global South," *Contexts*, vol. 11, no. 1, pp. 12–13.
Douglas, M. (1986) *How Institutions Think*, University of Syracuse Press, New York.
Emerald, E., Rinehart, R. and Garcia, A. (2016) *Global South Ethnographies: Minding the Senses*, Sense Publishers, Rotterdam.
Foucault, M. (1978) *History of Sexuality: An Introduction*, Penguin, New York.
Gupta, A. (1995) "Blurred Boundaries: The Discourse of Corruption, the Culture of Politics, and the Imagined State," *American Ethnologist*, vol. 22, no. 2, pp. 375–402.
Hunt, A. (1985) "The Theory of Critical Legal Studies," *Oxford Journal of Legal Studies*, vol. 6, no. 1, pp. 1–45.
IMF (2018) *IMF DataMapper: Gross Domestic Product (GDP)*, Available at: www.imf.org/external/datamapper/datasets/WEO/1 (Accessed 6 March 2019).
Kennedy, D. (1996) "Strategizing Strategic Behavior in Legal Interpretation," *Utah Law Review*, vol. 3, pp. 785–825.
Mattei, U. (2003) "A Theory of Imperial Law: A Study on US Hegemony and the Latin Resistance," *Indiana Journal of Global Legal Studies*, vol. 10, no. 1, pp. 383–448.
Merry, S. (1988) "Legal Pluralism," *Law and Society Review*, vol. 22, no. 5, pp. 869–896.
Merry, S. (2003) "Human Rights Law and Demonization of Culture (and Anthropology Along the Way)," *Political and Legal Anthropology Review*, vol. 26, no. 1, pp. 55–76.
Motta, S. and Nilsen, A. (2011) *Social Movements in the Global South: Dispossession, Development and Resistance*, Palgrave Macmillan, London.
Nader, L. and Grande, E. (2002) "Current Illusions and Delusions about Conflict Management: In Africa and Elsewhere," *Law and Society Inquiry*, vol. 27, no. 3, pp. 573–594.
Nelken, D. (1995) "Disclosing/Invoking Legal Culture: An Introduction," *Social and Legal Studies*, vol. 4, no. 4, pp. 435–452.
Poulantzas, N. (2014) *State, Power, Socialism*, Verso, London.
Quijano, A. and Ennis, M. (2000) "Coloniality of Power, Eurocentrism, and Latin America," *Nepantla: Views from the South*, vol. 1, no. 3, pp. 533–580.
Santos, B. (2016) "Epistemologies of the South and the Future," *From the European South: A Transdisciplinary Journal of Postcolonial Humanities*, vol. 1, pp. 17–29.
Santos, B. and Rodríguez Gavarito, C. (2005) *Law and Globalization from Below: Towards a Cosmopolitan Legality*, Cambridge University Press, Cambridge.
Spitzer, S. (1983) "Marxist Perspectives in the Sociology of Law," *Annual Review of Sociology*, vol. 9, no. 1, pp. 103–124.
Stumpf, J. (2006) "The Crimmigration Crisis: Immigrants, Crime, and Sovereign Power," *American University Law Review*, vol. 56, no. 2, pp. 367–418.
Willems, W. (2014) "Beyond Normative Dewesternization: Examining Media Culture from the Vantage Point of the Global South," *The Global South*, vol. 8, no. 1, pp. 7–23.

Part I

Cultural dynamics

Chapter 1

Criminalizing adultery in colonial India

Constructing the wife vs. the "other" in Islamic family law

Anisur Rahman

Introduction

On 19 February 1982, Sakina Bibi, a widow, filed a complaint with the Sub-Divisional Magistrate in Feni, a southern district in eastern Bangladesh, concerning her unwanted pregnancy. In her complaint, she accused Nurul Huq, the elder brother of her deceased husband, of developing an illicit sexual relationship with her. She also alleged that Huq had refused to marry her despite the fact that the affair had resulted in pregnancy and that he had forced her to have an abortion. Sakina's complaint resulted in criminal proceedings under section 497 of the Penal Code, or the prohibition against adultery. Section 497, which the British had first codified in the Indian Penal Code of 1860, criminalized consensual sexual intercourse between a man and the wife of another man. However, Huq contested the charge on the ground that Sakina was a widow, which the court promptly rejected. Unfazed, Huq went to the High Court Division (henceforth HCD) of the Supreme Court of Bangladesh (henceforth SCB) to quash the proceedings of the case (*Nurul Huq v. Bibi Sakina, Lex*/BDHC/0053/1985/Manupatra). In the HCD, the widowhood of Sakina became a crucial issue to determine the fate of the case. Since only the husband could file a complaint under section 497 of the Penal Code, Huq argued that a widow could not bring a charge for adultery, as she no longer had a husband. In addition, he argued that for a case to be successful under section 497, sexual intercourse must have taken place without the consent of her husband, who at this point was no longer alive to raise the claim. Finally, Huq argued that sexual intercourse with an unmarried woman, a prostitute, or widow did not constitute an offense of adultery. Ultimately, the HCD agreed with Huq, releasing him from detention and quashing the proceedings of the lower court. The decision of the SCB, as a result, gave rise to many important questions, including a) who was considered a "wife" under section 497, b) where did this proprietary right over the wife come from, and c) in which way did the past and the colonial construction of the law inform decisions related to adultery in the postcolonial South Asian nation of Bangladesh.

The *Nurul Huq v. Bibi Sakina* case revolves around section 497 of the Penal Code – a law that traces its history to British India. Although the prominent legal universalist T. B. Macaulay (1800–1859) played a pivotal role in drafting this colonial criminal law while he was chairing the first Law Commission in British India, to blame British morality alone without considering local values (Ali, 2010; Singha, 1998), economic and practical considerations (Chatterjee, 1999; Hyam, 1990), and how local values and ideas concerning gender become transmuted through the lens of another (Said, 1991; Stoler, 1995) would lead to an incomplete picture. Section 497 represents a provision of the criminal code that perpetuates traditional structures, such as patriarchy, its subsequent control over a woman's body, and how such traditions become entrenched, preserved, and perpetuated through the institution of the law. Although India in September 2018 in *Joseph Shine vs. Union of India*, WP(Crl.) No.194/17 (27 September 2018), removed Section 497 from its criminal code, Pakistan and Bangladesh have both preserved the provision, albeit in different ways.

This chapter explores the connection between the legal construction of the "wife" and criminalizing consensual sexual intercourse between a man and the wife of another man in British India. For this chapter, leading cases of different High Courts in colonial India, the Privy Council (the highest court of British India), and the Supreme Courts of Pakistan and Bangladesh have been examined in order to show the continuity of legal construction of the "wife" on the basis of the binary between licit and illicit sexual relationships. This chapter will first begin with a theoretical discussion about the role of the colonial government in controlling women's bodies, particularly in the context of marriage and adultery. Next, the chapter will explore colonial control over women's body and the family through the Privy Council's effort to define and construct the "wife" and in defining the boundaries of a legal sexual relationship. Then the chapter will discuss the way in which the binary of "licit" and "illicit" sexual relationships became the prevailing rationale in cases related to adultery in the High Courts of British India. In the last section, this chapter will focus on the way the colonial legal construction continued to inform the understanding of the offense of adultery in postcolonial states in South Asia.

Adultery in the British colony

Since 1772, colonial India was governed by Anglo-Hindu and Anglo-Mohammadan laws that were loosely based on religious texts interpreted by British and British-trained judges but informed by local *pandits* (Hindu scholars) and *mufties* (Islamic scholars). Things ultimately began to change in the first half of the 19th century. In 1833, Thomas Babbington (T. B.) Macauley served as the first law member of the Governor General's Council and on the Supreme Council of India between 1834 and 1838. As a utilitarian and legal universalist, Macauley strove to liberate Indians from what he saw as the restrictive grip of family, caste, and religious community and to synchronize laws between the different communities in India. He was harshly critical of local beliefs and customs, and in 1835, he produced his now infamous *Minute on Indian Education* piece in which he states, "A single shelf of a good European library was worth the whole native literature of India and Arabia" (Bureau of Education, 1920 [1965]). Following this line of thought, between 1828 and 1855, a series of British parliamentary acts were passed to revise the Anglo-Hindu and Anglo-Mohammadan laws, such as those relating to the right to religious conversion, widow remarriage, and right to create wills for inheritance. Ultimately, Governor General Dalhousie's egalitarian policy of promoting British values over local traditions and "treating all natives in much the same manner" helped to spur outrage and protest in colonial India, erupting into the Indian Mutiny of 1857. By 1858, the Government of India Act was passed in the Parliament of the United Kingdom (21 & 22 Vict. c. 106), liquidating the British East India Company and transferring control over the colony to the British Crown (Rudolph and Rudolph, 2000).

Thus, efforts to enforce universal values through the law encountered serious push back in the colony – and this was especially the case when it came to adultery. In colonial India, adultery was considered a significant crime because it served as a threat to male authority, family lineage, and native codes of honor. Under Islamic law, a man could send a person to his death if he found this person in the act of *zina* (unlawful sexual intercourse) with his wife or his slave. The woman, too, could be subject to death for the act (Singha, 1998, p. 144). Regulating adultery served the interest of the colonial government as well since it enforced the sanctity of marriage given the surge of Christian evangelicals in India by the late 18th century and the rise of social purity movements in the West by the mid-19th century (Hyam, 1990, pp. 119, 149). In a Christian world, adultery "overturned the 'natural' heterosexual relationship where the husband (as the 'head of the wife' as Paul instructed in Ephesians 5:23) was on top both mentally and physically, pleasure becoming sinful and intercourse only permitted for procreation" (Lawson, 1988, p. 14). Colonial economic interests, too, influenced the government's interest in leaving intact social institutions – such as slavery – that interfered or complicated the application of laws concerning adultery (Chatterjee, 1999, p. 21). In addition to engaging in the practice of trading slaves, many of the British employed slaves within their own households. Thus, "the simple reduction of the complex and different grades of slavery into 'marriage' relations by the Law Commission absolved the Company of any responsibility to legally end slave concubinage in the English officers' and soldiers' households" (ibid.). These cultural influences and practical necessities led the British to govern under a moral code that viewed local practices such as prostitution and slavery through a foreign lens, translating into laws and judicial opinions that imputed marriage when a slave was involved, or harsh and dismissive rulings when the case involved alimony or inheritance and concerned a prostitute.

Beyond the historical and economic concerns behind the criminalization of adultery lies the power of the law to translate expectations into tangible and enforceable practices, and to pass on such practices through the ages. In this regard, Foucault reminds us that the law is capable of "coding power [and] serving as its system of representation" (Foucault, 1978, p. 89). Particularly on the topic of adultery, Foucault's argument that sexuality served as a site of control, surveillance, and manipulation comes to life through the sordid details of adulterous affairs that are documented through the meticulous and public institution of the court. Yet Stoler (1995, p. 6) in her rereading of Foucault's *History of Sexuality* points out that he "systematically excludes and/or subsumes the fact of colonialism within it." Not only did the court serve as an instrument to assert state power over the body, but it also produced and inculcated a foreign set of values onto Indian society. Stoler's (1995) emphasis on race and Said's (1994) highlighting of the system of orientalist knowledge informing colonial law serve as running subtext to the cases explored in this chapter. Such an approach reminds us, however, that to ignore the important gender dynamic would create the violent displacement and silencing of women who become "caught between patriarchy and imperialism, subject-constitution and object-formation" (Spivak, 1988, p. 306). And that to do so would allow "the figure of the woman to disappear, not into a pristine nothingness, but a violent shuttling which is the displaced figuration of the 'third-world woman' caught between tradition and modernization" (ibid.). Thus, to interpret the law of adultery in colonial India as it pertains to Muslim communities would be incomplete if the reader were to ignore the intermingling of fluctuating understandings of Islamic beliefs and gender, orientalist interpretations of such beliefs, and practical realities of preserving order and control in the colonial enterprise.

Considering that law is "more than just a set of rules for regulating behavior" and is also a "structure of the political imagination" (Ruskola, 2013, p. 2), this chapter will explore the formation of the law on adultery for Muslim communities in colonial India historically to trace its manifestations and transmutations in the law today. While the law assumes that justice can be attained once and for all by the "fixing of identity and meaning," Menon (1999, p. 264) adds that "at particular historical moments, 'justice' is constituted by specific moral visions." How the courts treated women while adjudicating cases of adultery in the past not only shines light on the lineages and vestiges of colonial law on the institution of marriage and women's roles within it are conceptualized but also how such interpretations set the course for the crime of "adultery" today and into the future.

The privy council and the construction of the "wife" and "the other"

The Privy Council defined the term "wife" in a number of cases since the 1840s.[1] A review of these cases will show how Her Majesty's Council constructed Muslim marriage in a way that legalized the husband's ownership and domination over the wife. To do this, the Privy Council first constituted a marriage from an extended sexual relationship and then separated it from sexual relationship with others. Highlighting the duration of a sexual relationship, the Privy Council formed a binary sexual relationship – "wife" and "the other" – in order to indicate a "licit" or an "illicit" sexual relationship. In this section, two leading cases of the Privy Council relating to Muslim marriage have been examined to show the way the Privy Council constructed the "wife" in order to mean legal sexual relationships and to distinguish the wife from a prostitute or a concubine. The sexual relationship with the latter, according to the Privy Council, was illicit. These two cases are also important to show the way the legal construction of the "wife" legalized the husband's proprietary right over the wife.

In 1866, in the *Ashrufood Dowlah v. Hyder Hossein*, [1866] UKPC 35, the Privy Council attempted to answer an important question: could a court presume a Muslim marriage from an extended cohabitation in all circumstances? In this case, the marriage between the parents of Hyder Hossein Khan, the respondent, was challenged. Although the two lower courts – the Civil Court and the Judicial Commissioner of Lucknow – had pronounced different judgments, they agreed on the connection between sex and marriage. Highlighting the duration of cohabitation, the British courts in India distinguished sexual intercourse with the wife from that with a concubine. To them, while permanent cohabitation led to a presumption of marriage, a temporary cohabitation, in which the woman had opportunities to go outside the house (harem), did not lead to a similar presumption. Having suggested the binary permanent/temporary cohabitation, the colonial courts crafted oppositional categories, such as whether a woman was free or not free.[2] According to Mr. Fraser, the civil judge of Lucknow, the wife should not have the liberty to leave the harem. For him, the pregnancy of a free woman who had the liberty to leave the harem negated the presumption of a marriage. In order to determine the legal status of a child born of sexual intercourse with a concubine, Mr. Fraser, J. gave an analogy between a slave and a concubine. According to him, the legal status of a concubine was lower than that of a slave girl in Islamic legal traditions since the child from sexual intercourse between a master and a slave girl was entitled to a share in the property of the master. The rights afforded were somewhat similar to that of a child of a valid marriage. By comparing the status of a slave girl to that of a concubine, Mr. Fraser placed the wife and a slave on an equal footing. Highlighting the connection between lawful sex – sexual intercourse with the wife and a slave girl – the Civil Court of Lucknow held that temporary nature of cohabitation between a man and a free woman and subsequent birth of a child (in absence of a valid marriage) would not confer legitimacy to a child.

The facts of the case at hand, in brief, were that Ashrufood Dowlah, the appellant, claimed a share in the property of his deceased father, Nawab Ameenood Dowlah, the prime minister under the ex-king of Awadh. Hyder Hossein, the respondent, also claimed a share as co-heir in the property of the deceased vizier. Both of them were Shia' Muslim. The respondent based his claim on a *muta* (temporary) marriage of his mother with the deceased and the acknowledgment by his deceased father. Having denied both *muta* marriage and the alleged acknowledgment, the appellants challenged the legitimacy of Hyder Hossein. The Court of Civil Judge, Lucknow, did not find the sexual relations as a marriage between the parents of Hossein. The civil judge of Lucknow was assisted by a group of religious clergies who acted as a "jury" in the court. These religious clergies decided the legitimacy of Hyder Hossein while keeping in mind that only lawful sexual intercourse between a man and a wife conferred the legitimacy to a child. To them, Islam approved the sexual intercourse of a man with his slave and wife. In response to a query by the civil judge concerning what would then constitute proof of a legal status according to sharia, they replied,

> Had the Nawab distinctly stated the Defendant is to be his son, whether orally or in writing, that would have been conclusive; or had it been proved that the birth took place after marriage, that too would have been conclusive; or had the son been the issue of the Master by his slave girl, that also would create an heir.
>
> (*Ashrufood Dowlah*, Proceedings of the Civil Court of Lucknow/Judgment, 35.)

Since Hyder Hossein's mother was a free woman, a legal sexual relationship was required to establish his legitimacy in this case. Therefore, a marriage before impregnation or a clear acknowledgment from the father was crucial for the civil judge of Lucknow to determine Hossein's status as an official heir. The lower court found that the marriage between the parents of Hossein took place after his conception. The civil judge of Lucknow reached this conclusion by agreeing with the findings of the religious clerics who assisted the court as the jury and who found that Hossein was conceived out of wedlock. The civil judge of Lucknow, thereafter, decreed that Hossein was an illegitimate son and not an heir to Nawab Ameenood Dowlah's property.

On appeal, the judicial commissioner of Awadh reversed the decision of the civil judge of Lucknow. According to the judicial commissioner, neither the marriage nor the illegitimacy of Hossein was proven. Against the backdrop of the failure to prove all material facts, such as the date of the marriage and the date of the pregnancy, the judicial commissioner could not help presuming a marriage to fill the gap of the required evidence. Mr. George Campbell, the judicial commissioner, presumed the marriage from the facts of extended cohabitation: "I think it perfectly clear that deceased and defendant's mother *cohabited continuously together, that the Appellant [Hyder Hossein] was born during such cohabitation*" (*Ashrufood Dowlah*, Proceedings of the Court of Judicial Commissioner of Awadh/Judgment, 43. emphasis added).

Ultimately, Mr. Campbell's decision was challenged at the Privy Council. Her Majesty's Council opined that whether the presumption of an antecedent marriage compensated the defect was the fundamental question to be decided in this case. The Privy Council first highlighted the relationship between marriage (meaning lawful sexual intercourse) and the legitimacy of children. In the words of Sir Lawrence Peel, J.,

> Presumption of legitimacy from marriage follows the bed, and whilst the marriage lasts, the child of the woman is taken to be the husband's child, but this presumption follows the bed, and is not antedated by relation. An ante-nuptial child is illegitimate.
>
> (*Ashrufood Dowlah*, Judgment of the Privy Council, 11. Emphasis added.)

Her Majesty's Council used the phrase "legitimacy from marriage followed the bed" to indicate that only a marriage could lead to a legal sexual intercourse between a man and a free woman. Consequently, according to the Privy Council, a child born out of wedlock is illegitimate. However, Her Majesty's Council held that a Muslim marriage may be presumed (to confer legitimacy to a child) upon fulfillment of two conditions: a) it must not be after the conception of a child, and b) it must not be confounded with *concubinage*. If the facts of a case clearly suggested a *concubinage*, it would not lead to a presumption of marriage. For the Privy Council, a permanent nature of cohabitation was required to presume a marriage. In other words, a continuous control over the body of a woman was considered a distinguishing feature to determine who was the wife and how was the concubine.

The Privy Council, therefore, disagreed with Mr. Campbell, the judicial commissioner since his understanding of a Muslim marriage was not based on the nature of the cohabitation. According to the Privy Council, the woman was a free woman, unlike a slave or the wife, and used to go outside the harem. For Her Majesty's Council, a regular cohabitation could presuppose the husband's continuous control over the body of the woman. The fact that she was a free woman and used to go to market to shop instead of keeping to the tradition of staying behind the *purdah* (in the harem) destroyed the presumption that the deceased vizier had absolute control over her body. As a result, Her Majesty's Council held the legal presumption of the judicial commissioner unjustified.

The aforesaid discussion indicates that the Privy Council had clearly established a connection between marriage, the legitimacy of children, and the right to inheritance. The center of this triangle relationship was marriage. According to Her Majesty's Council, the nature of cohabitation – permanent and temporary – made Muslim marriage different from *concubinage*. The Privy Council's choice of words "permanent nature of sexual intercourse" could mean the man's absolute control over the person of a woman. In absence of such absolute control, the sexual relationship would be a *concubinage*. The control over the body of a woman, therefore, became the defining characteristic of (presuming) a Muslim marriage – a channel for lawful sexual intercourse. In other words, "lawful sex" became the crucial test for the Privy Council to determine who was, and who was not the "wife." Based on the binary sexual category – licit and illicit – the Privy Council clearly drew a line between sexual intercourse with the wife and with others. This binary category of sexual intercourse drove the Privy Council again not to presume a marriage in the following case despite the fact of extended cohabitation.

The wife vs. concubine/prostitute

In the *Jariut-ool-Butool v. Hosseinee Begum*, [1867] UKPC 6, the Privy Council categorically held that the extended cohabitation was not sufficient to construct a Muslim marriage through legal presumption if the fact of marriage was not proven. In this case, Jariut-ool-Butool, who was allegedly a prostitute, claimed that she had a valid marriage between herself and Mirza Abdollah Beg, a nobleman from Agra, northwestern province of India. In addition, she claimed that her husband executed a will in her favor before his death. She wanted to recover possession of the property of the late Mirza Abdollah by force of the deed of will. Her marriage was denied on the grounds that she was a prostitute, and she used to live with Mirza Abdollah as his mistress. Jariut-ool-Butool, on the contrary, claimed that she was a prostitute way before her marriage with Abdollah. The Court of Civil Judge of Jounpoor, the trial court, decreed the suit against her. Similarly, the *Sudder Diwanny Adawlut* (the Supreme Court of Revenue, henceforth "SDA") of northwestern province of India rejected her appeal. The SDA, unlike the Court of Civil Judge, took the fact of her extended cohabitation with late Mirza Abdollah into account. However, the SDA held that her marriage was not proved conclusively. The fact of her quitting prostitution and their living together as a man and wife was not proved either. As a result, the SDA not only abstained from presuming a marriage between them from an extended cohabitation but also held that the sexual intercourse between them was an illegal relationship according to Islamic law.

Dissatisfied, Jariut-ool-Butool filed an appeal against the decision of the SDA to the Privy Council, which had to deal with two important legal questions: a) whether a Muslim marriage could be presumed from extended cohabitation and b) when such presumption (if any) arose in this case since the appellant was a prostitute. In other words, "whether a concubine can be converted to a wife by judicial presumption through a lapse of time" was the main question. The Privy Council sought to determine the legal status of Jariut-ool-Butool first and then to investigate the veracity of her claimed marriage. Her Majesty's Council applied the ordinary principle of the law of evidence that the "ordinary legal presumption was that things remain in their original state" to determine her legal status. According to the Privy Council, Jariut-ool-Butool failed to prove her intermediary profession or means of maintaining her life before marriage with late Mirza Abdollah. Therefore, the Privy Council could not help but presume that she was a prostitute. Her Majesty's Council then suggested that the lower courts were justified to hold that Jariut-ool-Butool was a concubine, and her sexual intercourse with Mirza Abdollah was unlawful.

The forgone discussion indicates that the Privy Council had constructed marriage from an extended sexual relationship in which the husband enjoyed control, domination, and ownership over the person of the wife. In addition, the Privy Council, while distinguishing the wife from a concubine or prostitute, reduced her status from a free woman to an unfree one. Finally, having considered the marriage a means through which a legal sexual relationship could be established between a man and woman, the Privy Council defined a wife in a way in which the "wife" continued to be synonymously used to mean a licit sexual relationship. Such an understanding of marriage and the "wife" would come to determine the guilt of an accused for committing adultery in British India, which is the subject matter in the next section.

Marriage and adultery in British India

"I did not know that Kaniz Banoo was the wife of the plaintiff. I was in no way informed of the matter." Abdul Samad Sheikh invoked this defense in the High Court of Nagpur against his conviction for the offense of adultery. He went to the Nagpur High Court to have the decisions of the subordinate courts reviewed, which had convicted him of adultery and ordered him to pay damages. In *Abdul Samad v. Mohammad Ramzan* [1946] 33 A.I.R, Nagpur 393, Mohammad Ramzan Hussain, the husband of Kaniz Banoo, had filed a damage suit in a civil court accusing Samad of committing adultery with his wife. Although Mr. Vivian Bose, a judge in the High Court of Nagpur, had not discussed the findings of the two lower courts concerning the conviction on adultery, he regarded the decree of the court relating to the payment of damages unlawful. He opined that although adultery was an actionable claim, there was a disagreement among the authorities with regard to the way the action arises and what was the basis of that action. While there were some cases that focus on the loss of service, there were others that found that the offense of adultery constituted a tort against the husband. He referred to *Clerk and Lindsell on Torts* (1848–1898 [1937]), an authoritative text in continuous print since 1848, which suggested that although there was no bar in the strict sense, it was unusual to award damages for the offense of adultery where the marital status of the woman was unknown to the offender. Insisting that some special reasons were required to disregard the general rule, Mr. Bose overruled the decisions of two subordinate courts relating to the payment of damages for adultery.

Although the payment of damages was ultimately overturned, the forgone discussion indicates that the offense of adultery was considered a kind of wrong which incur loss to the husband for which the latter might claim compensation. As a result, the courts sought to remedy the loss of the husband. Although the appeal was allowed, in this case, the idea of providing damages to the husband for violation of his rights was not entirely abandoned. By allowing a husband to seek recourse at the court for the violation of his marital rights, the colonial courts established a connection between marriage and the offense of adultery.

The importance of marriage in order to prove adultery was reiterated in *Aziz Khan v. Ekram Hussain* case, A.I.R. (1937) Patna 219, in which the court held that the alleged marriage must be proven in the strict sense to convict a person for the offense of adultery. In this case, Aziz brought a charge for adultery against Ekram. The latter, however, defended the charge by insisting that there was a divorce between Aziz and his wife, Sayidan. Although the divorce was not proven, the lower court emphasized the lack of evidence of a marriage between Aziz and Sayidan. As the marriage was not proven in the subordinate courts, Ekram was acquitted of the charge. However, the High Court of Patna considered the deposition of the husband and the wife as the proof of their marriage and thereby overruled the decisions of the subordinate courts.

It, therefore, can be said that the courts in British India contributed to establishing a relation between marriage and the offense of adultery. In other words, adultery was considered an offense against marriage: criminalizing sexual intercourse with the wife of another man. Such a construction of an offense subdued a married woman's choice of sexual intercourse for the sake of marriage. Consequently, where marriage existed, the plea that there was consent from the wife was not sufficient to escape from the charge of an adultery. In *Gul Mohammad v. Emperor*, A.I.R (1946) 121, the High Court of Nagpur explicitly held that the wife's consent to a sexual intercourse was not a defense for an offense of adultery.

In this case, Gindia, the wife of Babulal, was forced to convert to Islam to be married to Gul Mohammad. A family friend of Gindia's, Mohammad deceitfully confined her before the forced conversion and marriage. He had sexual intercourse with her before she was rescued by police upon a warrant issued by a local Magistrate. The latter convicted Mohammad for adultery, which was confirmed by the additional session judge. Mohammad then went to the High Court of Nagpur for final redress. In the High Court, the counsel for Gul Mohammad defended the charge on two points relating to *locus standi* and effect of the second marriage. With regard to the right to bring a charge for adultery, it was argued that after the subsequent marriage of Gindia, the right of Babulal, as the husband, was ceased to file a complaint about adultery. It was also opined that after the conversion and marriage, Gindia actually consented to the sexual intercourse with Mohammad and thereby could not be considered adulterous. Consequently, the court had to examine the status of Gindia's previous marriage and whether consent of the wife served as grounds for acquitting a person from the charge of an adultery.

Mr. Sen, the presiding judge in the High Court of Nagpur, held that the conversion of a Hindu wife to Islam did not automatically dissolve her previous marriage. It was also observed that a Hindu wife could not contract a marriage during the lifetime of the husband. Consequently, to Mr. Sen, the marriage between Gindia and Babulal was still in force, and the latter continued to be the husband of Gindia. The court further insisted that Gul Mohammad was aware of the fact that Gindia was the wife of Babulal when he had sexual intercourse with her. Convicting Mohammad for adultery, Mr. Sen held "as the marriage of Gindia with Babulal was not dissolved, sexual intercourse by the accused with or without her consent was an offence under section 497 of the Penal Code" (*Gul Mohammad, 123*).

The review of cases here clearly indicated a connection between marriage and the offense of adultery. The centrality of marriage to convict a person for adultery reinforces the idea that criminalizing sexual intercourse in British India was actually to protect the husband's proprietary rights over the wife within the institution of marriage. As a result, the husband is required to actively prevent another man from violating his marital rights, which would inform the judicial decisions in the postcolonial states in South Asia. In the final section, how such requirements live on in the postcolonial nations of Pakistan and Bangladesh will be explored.

Postcolonial interpretations of marriage and adultery in Pakistan and Bangladesh

While the cases noted earlier demonstrate control over the woman's body and how adultery laws protected a man's right to his woman over other men, India received its independence in 1947, and these laws no longer needed to apply to Indian citizens and those living on the South Asian continent. But as mentioned in earlier, it took nearly 71 years for post-independent India to strike down Section 497. Moreover, the law is still in place, and in some cases, it is modified and enhanced in modern-day Pakistan and Bangladesh. This next section will review the development of Section 497 in these two Muslim nations.

In *Ali Newaz Gardezi v. Muhammad Yusuf* [1963] PLD, SC, 55, the Supreme Court of Pakistan acquitted Yusuf from a charge of adultery as Gardezi had not strongly resisted the latter from committing adultery with his wife. Being "enticed" by Muhammad Yusuf, a military official, Christa Renate, the wife of Gardezi, developed a relationship with Yusuf. She met him at Quetta (the largest city in the province of Balochistan) upon returning from Europe to Pakistan with her husband. Gardezi first came to know of the friendly relationship between his wife and Yusuf, and how it turned into a mutual infatuation through an intercepted letter. While he tried his best to get his wife to forget Yusuf, Renate demanded Gardezi sign a divorce letter. When he refused, she left the home for Quetta and married Yusuf on 2 January 1962, in accordance with sharia. On 5 January 1962, Gardezi filed a case against Yusuf in the Court of Additional District Magistrate, Lahore, for taking his wife away and for adultery. It was eventually transferred to the High Court of West Pakistan (HCWP). The single judge of the HCWP found Yusuf guilty of adultery as Renate continued to be the wife of Gardezi. On appeal, a three-judge bench of the same court reversed the decision of the single judge and set the conviction aside. Gardezi then filed an appeal to the Supreme Court of Pakistan (SCP).

The court focused on the evidence that Gardezi was informed of the relationship between Yusuf and his wife since their first meeting at Quetta. The court noted that even though he was aware of the contact, Gardezi allowed their regular correspondence on the phone or via telegram. Gardezi, according to the SCP, was an "accommodating husband" who allowed his wife to carry on a relationship with another man. Gardezi, opined the SCP, not only neglected the growing relationship between Yusuf and his wife but also willfully refrained from taking any action to prevent Yusuf from committing adultery with her. In addition, the SCP applied the common law principle of *volenti non fit injuria* ("to a willing person, injury is not done") to hold that since Gardezi passively assented to that adulterous relationships between Yusuf and his wife, Yusuf could not be held guilty for adultery in this case. In other words, because Gardezi, through his actions, assented to the loss of his marital rights, he could not now go to the courts to take recourse.

Although in the end the court refused to apply Section 497 in this case, it still relied on evidence that the husband accommodated the relationship, almost as if he inadvertently released his wife from his dominion. And the law to this day is still enforced in Pakistan. The crime of adultery was eventually enhanced in 1979 with the Islamization of Pakistan's laws. In particular, the Section 497 part of the code was renamed "The Offence of Zina (Enforcement of Hudood) Ordinance (VII of 1979)" and defined as fornication, adultery, and *zina bil jabbar* (rape). For *zina liable to had*, otherwise known as adultery, the punishment originally found in Section 497, which was punishable by imprisonment of up to five years and a fine under the Hudood laws, was now subject to death by stoning for the adulterer and public whipping of 100 lashes for a fornicator. Moreover, the ordinance made it exceptionally difficult and dangerous to prove an allegation of rape. As a result, in 1979, before the ordinances went into effect, there were 70 women held in Pakistani prisons. By 1988, there were 6,000 (Ashfaq, 2006). According to a 2015 report by the Asian Development Bank, "There is considerable evidence that this legislation has negatively impacted Pakistani women's lives and made them more vulnerable to extreme violence. Today, the majority of women in prison have been charged under the Hudood Ordinance" (ADB, 2015, p. 11). Many times, while men escape the charge for adultery, in the same cases, women are convicted for fornication.

One could argue that the situation in Bangladesh is moving in a different direction. As illustrated in the *Nurul Huq v. Bibi Sakina* case in the introduction, Section 497 was never modified in Bangladesh's Penal Code and remains in force to this day. At the same time, however, some of these laws, or the concepts that are essential to these laws – such as marriage – have been interpreted to enhance women's rights. In *Mst. Momtaz Begum vs. Anowar Hossain*, [2011] 40 CLCAD 5522, Momtaz Begum took Anowar Hossain to court with a claim of dower money and maintenance. She claimed that despite a failure to register their marriage, they had been living together, and the marriage was consummated accordingly. Having considered the fact of their "living together," the trial court (Family Court) presumed a marriage between them and decreed the suit. The High Court, the first appellate bench of the SCB, however, rejected the trial court's decision with a suggestion that "mere living together did not bring her within the bounds of marriage." Moreover, the HCD considered it adultery. Momtaz Begum eventually appealed her case to the Appellate Division (AD), the court of final appeal in Bangladesh. Reversing the High Court, it opined that the High Court could have presumed the marriage from the facts instead of relying overwhelmingly on the definition of marriage under Islamic law. It further observed that no religious ceremony is required to contract a valid Muslim marriage, and if there is continuous cohabitation between a man and a woman as husband and wife, there is a presumptive marriage if they are not under prohibited degree. In addition, the SCB suggested that marriage resulted in a "relation arising out of permanent contract for sexual intercourse and procreation of children between the parties to the marriage." Thus, while marriage is still key in the assumption of rights, and cohabitation and man's control over the woman is still examined, these factors have been interpreted loosely to impute responsibility when women are purportedly wronged.

Legal observers saw this as a win for woman's rights, with one newspaper article entitled "An Incentive to Promote Women's Rights" stating,

> As a consequence of this newly introduced and established doctrine the underprivileged women of our country will have access to the rights like the confirmation of *Mahr* (dower), the establishment of descent or paternity, the necessity for the wife observing *iddat* (required waiting period before marriage after divorce or widowhood), [and] the wife's right to maintenance and residence during iddat.
>
> (Abrar, 2014)

The same author has elsewhere written piece that discussed how the law served as "a contemporary and classical doctrine to promote and ensure women's rights" (Abrar, no date). Lastly, it has been argued that the judgment of the Supreme Court of Bangladesh in *Momtaz Begum vs. Anowar Hossain* can be considered an endeavor to widen the scope of marriage in order to accommodate sexual desire of a large number of people and to protect women from deception and offspring from being born out of wedlock (Rahman, in progress). Furthermore, the case also demonstrates a continuity of the legal orientalist visions of Islamic law by relying heavily on Privy Council definitions of marriage (ibid.).

Conclusion

The review of cases in this chapter suggests that in British India adultery was a channel to establish domination of the husband over the wife, and in doing so, it turned women into chattel upon which a violation constituted a tort against its owner, the husband. In this regard, women become the quintessential subalterns whose bodies and sexuality do not belong to them, are subject to control or discipline, and are only relevant when necessary to determine whether an offense took place against a husband. Kecia Ali (2010) argues that legitimacy of women's sexuality within male control and man's licit sexual intercourse in the beneath of his absolute control and domination. "Women's sexuality," she argues, "was licit only within the confines of man's control, and a man's sexual activity was licit only with women over whom he had exclusive domination" (Ali, 2010, p. 190). Furthermore, this arrangement was not the product of an oppressive religious regime but rather emerges through a confluence of tradition, foreign interpretations of Islam, and the finality of entrenching such concepts in the law. It is from here, that postcolonial states such as Pakistan and Bangladesh build their jurisprudence – either relying on an arguably legally orientalist interpretation of Islam to "liberate" women, as in Bangladesh, or enhancing such entrenched laws through the Hudood as seen in Pakistan.

The genealogy of criminalizing consensual sexual relationships between a man and the wife of another man shows that adultery laws are not simply an imposition of Victorian sexual morality of licit and illicit sexual relationship. Adultery laws in South Asia were not the product of legal universalism alone – laws on adultery emerged out of political compromise, economic efficiency, and legal orientalism. Through the institution of the law, they become entrenched and form important categories that affect the intimate lives of the family. Controlling women's sexuality becomes essential to the definition of who is a "wife," a "legitimate" mother, or an equal partner worthy of the rights and protections of the law. At the same time, its boundaries exclude women who refuse to surrender full control of their bodies, such as concubines or prostitutes. While things are changing in the Islamic nations of Pakistan and Bangladesh, these colonial categories still define the scope of such change – whether through reliance on the institution of marriage or enhancing punishments to fend off changes to it. Thus, the influences of the past are strong and everlasting, while the rights of citizens today rely on their incremental change.

Notes

1 Following the Hastings's Plan of 1772, a significant change was introduced in the administration of the justice system. A court of a civil nature, such as the *Diwani Adalat,* and a court of a criminal nature, for example, the *Nizamat Adalat*, was established in each *collectorate* being presided over by the *diwan* (collector) in the former case, and by the *qazi* – subject to the supervision of the collector – in the latter case. The chief civil court, the *Sadar Diwani Adalat*, was presided over by the governor general and council, and the chief criminal court, the *Sadar Nizamat Adalat*, was presided over by a *Darogah Adalat.* In 1774, the Supreme Court was established in India to protect Indians from sufferings caused by the company officials as well as from the tyranny of the company government. It was replaced by the High Courts in 1861. From these High Courts, appeals were passed on to the Privy Council. Therefore, the judicial reorganization ended up with the Privy Council as the final legal authority in British India with jurisdiction. The Judicial Committee of the Privy Council, which was established by an act of Parliament in 1833, was the highest court in India until January 1950. It was presided over by the same judges who heard appeals in the House of Lords. The Privy Council did not pronounce a judgment, but instead, it merely advised the Crown to give a ruling on a particular issue.

2 With the words "permanent cohabitation," the British courts in India implied a sexual relationship between a man and a woman, where the latter was unable to go outside the house. In other words, it presupposed a continuous possession over the body of the woman.

References

Cases

Abdul Samad v. Mohammad Ramzan [1946] 33 A.I.R, Nagpur 393.
Ali Newaz Gardezi v. Muhammad Yusuf [1963] PLD, SC, 55.
Ashrufood Dowlah v. Hyder Hossein [1866] UKPC 35.
Aziz Khan v. Ekram Hussain case, A.I.R. [1937].
Gul Mohammad v. Emperor, A.I.R. [1946] 121.
Jariut-ool-Butool v. Hosseinee Begum [1867] UKPC 6.
Nurul Huq v. Bibi Sakina, Lex/BDHC/0053/1985/Manupatra.
Mist. Momtaz Begum v. Anwar Hossain [2011] 40 CLCAD, 5522.

Books and articles

Abrar, M.S. (no date), 'Presumption of Marriage in Muslim Family Law: A Contemporary and Classical Doctrine to Promote and Ensure Women's Rights,' uploaded to Academia.edu. Available at: www.academia.edu/10695375/Presumption_of_Marriage_in_Muslim_Family_law_A_contemporary_and_classical_doctrine_to_promote_and_ensure_women_s_rights

Abrar, M.S. (2014) 'An Incentive to Promote Women's Rights,' *Daily Star* (Bangladesh), 28 January.

Ali, K. (2010) *Marriage and Slavery in Early Islam*. Cambridge, MA: Harvard University Press.

Ashfaq, A. (2006) 'Voices from Prison and a Call for Repeal: The Hudood Laws of Pakistan,' *New Politics*, 10 (4).

Asian Development Bank (ADB) (2015) 'Women in Pakistan,' Country Briefing Paper, 19 April.

Bureau of Education (1965) *Selections from Educational Records, Part I (1781–1839)*. Edited by H. Sharp. Calcutta: Superintendent, Government Printing, 1920. Reprint. Delhi: National Archives of India, pp. 107–117.

Chatterjee, I. (1999) *Gender, Slavery and Law in Colonial India*. New Delhi: Oxford University Press.

Clerk, J. F. and Lindsell, W. H. B. (1848–1898 [1937]) *Clerk and Lindsell on Torts*, 9th ed./ under the general editorship of Harold Potter. Edited by C. Odgers . . . [et al.]. London: Sweet & Maxwell.

Foucault, M. (1978) *History of Sexuality: An Introduction*. New York: Penguin.

Hyam, R. (1990) *Empire and Sexuality: The British Experience*. Manchester: Manchester University Press.

Lawson, A. (1988) *Adultery: An Analysis of Love and Betrayal*. New York: Basic Books.

Menon, N. (1999) *Gender and Politics in India*. New York: Oxford University Press.

Rahman, A. (In Progress) 'Regulating Sexuality through Legitimizing Marriage and Children in Bangladesh,' Manuscript with author.

Rudolph, S. H. and Rudolph, L. I. (2000) 'Living with Difference in India,' *The Political Quarterly*, 71, pp. 20–38.

Ruskola, T. (2013) *Legal Orientalism: China, the United States, and Modern Law*. Cambridge, MA: Harvard University Press.

Said, E. (1994) *Orientalism*. New York: Penguin.

Singha, R. (1998) *A Despotism of Law: Crime and Justice in Early Colonial India*. New Delhi: Oxford University Press.

Spivak, G. (1988) 'Can the Subaltern Speak?,' Reprinted in Nelson, C. and Grossberg, L. (eds.). *Marxist Interpretations of Culture*. New York: MacMillan, pp. 271–313.

Stoler, A. L. (1995) *Race and the Education of Desire: Foucault's History of Sexuality and the Colonial Order of Things*. Durham: Duke University Press.

Chapter 2

"First world problems" in the "third world"?

LGBT rights in Singapore

George Radics

Introduction

Singapore's founding prime minister Lee Kuan Yew in his memoir *From Third World to First: The Singapore Story* discussed how the former British colonial trading post became transformed into a global metropolis with the world's busiest port of trade and the fourth highest per capita real income that today is consistently ranked among the top-ten nations in the United Nation's Human Development Index. This transformation arguably is a result of Singapore's dedication to free and open markets, making it one of the most "globalized" nations on earth. While economically, the nation remains open, politically and socially, Singapore is somewhat conservative. In the 1990s, Lee Kuan Yew championed the "Asian values" discourse, which argued that individual political rights were unnecessary luxuries that should come after the rights of the community, the economy, and the state. Thus, while economically, the nation flourishes, many minorities suffer in silence as majoritarian and neoliberal economic policies dominate the social landscape, with incremental progressive developments taking place when such policies affect the financial well-being of the nation. The LGBT community, in particular, serves as a perfect example of a minority group whose rights ebb and flow with the political and economic conditions of the nation. Moreover, as Singapore's economy continues to grow, the purchasing power and global outlook of gay and straight Singaporeans alike is beginning to clash with those who cling to the "Asian values" rhetoric. Here, the argument that LGBT rights are human rights is depicted as the "political claims of a narrow interest group masquerading as legal entitlements" pursued by those who "seek to copy the sexual libertine ethos of the wild West" (Thio, 2007, p. 2242). While Singapore is not typically considered a part of the Global South, this chapter highlights how the nation's position in the Global South explains its complicated relationship with LGBT rights and how its wealth and development are part of the reason Singapore serves as a unique case study for this volume.

In spite of its global status as a cosmopolitan and developed nation, Singapore is among the minority of countries that still criminalize homosexuality.

Section 377A of its Penal Code criminalizes sodomy between men, introducing a whole set of problems for the nation's multiracial and multireligious LGBT community. To understand the conditions behind Section 377A, this chapter will first review the historical conditions found in Singapore and how these conditions shaped attitudes toward LGBT rights. It will then move on to explore the country's unique conditions, such as its emphasis on economic security over political freedom, reaction against the West through emphasizing "Asian values," and status as a wealthy, cosmopolitan, and multicultural society. In the final section, the chapter will briefly discuss how access to new technology may complicate traditional family configurations, challenging Singapore's conservative views, particularly as it pertains to gay parenting. It will also discuss the intersectionality of race, class, and minorities within the LGBT community by examining the impact of Section 377A on gay Malays and transgender Singaporeans.

Criminalization of homosexuality in Singapore

LGBT organizations in the North can be traced to as far back as Weimar Germany, though their real influence began to spread after World War II (*see* Bauer, 2017). While LGBT organizations initially pursued relatively conservative agendas, continued repression spurred radicalization by the 1960s (Weiss, 2007). The changing social context in Euro-America provided space for assertive, proactive, and even militant LGBT organizations to thrive, while also allowing more conservative, or self-described "pragmatic" organizations, to entrench themselves in the political center, seeking and winning many policy and legal reforms (Faderman, 2015). By the end of the 1970s and early 1980s, much of the Global North celebrated Gay Pride events initially commemorating the iconic Stonewall riots in New York and eventually celebrating gay social movements more generally. Although the expansion of LGBT rights in other nations of the Global North may have been a response to local conditions, their emergence happened in tandem with, or immediately before or after, the United States. This is perhaps because many of the conditions were similar: the postwar baby boom, a growing cultural revolution, or shifting sentiments against heavy-handed efforts by the church or state to enforce outdated social mores (May, 1988; Edsall, 2003). This was not, however, the story that Global South nations like Singapore experienced.

One of the major differences between the Global North and the Global South was the former's colonization over the latter. Criminalization of homosexual relations and non-cisnormative behaviors was one of the lasting legacies of colonial rule, with the roots of Singapore's criminalization of homosexuality tracing back to the British. Beginning in 1861, the British passed Section 377 of the Indian Penal Code prohibiting sexual activities "against the order of nature" – a law that ultimately reached much of its empire and was only struck down by the Supreme Court of India in September 2018 (*Navtej Singh Johar v.*

Union of India, W.P [Crl.] No. 76 of 2016). In Singapore's case, for reasons still debated, in 1938, the Straits colonies enacted Section 377A of the Penal Code, a subsection and derivative of Section 377 of the Indian Penal Code of 1860 (*see* Radics, 2013, pp. 60–64). Section 377A was based on Section 11 of the Criminal Law Amendment Act 1885 (United Kingdom), otherwise known as the Labouchere Amendment, a law that criminalized sodomy between men, but was removed from the criminal code in 1967. By the time the United Kingdom repealed Section 11, Singapore was an independent nation grappling with serious problems such as expulsion from Malaysia, interracial violence, and a struggling economy – all issues that prevented it from reviewing the provisions within its own criminal code. It was not until the 1980s that Section 377A was back in the limelight with the raiding of gay bars and arrests of men in gay cruising areas through entrapment. In 2007, when Section 377 of the Singaporean Penal Code was reviewed by Parliament for removal, Section 377A received serious attention and debate. Ultimately, Section 377 was repealed and Section 377A was retained. The law was challenged again in 2010, this time in the courts, but the challenge was shot down and the law was retained.

In defending the ongoing criminalization of homosexuality, the government falls back on the argument that Singapore is a "conservative" society, uninterested in the LGBT rights of the "wild wild West." Yet this overly simplified explanation obfuscates a much deeper and more complex situation behind the criminalization of homosexuality in Singapore. This chapter will explore LGBT rights in Singapore along the themes of 1) economic security over political freedom, 2) responding to Western pressures through the "Asian values" discourse, and 3) globalization, cosmopolitanism, and multiculturalism.

Economic security over political freedom

At the end of World War II, after over 140 years of British rule, colonial Malaya was granted its independence in 1963, with Singapore splitting from Malaysia two years later. This was a challenging period for Singapore. In 1965, it was a tiny city-state expelled from its larger neighbor, reliant on a few staples of production with an inconsiderable local market and a swelling immigrant population. To survive, Singapore ruthlessly pursued economic growth "over all else" and was considered a "developmental state," or a nation that relied on state-led macroeconomc planning (Pereira, 2008). The nation became obsessed with development, relying on the tools of control left behind by the British to organize and discipline its diverse population. Strict labor legislation and control of trade unions made the island a source of cheap labor. To fast-track decision making, political dissent was restricted, the media was rigorously regulated, and the branches of government were streamlined. The People's Action Party, the ruling party since independence, pursued free-market principles to encourage competition and to assuage its ethnically diverse population by indicating that merit, and not background, would determine one's worth in the new society. To this end, Stewart Chang describes Singapore's "exceptional" status as a nation different from the West for being an "independently successful Asian country that was able to evolve differently from the liberal democratic model" and different from the region because it is "more developed than other nations in the region [and because it achieved] this exceptional standing [through] its embrace of Western capitalism" (Chang, 2016, p. 77).

In this context, economic growth was prioritized over political freedom. According to Cherian George, "Put simply, no existing state can match [Singapore's] record of political stability combined with high standards of socio-economic development" (George, 2007). He adds, however, that even though Singapore is among the top-ten, most-developed countries in the world, on a scale from 1 to 7, it receives a "4," in Freedom House's rating of civil liberties and is the only developed nation not rated "1" (George, 2017). More disparagingly, Jothie Rajah argues that Singapore is a nation that experiences "rule by law" as opposed to "rule of law." Through the Vandalism Act, the Press Act, the 1986 amendments to the Legal Profession Act, the Religious Harmony Act, and the Public Order Act, Rajah argues that in Singapore, "the courts have been constrained, civil society dismantled, and basic legal freedoms disregarded" (Rajah, 2012, p. 14). Chua Beng Huat adds that there are other laws that stifle free speech, such as the Internal Security Act, which provides the government the power to detain and interrogate those considered a national threat, and the Societies Act that delimits "political" activities narrowly to the purview of political parties (Chua, 2002). Thus, unlike in the West, where the 1960s and 1970s led to an expansion of political and civil rights, in Singapore, due to its desire to expedite economic growth, British laws that were meant to control the colony were utilized and enhanced from independence to the present to restrict political freedoms.

Since political activism was severely restricted, and sexual expression was considered less important than economic issues, rights for LGBT people were rarely demanded. Homosexuality was deemed immoral and subject to shame, or simply ignored, rather than acknowledged, let alone celebrated. When Section 377A of the Penal Code was adopted in 1938, a number of high-profile cases made the front-page news within a year of the law's implementation (see Radics, 2013). Interest in the matter waned, however, as the region became drawn into war. By the 1980s, after Singaporeans had experienced over a decade of rapid economic growth, society was less consumed with hand-to-mouth issues. Political crises had subsided, and the wars in Southeast Asia were over. Because the government became concerned that Singaporean values were becoming wayward due to the influx of wealth and new vices, homosexuality became an issue again, with the government intervening with a heavy hand. According to Wai-Teng Leong (1997), from the early 1980s to the 1990s, arrests for homosexual activities increased and were procured through entrapment. Since Section 377A involves two willing parties, men arrested for "homosexual acts" with undercover agents were mostly tried under Section 354 (molest or outrage of modesty). Punishment for this offense ranged from two to six months imprisonment and three strokes of the cane. Section 294(a) of the Penal Code was also used. Originally meant to be used for "obscene songs," it was wide enough to include the commission of any obscene act in any public place to the annoyance of others, such as a person using a gesture to proposition sex. Fines under this section ranged between S$200–S$800. Moreover, to further shame those caught, their names, professions, and ages were published in the local newspapers.

i. An opening for change – Rascals bar raid

While troubling, the oppressive situation also provided opportunities for change, leading to Singapore's "Stonewall" moment. In addition to targeting popular "cruising" areas in the 1990s, police also frequently raided gay businesses. On 30 May 1993, the police raided a disco called Rascals on Beach Road in an area where many popular gay bars and clubs were located. That evening, a plainclothes police officer demanded that the crowd "shut up!" and threatened to beat them. All patrons were instructed to produce their identification documents, and those who did not carry their IDs with them were hauled to the police station and made to squat outside. The next morning, everyone was released without charge. Outraged by this situation, a young lawyer wrote to the police stating, "It is particularly disturbing to find Singapore law enforcement officers behaving rudely towards and verbally threatening citizens who have not committed any offenses" (Chua, 2014, p. 4).

After a month, the young lawyer received a phone call from the assistant superintendent of the Beach Road police station stating that internal trainings had taken place and assuring him that what happened at Rascals would not happen again. Afterward, an official letter was sent to the lawyer stating that there were complaints of overcrowding and false IDs being used and that the measures taken that evening were meant to address such complaints. The letter was also apologetic for the "lack of tact in dealing with the situation" (Chua, 2014, p. 5). The civil exchange between the parties provided hope to the nascent community of gay organizers that they could negotiate with the government, and out of this period, community-based education, forums, and other community building activities began to emerge. What transpired at Rascals that evening, according to Lynette Chua, is "often hail[ed] . . . as Singapore's Stonewall . . . galvanizing a fledgling gay movement that was quietly taking shape in the early 1990s" (Chua 2014, p. 3).

ii. Pragmatic resistance

In a nation where political voice is exchanged for economic well-being, change happens slowly, trepidatiously, and organically – providing scholars of social movements a unique case study of how change happens in a mostly functional and paternalistic authoritarian government. Although a "Stonewall" moment, the Rascals incident was not a direct result of the events in New York City 35 years earlier, nor were foreign parties involved. Instead, Rascals constituted a strategic rupture in which political activists saw an opening for change, seized it, but were very careful never to break any of the numerous laws discussed earlier. Given Singapore's unique political situation, Lynette Chua (2012) argues that LGBT activists in the country must engage in "pragmatic resistance." Pragmatic resistance requires the four steps of "strategic adaptation," which are that actors 1) remain nonconfrontational, allowing the government to decide without forcing both parties into a winner-take-all scenario; 2) preserve social stability, never challenging society head on; 3) perpetuate the ruling party by deferring to its authority; and, finally, 4) preserve their own legal legitimacy by never breaking the law. While this may seem depressingly slow and feeble, the approach shifts the attention of law and society and social movement studies away from overt and public forms of collective mobilization in Western liberal democracies onto alternative forms of strategies and tactics. Moreover, although the approach reinforces the existing power arrangement, it also allows for the coexistence of the organizations that advocate for the repeal of 377A, Pink Dot SG (an event akin to Gay Pride); a gay community library with year-round social events; and an openly gay counseling center that occupies the second floor of a shophouse in Singapore's significant historical and cultural enclave of Chinatown (Chua, 2012, p. 742).

Although the government refuses to endorse these LGBT groups, it allows them to exist; and instead of intentionally restricting the rights of LGBT people, it is simply upholding the traditional values and beliefs of a conservative "Asian" society. "Asian values" were proclaimed as a justification for the political arrangement in this section. As we will see in the next section, it also serves as the justification behind Section 377A of the Penal Code, as well as for exercising restrictions on Singapore's Pink Dot.

Protecting society from the "evil" West: Asian values

By the 1990s, the changing patterns of consumption, rise of nontraditional lifestyle choices, and the development of new expectations on the government all brought about by two decades of rapid development and the increasing socioeconomic status of Singaporeans led some to believe that the nation was experiencing a period of moral degradation. As a result, government elites began to champion "Asian values" as an alternative development model to Western liberal democracies. "Asian values" emphasize the shift from a focus on democracy, to one of social discipline, as the precursor for economic growth (Thompson, 2004). This had profound effects, transforming an obsession with development to an obsession with preserving cultural values. Combined with the fear of AIDS, the government took a harsher stance on "divergent" and "Western" values – such as same-sex relationships (Leong, 1997). Moreover, "Asian values" were invoked as a form of developmentalism in Southeast Asia, with the claim that until prosperity is achieved, democracy remains an unaffordable luxury. This Protestant-ethic-like form of "Asian values" attributed high growth rates to hard work, frugality, discipline, and teamwork that only a "disciplined" regime could provide during the early stages of development. "Asian values" also underscore the legitimacy of cultural particularism, which informs the understanding of human rights within a neo-communitarian context, where group interests trump individual rights and consensus, and harmony is valorized over contention and potential destabilization (see Chang, 2014, pp. 320–321).

Ultimately, however, the government's goal of economic development clashed with its newly constructed discourse of "Asian values." Although discipline and order may have been required in an industrializing economy of the 20th century, to remain competitive in the creative economy of the 21st century, the government had to ease restrictions. As a result, by the early 2000s, the state became more tolerant of same-sex relations, and certain privileges afforded to all citizens were suddenly afforded to lesbians, gays, and bisexuals. Plays that had been banned for having gay characters were now being shown, with some of the playwrights even being commissioned by the government to raise awareness of issues affecting the gay community, such as HIV/AIDS. Although the government withdrew its support of these commissioned plays for depicting homosexuality as "normal," the theater movement continued to produce plays that addressed gay issues in Singapore (Lim, 2005). By the early 2000s, the government began to express an increasingly tolerant approach to same-sex relations by announcing that gays would be allowed to work in the civil service (Tan, 2009). Such advances demonstrated Singapore's attempt to pragmatically give its image a "makeover" from its previous persona of a straitlaced and disciplined society, to one that was more creative, open, and diverse. While this loosening up provided spaces for change, conservative "Asian values" were used as a check on rapid societal transformations all under the guise of protecting Singapore from the evils of Western moral degradation.

i. Pink Dot SG

As part of the government's attempt to reinvent itself as a more open society, in 2000, it created the "Speaker's Corner" in Hong Lim Park, a space where citizens could apply for a permit to express their views. By 2008, rules were relaxed further to allow for preapproved public demonstrations by Singaporean citizens and permanent residents. At this time, gay organizers began to consider the idea of bringing something similar to Gay Pride to Singapore. In 2009, Pink Dot was established to provide gay and straight participants a site to congregate and wear pink to show their support of the LGBT community in Singapore.

In 2009, it was reported that approximately 2,500 people participated to show their support: the largest number of people to ever congregate in Hong Lim Park since Speaker's Corner was launched (PinkDot.sg, 2015). By 2015, the number of participants increased more than tenfold to 28,000 individuals (ibid.). Pink Dot has gained international attention and sponsorship from major corporations such as Twitter, Cathay Cinemas, Bloomberg, Google, UK banking group Barclays, and US bank Goldman Sachs. Though Pink Dot became an important success, resistance to the event has grown as well. In 2014, Singapore's minister for social and family development, Chan Chun Sing, publicly reprimanded Goldman Sachs for its support for LGBT matters in Singapore. He is quoted as saying, "Singapore and Singaporeans will decide on the norms for our society. Foreign companies here should respect local culture and context" (Tan, 2015). Moreover, various religious communities encouraged their constituents to wear white in protest of Pink Dot and to stand in solidarity with "traditional family values" (Ng, 2014).

In 2017, the government made amendments to the Public Order Act (Chapter 257A, 2012 Reprint) to ban foreigner participation in political events, particularly those to be held at Speaker's Corner, such as Pink Dot. In particular, the proposed change in Section 7 states,

> (2). The Commissioner may refuse to grant a permit for a public assembly or public procession in respect of which notice under section 6 has been given if he has reasonable ground for apprehending that the proposed assembly or procession may –
>
> . . . .
>
> (*h*) be directed toward a political end and be organized by, or involve the participation of, any of the following persons:
>
> (i) an entity that is not a Singapore entity;
> (ii) an individual who is not a citizen of Singapore.

While discussing the changes, Minister of Law K. Shanmugam added, "These amendments do not impact on Singaporeans. These are directed at foreigners and foreign entities" (Public Order Act [POA] Debates, 2017). Nominated member of Parliament Kok Heng Leun expressed his concerns regarding the proposed changes stating, "The new amendments have the potential to incite more fear and create more barriers for civil society to engage with foreign experts" (ibid.). He added,

> We should also not inhibit concerned individuals or civil society from initiating engagement. Bottom up is not always a bad thing. It is time for the Government to trust its people. Let Singaporeans strive to find solutions for important issues without Government interference.
>
> (ibid.)

Member of Parliament Louis Ng added, "With society evolving, topics that were once deemed contentious or taboo have, with time, become necessary conversations. Who decides when a matter becomes a matter of public controversy?" (ibid.).

In response, Mr. Shanmugam stated,

> The key condition [for denying a permit is that the] event is not being organised by a Singapore entity or individuals who are not citizens of Singapore. Essentially, foreign involvement. Now, what has that got to do with bottomup, topdown trust in citizenry, empowered citizenship?
>
> (ibid.)

He added, regarding LGBT issues, "The Government is neutral on this point. . . . But whether it is pro-LGBT or opposing LGBT, it is a matter for Singaporeans to decide" (ibid.). While Pink Dot organizers were able to raise local sponsorship from 5 local businesses in 2016 to over 100 in 2017, human rights activist Jolovan Wham stated, "We are influenced by foreign ideas and cultures all the time. . . . The Government is worried about the expansion of our civil and political space" (Kok, 2016a). Leow Yangfa, executive director of LGBT counseling group Oogachaga, saw the move as a clampdown on LGBT groups and is worried that companies may become reluctant to support LGBT groups in the future (ibid.).

ii. Judicial challenge to 377A

In 2007, after nearly 140 years, Section 377 of the Penal Code regarding the criminalization of "carnal intercourse against the order of nature" was repealed. Its repeal was the product of overwhelming support from society, which interpreted Section 377 as antiquated and no longer representing the values of modern Singapore. Attempts to repeal Section 377A, the provision that specifically criminalizes gay male sex, however, did not receive the same support. Member of Parliament Siew Kum Hong submitted a public petition signed by 2,519 Singaporeans who wanted 377A repealed and presented a stirring speech requesting that members of Parliament vote against the Penal Code (Amendment) Bill, which repealed 377 and retained Section 377A (Radics, 2013, p. 80). However, over 15,560 Singaporeans signed a petition to retain Section 377A, and in the end, Parliament decided to maintain Section 377A to placate "conservative" Singaporeans (ibid.). Addressing Parliament, Prime Minister Lee Hsien Loong stated,

> Among the conservative Singaporeans, the deep concerns over the moral values of society will remain and, among the gay rights' activists, abolition is not going to give them what they want because what they want is not just to be freed from section 377A, but more space and full acceptance by other Singaporeans. . . . And when it comes to these issues, the majority of Singaporeans will strenuously oppose these follow-up moves

> by the gay campaigners and many who are not anti-gay will be against this agenda, and I think for good reason.
>
> (Lee, 2007: Line 2397)

Section 377A, therefore, remained in force while Section 377 was repealed. Prime Minister Lee, however, noted in his speech, "There are gay bars and clubs. . . . The Government does not act as moral policemen. And we do not proactively enforce section 377A" (Radics, 2013, p. 81). Therefore, Section 377A was to be, in effect, an "unenforced" offense.

Prime Minister Lee Hsien Loong's words were put to the test just three years later. On 9 March 2010, Tan Eng Hong was found committing an act of "gross indecency" in a public restroom and was charged under 377A of the Penal Code. Tan felt that he had been treated unjustly because of his sexuality. He resented the fact that he was handcuffed and placed in jail for an act between two consenting adults, causing harm to no one (Radics, 2013, p. 82). While the other man he was caught with refused to challenge the law, and much of the gay community chastised Tan for taking on the case, he approached prominent human rights attorney M. Ravi and decided to challenge the constitutionality of Section 377A.

In September 2010, Tan filed suit, arguing that Section 377A was inconsistent with Singapore's constitutional provisions regarding liberty, equal protection, and freedom of association (*Tan Eng Hong v. Attorney General*, [2011] SGHC 56). State counsel for the attorney general informed Tan that the charge against him had been amended to a charge of public obscenity under Section 294(a) of the Penal Code and then moved to dismiss Tan's suit. The case was dismissed.

In June 2011, Tan appealed all the way to the Court of Appeal, Singapore's highest court. Reversing the High Court, the Court of Appeal held that every constitutional right is a personal right and that a "violation of constitutional rights *may* be brought about by the very existence of an allegedly unconstitutional law in the statute books . . . and/or by a real and credible threat of prosecution under an allegedly unconstitutional law" (*Tan Eng Hong*, [2012] SGCA 45, at [115]). The Court further found that Tan's case should not have been thrown out because Section 377A is arguably inconsistent with Singapore's constitutional guarantees of equal protection under the law. The Court of Appeal's judgment in *Tan Eng Hong v. Attorney General* was a landmark decision. It declared that a person can challenge legislation for being in violation of a constitutional right and opened the door for Singaporeans who were personally affected by unconstitutional laws to file suit even without being prosecuted under the law. The case was then sent back to the High Court to determine whether 377A was inconsistent with the equal protection provision of the Constitution.

After the court opened the door for all Singaporeans to challenge unconstitutional laws, a gay couple, Lim Meng Suang and Kenneth Chee Mun-Leon, filed suit seeking a declaration that Section 377A of the Penal Code was unconstitutional. They argued that on the basis of being in a romantic and sexual relationship for the past 15 years, they were affected by the law and therefore could challenge it (*Lim Meng Suang and another v. Attorney General*, [2013] SGHC 73). In a separate hearing, Tan also presented his arguments at the High Court (*Tan Eng Hong v. Attorney General*, [2013] SGHC 199). Justice Quentin Loh of the High Court ultimately ruled against both parties, and in July 2014, the Court of Appeal heard both appeals in a consolidated review.

The Court of Appeal affirmed the rulings of the High Court (*Lim Meng Suang and another v Attorney General and another appeal and another matter*, [2014] SGCA 53). In affirming the High Court, the Court of Appeal focused on arguments concerning the deprivation of liberty (Article 9 of the Constitution Republic of Singapore [1999 Reprint]) and that it violates constitutionally provided equal protections under the law (Article 12). The Court held that Article 9 mainly pertains to capital punishment and incarceration. The Court added that the law is not invalid for being excessively vague since the language is clear: sexual acts between males are criminal. In addressing the equal protection clause, the Court found that the purpose of the law was to prosecute gay male acts generally and that while Section 377 covered "carnal intercourse against the order of nature," 377A took this a step further to include the lesser offense of "gross indecency," which, in effect, broadened the scope of criminal activity. Lastly, the law was meant to enforce "morals of the community" by targeting acts that were deemed particularly offensive, such as gay male sex, and prohibiting such activities not only in public but also in private. Ultimately, the Court held that the law was constitutional, and it was up to the legislature to determine whether the offense should be abolished.

Multiculturalism, modernity, and cosmopolitanism

As can be expected, many were disappointed with the Court's decision. LGBT organizations in Singapore issued a joint statement expressing their discontent and declared, "We are greatly shocked and disappointed by the Court of Appeal's ruling" (Joint Statement, 2014). They added, "While we appreciate the Court's position that it cannot assist in providing a judicial remedy to what it views as a legislative issue, we cannot accept its narrow interpretation of the constitution in this regard" (ibid.). The Association of Women for Action and Research (AWARE) focused on the Court's narrow interpretation of the equal protection clause, asserting that the Court's decision not only deprived the gay community of constitutional protections but also may have violated Singapore's legal obligations under the Convention on the Elimination of All Forms of Discrimination Against Women (CEDAW) since a narrow interpretation may also exclude women who are not explicitly a protected class under that clause of the constitution (Goh, 2014). What these views demonstrate is that in spite of a very strong state that restricts channels of free speech, civil society continues to assert its voice and challenge the status quo – a status quo the government refuses to change, even if it is out of synch with Singapore's past and rapidly changing present.

While the Singapore government fiercely protects certain rights of religious and racial minorities, LGBT issues are still considered politically sensitive topics that the government refuses to take a position on. However, Southeast Asia has always experienced porous sexual categories, and as late as the 1970s, Singapore served as the first and most advanced country in Asia to conduct sexual reassignment surgery. This final section will discuss the unique situation Singapore finds itself in as a diverse nation with a history of sexual diversity, grappling to cling to "traditional" values when Singapore's cosmopolitan nature is allowing its LGBT community access to assistive reproductive technology, and when its own past is more in line with practices found in the "West." It will first review the recent *Re UKM* [2018] SGFC 20 in which a gay man was denied the right to adopt a child he fathered through surrogacy and *in vitro* fertilization services (IVF) in the United States. Up to this point in this chapter, much of the discussion has been about Chinese gay males given the fact that the Chinese are the predominant ethnic group in Singapore and that the legal restrictions target gay men. The final section will therefore conclude with a discussion on the situation for minorities among the LGBT community, such as gay Muslims and transgender people.

i. Access to assistive reproductive technology

A consequence of Singapore's advanced development is the facility and access to advanced technologies that have the potential to go beyond traditional conception methods. Such technology can allow the unmarried and those who cannot conceive the opportunity to raise a child of their own genetic makeup. In anticipation of such technology, the government passed the Status of Children (Assisted Reproduction Technology) Act (Chapter 317a) to address this issue. The law, however, is complicated by the fact that such technology runs afoul of Singapore's policy to promote children only within wedlock, as well as its policy against same-sex partnerships. In 2013, before the enactment of the law in 2014, a gay medical doctor and his partner of 13 years were able to give birth to a son through IVF and surrogacy. Upon birth, the child attained US citizenship, with the surrogate and her partner relinquishing all rights to the child. Shortly after the child's birth, the gay couple returned home to Singapore and applied for Singaporean citizenship for their child, but the application was denied after eight months. The doctor then pursued adoption to give him sole rights and responsibility to the child and to remove the child's "illegitimate" label under Singaporean law. The couple also did this in hopes that that this would make it easier for the child to receive Singapore citizenship. Their application was denied after six months, with the director of social welfare in her role as guardian-in adoption (GIA) stating that it was the position of Singaporean public policy that parenthood is encouraged within marriage, as it is within the interest of the child to grow up with a mother and a father. The GIA added that gay marriage is not allowed in Singapore and that it would be contrary to public policy to allow for the adoption of a child when the applicant is in a same-sex relationship. The doctor and his partner appealed the GIA's decision.

Judge Shobha Nair of the Family Court issued her ruling the day after Christmas, dismissing the couple's appeal. In her written opinion, released in March, she relied on the government's policy of not recognizing same-sex partnerships and stated,

> This application is in reality an attempt to obtain a desired result – that is, formalizing the parent-child relationship in order to obtain certain benefits such as citizenship rights, by walking through the back door of the system when the front door was firmly shut.
>
> (*Re UKM*, at [33])

On appeal, although the Court of Appeal acknowledged that "the government is opposed to the advancement of any right claimed by a homosexual for the purpose of forming a same-sex family unit" (*UKM v Attorney General*, at [202]), Justice Menon reversed the Family Court after a lengthy discussion on balancing the welfare of the child against the government's stated policy. The Court found that allowing the adoption in this case facilitated citizenship and all the rights attached, including intestacy. Justice Menon was careful to point out that "our decision is a decision on the particular facts of this case, and should not be taken as an endorsement of what the appellant and his partner set out to do" (*UKM v Attorney General*, at [249]).

With the advent of new reproductive technology, and Singaporean access to it, the government will have to continue to make exceptions for the LGBT community or explicitly restrict LGBT access altogether. The tension between idealized family structures and Singapore's actual history, or "traditional" child-rearing versus technology and new family structures, will continue to bear down on Singapore—a nation that tries to preserve its "culture" and "tradition" when its material conditions make it more akin to a developed country with low fertility rates, a rising middle class with an outwardly looking mind-set, and access to assistive reproductive technology.

ii. Gay Malays and transgender Singaporeans

As a wealthy and developed country in the Global South, Singapore's changing demography and the strong economic position of many of its citizens places it in a unique situation among countries of the South. Yet not all of Singapore's citizens experience these conditions in the same way. In particular, many Malay

Singaporeans experience the double burden of racial discrimination on top of the existing pressures to conform to the "Asian values" rhetoric. Also, as part of a region that experienced vast sexual plurality and that only a few short decades ago was internationally known for its transgender nightlife and advanced technology in gender reassignment surgery, transgender people in Singapore are discriminated against by both society at large and the gay community. Although this final section will not focus on legal issues facing this community, it will discuss the social consequences for minorities living in the shadow of the criminalization of homosexuality.

In 2014, Associate Professor Syed Khairudin Aljunied in the Department of Malay Studies at the National University Singapore (NUS) posted a Facebook comment in which he responded to a question regarding his position on how "liberal Islam . . . is now supporting the lesbian movement." In answering the question, he stated,

> Scholars and religious teachers . . . Parents and school teachers . . . [and] the youths must assist . . . to spread the message of true Islam in all media platforms [and] make the pure message of Islam viral to cleanse the impurities of liberal Islam and lesbianism. Together, we will stop these cancers in their track!
>
> (Ibrahim, 2016, p. 961)

Aljunied's post may have been responding to a widely circulated blog post by a Malay Singaporean student who had discussed the difficulty of being a lesbian in Singapore (Fikri, 2013). Other sources believe that the debate was sparked by the Singapore's Health Promotion Board's recent FAQ response that being LGBT was not a mental illness.

After Aljunied's post was made public, three students at NUS circulated a petition calling on him to withdraw his statements, apologize, and go for counseling to gain an understanding of LGBT issues. Shortly thereafter, another petition in support of Aljunied chastised the authors of the first petition, stating that the students were intimidating Aljunied and that they had violated their "duty to provide a safe academic environment for teachers" (Rejal, 2014). Ultimately, the university counseled Aljunied and stated that his post "contained provocative, inappropriate and offensive language" (Lee, 2014). Aljunied later acknowledged that his original post "reflected poor judgment in the tone and choice of words" (ibid.). But even though he acknowledged poor judgment, his post received an outpour of support with many Muslim organizations endorsing his statements, citing religious texts for support. The petition supporting Aljunied also led to over a thousand signatures, with accompanying threats to the original three students who protested his post, forcing them to retract their petition against him. Aljunied's supporters went on to accuse the LGBT community at large of using intimidation tactics and argued that they were restricting freedom of speech. Support for Aljunied triggered strong statements that criticized even the LGBT community outside of Singapore, stating, "It is unfortunate that the global LGBT movement has infected Singapore to the extent that some citizens have become confused about what a family unit is" (FMSA, 2014).

Nur Amali Ibrahim very astutely explains the sudden surge of homophobia in the Malay community as a reaction to other issues – such as the state's depiction of the community as insular, prone to fundamentalism, and suffering from a cultural deficit. Ibrahim also argues that the recent homophobic turn has been used by Malay men in particular to redefine Malay-Muslim masculinity, which is often depicted as inadequate. This exacerbates what Joseph Toh calls the "triple jeopardy," which gay Malays must endure when they believe their religion condemns homosexuality, their co-ethnics treats them as a threat, and Singapore at large sees Malays as less successful or desirable (Toh, 2002). Norhazlina Bte Md Yusop (2004) highlights how the enormous social pressures on the Malay community can render homosexuality a corollary issue, inhibiting frank and useful discussions on the topic, and perpetuating stereotypes and ignorance. When ignorance is maintained, the triple jeopardy LGBT Malays face becomes even more oppressive, as pressures on the Malay community mount, and it continues to be seen as suffering from a cultural deficit.

Although not always subject to the pressures of religion, transgender Singaporeans also suffer from marginalization at the hands of both society and the gay community. Transgender people have a long presence and history in Singapore and the region in general. Michael Peletz's survey of Southeast Asia from the 15th to the 21st centuries found that historically, the region was flexible and pluralistic in matters of gender and sexuality (Peletz, 2009; 2006). In neighboring Indonesia, for instance, historically, the Bugis ethnic group recognized and accepted five genders: males, females, transgender males, transgender females, and androgynous persons (Davies, 2007). In modern Singapore, although homosexuality is criminalized, transsexuality is a state-sanctioned practice where people can obtain government-subsidized sexual reassignment surgery (SRS) and legally change their assigned gender. The first SRS in Asia took place in Singapore in 1971, five years after the country gained independence, with public hospitals subsequently dealing with hundreds of cases every year (Yeo, 1971; Hoe, 2014). From the 1950s to the 1970s, transgender and transsexual nightlife in Singapore was notorious, serving as a popular tourist attraction for Western sailors and soldiers on military leave (Yue, 2017). The center of this nightlife was Bugis Street, at the time referred to as "Singapore's most famous street" and "one of the must see places in international tourist magazines" (Cheah et al., 1985).

In spite of this colorful and rich history, transgender Singaporeans continue to face discrimination and physical violence. According to Leow Yangfa, transgender Singaporeans suffer from bullying and discrimination in school, employment and housing discrimination, a lack of information and professional support in community and social service settings, and difficulty accessing affordable, trans-affirming health-care services, including sexual and mental health services (Kok, 2016b). Although SRS is recognized in Singapore and transsexuals can change their gender on government-issued identity cards after surgery – and can get married based on their listed gender since 1996 (see Women's Charter, Section 12(3)(b)) – the doctors able to perform SRS in Singapore are no longer available, and the procedure is costly to perform abroad. Furthermore, without the costly and painful procedure, transgender Singaporeans are subjected to the increasingly heteronormative standards set by the state and enforced through Section 377A. In 2016, the situation was so severe for one preoperative transgender woman that she was recently granted asylum in the United Kingdom to protect her from forced conscription into National Service (*The Straits Times*, 2016). Similar to gay Malays, transgender Singaporeans must fight against pervasive stereotypes, and the community must grapple with increasing economic disparity between the rich and poor (Guo, 2016).

Conclusion

The rise of LGBT rights in the Global North is the product of decades of struggle that is far from over. However, as seen in this chapter, the conditions behind the emergence of LGBT social movements in the Global North are very different from the conditions found in the Global South. After centuries of colonization, tumultuous periods of war, chaos after independence, and the continual process of redefining itself in the shadow if its colonial past, nations of the Global South did not experience the 20th century – the formative period in LGBT activism – in the same way the North did. Singapore is a perfect example of this. To build its reserves while containing the chaos it encountered upon independence, Singapore opened its borders to international trade while carefully managing its social and political landscape. Relying on tools of control left behind by the British, Section 377A was but one mechanism of control used to manage its population. Justified by the desire to preserve "traditional" Asian values in the face of a purportedly neocolonial Western human rights discourse, Section 377A continues to restrict the rights of the LGBT community in a nation that is highly connected to a world whose values are generally moving toward inclusivity and openness.

The tension between "tradition" and being a global node in a rapidly changing world can be seen in the continued success of Pink Dot SG, numerous court challenges against 377A, and the growth of LGBT advocacy and support organizations, as well as the pushback from the state and many religious organizations. This conflict is fraught with racial, class, and religious implications that go beyond LGBT issues. Nevertheless, challenges to decriminalize homosexuality in Singapore push on. In September 2018, in response to the Indian Supreme Court's decision to strike down Section 377 of their Penal

Code, veteran Singaporean diplomat Tommy Koh called on the gay community to renew its challenge to Section 377A in Singaporean courts (Channel News Asia, 2018). After the Indian Supreme Court decision, two constitutional challenges against Section 377A were filed (see Lum, 2018). The renewed challenges provides hope that things will change for the better in Singapore, but also demonstrates how the nation has a long way to go before all its citizens can reap the benefits of the success of the country's development. It additionally highlights how resolving the multitude of issues – from national development, economic growth, and managing incredibly diverse populations – is never a straightforward process in the Global South, regardless of one's economic progress.

References

Cases

Lim Meng Suang and another v. Attorney General, [2013] SGHC 73 (H.C.)(Singapore).
Lim Meng Suang and another v. Attorney General and another appeal and another matter, [2014] SGCA 53 (C.A.)(Singapore).
Re UKM, [2018] SGFC 20 (Family Court)(Singpore).
Tan Eng Hong v. Attorney General, [2011] SGHC 56 (H.C.)(Singapore).
Tan Eng Hong v. Attorney General, [2012] SGCA 45 (C.A.)(Singapore).
Tan Eng Hong v. Attorney General, [2013] SGHC 199 (H.C.)(Singapore).

Parliamentary debates

"Public Order Act: Second Reading Bills," Singapore Parliamentary Debate Official Report, Vol. 94 (April 3, 2017).
"Statement of Prime Minister Lee Hsien Loong," Singapore Parliamentary Debate Official Report, Vol. 83 (October 23, 2007).
"Statement of Prof. Li-Ann Thio," Singapore Parliamentary Debate Official Report, Vol. 83 (October 23, 2007).

Laws (Singapore)

Constitution of the Republic of Singapore (1999 Reprint).
Penal Code, Chapter 224 (2008 Revised Edition).
Public Order Act, Chapter 257A (2012 Reprint).
Women's Charter, Chapter 353 (2009 Revised Edition).

Books and articles

Bauer, H. (2017) *The Hirschfeld Archives: Violence, Death, and Modern Queer Culture*. Philadelphia: Temple University Press.

Chang, S. (2016) 'Legacies of Exceptionalism and the Future of Gay Rights in Singapore,' *Hong Kong Law Journal*, (46) 1, pp. 71–87.

Chang, S. (2014) 'The Postcolonial Problem for Global Gay Rights,' *Boston University International Law Journal*, (32), pp. 309–354.

Channel News Asia (2018) 'Veteran Singapore Diplomat Tommy Koh Calls for Gay Community to Challenge Sex Ban,' *Channel News Asia*, 7 September [Online]. Available at: www.channelnewsasia.com/news/singapore/diplomat-tommy-koh-calls-for-gay-community-ban-377a-10693594 (Accessed on: 11 October 2018).

Cheah, P., Ang, L.W., and Toh, D. (1985) 'The Street That Wouldn't Sleep,' *The Straits Times*, 11 October, p. 16.

Chua, B.H. (2002) *Communitarian Ideology and Democracy in Singapore*. London: Routledge.

Chua, L.J. (2014) *Mobilizing Gay Singapore: Rights and Resistance in an Authoritarian State*. Philadelphia: Temple University Press.

Chua, L.J. (2012) 'Pragmatic Resistance, Law, and Social Movements in Authoritarian States: The Case of Gay Collective Action in Singapore,' *Law & Society Review*, (46) 4, pp. 713–748.

Davies, S.G. (2007) *Challenging Gender Norms: Five Genders among Bugis in Indonesia*. Belmont, CA: Thomson Wadsworth.

Edsall, N.C. (2003) *Toward Stonewall: Homosexuality and Society in the Modern Western World*. Charlottesville: University of Virginia Press.

Faderman, L. (2015) *The Gay Revolution: The Story of the Struggle*. New York: Simon & Schuster.

Fellowship of Muslim Students Association (2014) 'Official Statement: FMSA Position on Letter of Concern to NUS Provost on Associate Professor Dr. Syed Muhd Khairudin Aljunied,' 3 March. Available at: www.scribd.com/document/215188280/FMSA-Position-on-NUS-Concern (Accessed on: 11 October 2018).

Fikri (2013) 'Fear and Loathing (as a 21-Year Old Queer) in Singapore,' *Autostraddle*, 30 August [Online]. Available at: www.autostraddle.com/things-i-fear-queer-singapore-190094 (Accessed on: 12 October 2018).

George, C. (2017) 'Neoliberal "Good Governance" in Lieu of Rights: Lee Kuan Yew's Singapore Experiment,' in M. Price & N. Stremlau (Eds.), *Speech and Society in Turbulent Times: Freedom of Expression in Comparative Perspective*. Cambridge: Cambridge University Press, pp. 114–130.

George, C. (2007) 'Consolidating Authoritarian Rule: Calibrated Coercion in Singapore,' *Pacific Review*, (20) 2, pp. 127–145.

Goh, L.S. (2014) 'S377A Ruling Contradicts Govt Position on Equality,' *Today*, 17 November [Online]. Available at: www.todayonline.com/voices/s377a-ruling-contradicts-govt-position-equality (Accessed on: 9 October 2018).

Guo, M. (2016) *More Than My Genitalia*. Honours Thesis. National University of Singapore.

Hoe Pei Chan (2014) 'Sex Change Operations Dwindling in Singapore,' *The Straits Times*, 28 December.

Ibrahim, N.A. (2016) 'Homophobic Muslims: Emerging Trends in Multireligious Singapore,' *Comparative Studies in Society and History*, (58) 4.

Joint Statement (2014) 'Court of Appeal's Verdict on 377a Constitutional Challenge: A Missed Opportunity,' 30 October. Available at: http://pinkdot.sg/court-of-appeals-verdict-on-377a-constitutional-challenge-a-missed-opportunity/ (Accessed on: 9 October 2018).

Kok, X.H. (2016a) 'Pink Dot Just "Catalyst for Speakers" Corner Reminder,' *Straits Times*, 31 October. Available at: www.straitstimes.com/singapore/pink-dot-just-catalyst-for-speakers-corner-reminder (Accessed on: 9 October 2018).

Kok, X.H. (2016b) 'Recognised Legally, But Challenges Remain,' *Straits Times*, 19 September.

Lee, P. (2014) 'NUS Professor "Counselled" by University for Facebook Posting on Lesbianism,' *The Straits Times*, 5 March [Online]. Available at: www.straitstimes.com/singapore/nus-professor-counselled-by-university-for-facebook-posting-on-lesbianism (Accessed on: 11 October 2018).

Leong, W.T. (1997) 'Singapore,' in D.J. West, et al. (Eds.), *Sociolegal Control of Homosexuality: A Multi-Nation Comparison*. New York: Plenum Press.

Lim, E.B. (2005) 'Glocalqueering in New Asia: The Politics of Performing Gay in Singapore,' *Theatre Journal*, 57.

Lum, S. (2018) 'Court Challenge Filed by Singapore DJ against Section 377A,' *The New Paper*, 12 September [Online]. Available at: www.tnp.sg/news/singapore/court-challenge-filed-singapore-dj-against-section-377a (Accessed on: 11 October 2018).

May, E.T. (1988) *Homeward Bound: American Families in the Cold War Era*. New York: Basic Books.

Ng, J.Y. (2014) 'Thousands Wear White at Church Service to Defend Family Values,' *Today Online*, 30 June [Online]. Available at: www.todayonline.com/singapore/thousands-wear-white-church-service-defend-family-values (Accessed on: 9 October 2018).

Norhazlina Bte Md Yusop (2004) *Same Sex Sexuality and Islam in Singapore*. Masters Thesis. National University of Singapore.

Peletz, M. (2009) *Gender Pluralism: Southeast Asia since Early Modern Times*. New York: Routledge.

Peletz, M. (2006) 'Transgenderism and Gender Pluralism in Southeast Asia since Early Modern Times,' *Current Anthropology*, (47) 2.

Pereira, A. (2008) 'Whither the Developmental State? Explaining Singapore's Continued Developmentalism,' *Third World Quarterly*, (29) 6, pp. 1189–1203.

PinkDot.sg (2015) 'Press Release: A LOVE Note, from 28,000 at Hong Lim Park to Reaffirm Their Support for the Freedom to Love'. Available at: https://web.archive.org/web/20160330225247/http://pinkdot.sg/alovenotefrom28000/ (Accessed on: 9 October 2018).

Radics, G.B. (2013) 'Decolonizing Singapore's Sex Laws: Tracing Section 377A of Singapore's Penal Code,' *Columbia Human Rights Law Review*, (45) 1, pp. 57–99.

Rajah, J. (2012) *Authoritarian Rule of Law: Legislation, Discourse and Legitimacy in Singapore* (Cambridge Studies in Law and Society). Cambridge: Cambridge University Press.

Rejal, K. (2014) 'Letter of Concern Regarding Benjamin Seet, Melissa Tsang and Khairulanwar Zaini,' *The Petition Site*, 1 March [Online]. Available at: www.thepetitionsite.com/357/463/602/concern-over-academic-expression-and-religious-freedom-jeopardized-by-lbgt-activist-singapore/ (Accessed on: 11 October 2018).

The Straits Times (2016) 'Singaporean Transgender Woman Seeking to Avoid In-Camp Training Granted Asylum in UK,' *The Straits Times*, 29 April [Online]. Available at: www.straitstimes.com/singapore/singaporean-transgender-woman-seeking-to-avoid-in-camp-training-granted-asylum-in-uk (Accessed on: 11 October 2018).

Tan, C.K.K. (2009) 'But They Are Like You and Me: Gay Civil Servants and Citizenship in a Cosmopolitanizing Singapore,' *City and Society*, (21) 1, pp. 133–154.

Tan, S. (2015) 'Respect Local Culture: Singapore Minister Rebukes US Investment Bank for LGBT Recruitment Drive,' *GayStarNews.com*, 3 May [Online]. Available at: www.gaystarnews.com/article/respect-local-culture-singapore-minister-rebukes-us-investment-bank-lgbt-recruitment-drive03/ (Accessed on: 9 October 2018).

Thompson, M. (2004) 'Pacific Asia after "Asian Values": Authoritarianism, Democracy, and "Good Governance",' *Third World Quarterly*, (25) 6, pp. 1079.

Toh, J. (2002) *Muslim by Birth, Malay by Society, Gay by Choice*. Honours Thesis. National University of Singapore.
Weiss, J. (2007) 'Lesbian, Gay, Bisexual, and Transgender (LGBT) Movement,' in G. L. Anderson & K. G. Herr (Eds.), *Encyclopedia of Activism and Social Justice*. Thousand Oaks, CA: Sage Publications 1, pp. 846–848.
Yeo, J. (1971) 'First Sex Change Surgery in Singapore,' *The Straits Times*, 31 July, p. 17.
Yue, A. (2017) 'Trans-Singapore: Some Notes towards Queer Asia as Method,' *Inter-Asia Cultural Studies*, (18) 1, pp. 10–24.

Chapter 3

Privacy in public spaces

The transformative potential of *Navtej Johar V. Union of India*

Danish Sheikh

Introduction

On the night before the Supreme Court read down Section 377 of the Indian Penal Code and decriminalized the intimate lives of LGBTQ individuals, I shared an auto-rickshaw ride with a lover. It was late, the streets were empty, our fingers were entwined. As the auto came to a halt, he leaned in and kissed me tenderly. It should have been a casual moment of intimacy, a final grace note to a lovely evening. Instead, I felt my body go rigid with panic. It is one thing to slide into the easy anonymity that comes from holding hands with a member of the same sex in public spaces, delinked as it is from desire in the public imagination. The kiss in that moment, however, was an act of rupturing that veil and dragging our sexuality out into the open, to render what was safely private now suddenly vulnerable in public.

About 12 hours after this moment, I walked out of Court Room No. 1 onto the lawns of the Supreme Court. I saw his face in the crowd of reporters, his expression mirroring the dazed happiness on mine. We kissed right there, a near inevitable impulse to the rush of victory. This was a vastly more public space in theory, but at that moment, it felt as safe as any corner of his living room. As we disengaged, I heard a cry of annoyance from a man. "Sir, please, do it again properly?" a reporter asked us, camera in hand. We refused, incredulous, balking at the prospect of our display of intimacy being featured in a national newspaper. Overnight, our terms of engagement with the world seemed to have transformed.

When the Supreme Court of India rendered its decision in *Navtej Johar v. Union of India*, it had many possible routes toward decriminalization. It could have picked constitutional doctrine on equality and nondiscrimination, spoken of the right to health, or landed on the right to privacy. It ultimately chose to feature all these elements in its decision and in some cases read these rights in the widest ambit possible. For the purpose of this chapter, I am interested in *Navtej Johar's* articulation of the right to privacy and its concomitant engagement with the public-private divide. I will argue that the Court opened out – or followed upon – a transformative manner of thinking about privacy. In the hands of the Court, privacy becomes a way to think about transforming the public sphere. It becomes a way to link the struggles of LGBTQ individuals with those of other persons navigating the right to intimate partnerships. It also allows the judiciary a space to shed some of the trappings associated with its institutional role.

The broader litigation that this decision has brought to a successful close is a longer story involving a range of lawyers, activists, and queer persons who came together as part of a movement to strike down the law. In my own capacity, I have been engaged with this litigation across multiple capacities: as a member of the litigation team at one point, as a member of a research team examining the impact of Section 377 at another, and as a theater practitioner who used the stage as a tool of advocacy and activism. I draw upon these different spheres in examining the public-private discourse that emerges in the process of the litigation. I will begin by examining the roots of the law as it was enacted in the Indian Penal and then look at the litigation and advocacy that featured a series of public debates over the notion of sexuality and privacy, which finally led to the *Navtej Johar* decision. Finally, I will discuss the ways in which the engagement with LGBT rights has broken open the space of the public-private divide, effectively enshrining a right to privacy that inheres in public spaces.

Prior to embarking on the story of this litigation, it will be useful to tease apart the different ways in which we might articulate public and private spheres. Michael Warner's *Publics and Counterpublics* (2005) gives us a useful theoretical framework to think about notions of public, private, and the porous boundaries between these realms. First, the veil between public and private is an illusory line to draw. As Warner notes,

> Different senses of public or private intermingle constantly: a private conversation can take place in public form; a kitchen can become a public gathering place; a private bedroom can be a public and commercial space, as in a hotel; a radio can bring public discussion into a bathroom, and so on.
> (Warner, 2005)

Next, the public display of private intimacy has different consequences for different sexualities. Warner notes that acts such as kissing or holding hands in public view by same-sex couples commonly incite disgust, even violence, while similar intimacy by mixed-sex persons is largely rendered ordinary (Warner, 2005). This view doesn't entirely translate when it comes to the Indian context, as I hint at in the beginning of this chapter. There is at least some degree of invisibility that same-sex intimacy can enjoy in the public sphere as evinced by the constant public holding of hands by same-sex individuals. The reason this is tolerated, however, is the same reason that public displays of intimacy by mixed-sex persons might be frowned upon in the country: there is little in the way of assumption of a sexual space when it comes to these public displays of same-sex affection.

Finally, Warner finds that "public and private are bound up with elementary relations to language as well as to body" (Warner, 2005). Degrees of formality in speech track onto a continuum of publicness in this view. This tension between public versus private, I will go on to show, pervades in and is productively worked through the *Navtej Singh Johar* decision.

Criminalizing sexuality and the public-private debate

Section 377 of the Indian Penal Code criminalizes "carnal intercourse against the order of nature." While the words of the statute do not explicitly target the LGBTQ community, the provision has been used largely to persecute community members since its inception in the Penal Code in 1860 (International Commission of Jurists, 2017). In many instances, this persecution would take the form of harassment, physical abuse, and blackmail of LGBTQ persons, by both state and non-state institutions (International Commission of Jurists, 2017).[1]

The constitutionality of this provision was challenged for the first time in 1994 by AIDS Bhedbhav Virodhi Andolan (ABVA), a human rights activist group. ABVA filed a petition before the Delhi High Court, which was ultimately disposed of silently after years of deferred hearings (Narrain, 2004). In December 2001, a fresh petition was filed before the same court by Naz Foundation, a nongovernmental organization working in the field of HIV/AIDS intervention and prevention. As an organization that worked with gay and MSM (men who have sex with men) individuals,[2] Naz Foundation's petition made the case that its HIV/AIDS prevention efforts were impaired by discriminatory attitudes exhibited by state agencies toward sexuality minorities. Unless the self-respect and dignity of sexuality minorities were restored by doing away with discriminatory laws such as Section 377, it would not be possible to promote HIV/AIDS prevention in the community.[3]

In her ethnography of queer activism in India, Naisargi Dave notes one major critique of the petition that emerged from within the queer community in the country (Dave, 2012). The petition asked for consensual sexual acts covered under Section 377 to be decriminalized in private: this left out numerous individuals who were unable to inhabit private spaces owing to their differential socioeconomic status. In this case, privacy was a privilege available to those who could afford it. The critique of a privacy-based argument wasn't confined to class bias, either. Women's groups also opposed this focus on privacy. If one of the major struggles of the women's movement was to remove impunity within the private sphere, it was argued that enabling a privacy-based argument in this manner would bolster the ideological foundations they had been actively fighting against for decades.

In 2009, the Delhi High Court delivered its verdict in *Naz Foundation v. Union of India* (2009), effectively decriminalizing the intimate lives of queer individuals in the country. The judgment was a landmark moment that was celebrated by members of the community as well as the broader civil society. It did, however, reflect the ambivalence on privacy that had caused such heated debates in the first place. On the one hand, the Court defined the right to privacy to include a protection of acts done in private spaces (zonal privacy) as well as the exercise of private choices (decisional privacy). This latter point located privacy in personhood as opposed to space, notionally extending privacy to a protection of private will (*Naz Foundation v. Union of India*, 2009). This expansive notion of privacy, which would have certainly dealt with some of the critiques raised, was not reflected in the final declaration of the Court. In its holding, the Court read down Section 377 to exclude from its ambit consensual sexual acts between adults "in private."

The Delhi High Court's decision was subsequently appealed before the Supreme Court, India's Highest Court of Appeal. In a decision that has been considered one of the lowest moments of the Indian judiciary – another bench of the Court referred to this decision as a "discordant note" – the Supreme Court in 2014 reversed *Naz Foundation* and upheld the constitutionality of Section 377. *Suresh Kumar Koushal v. Union of India's* reasoning was plagued by gaps in logic, with its rejection of the constitutional right to privacy as it pertained to LGBT individuals particularly bereft of a rational basis. The Court recounted in detail the evolution of the right in constitutional jurisprudence and then went on to dismiss its application in the case at hand in a single line. Even if it were true that Section 377 has been used to perpetrate harassment, blackmail torture of persons belonging to the LGBT community, the Court said, "This treatment is neither mandated by the section nor condoned by it and the mere fact that the section is mixed by police authorities and others is not a reflection of the vires of the section."

The Delhi High Court had thus provided protection to LGBT individuals, even as it had circumscribed this protection within a conventional zone of privacy. With the *Suresh Kumar Koushal* decision, the intimate lives of LGBT individuals whether in public or private were once again subject to criminalization. I will show how the various responses to the *Koushal* decision pushed for a reimagination of the lines between public and private, generating discourse that would lead to a transformative decision in *Navtej Johar*.

The backlash to Koushal

Suresh Kumar Koushal v. Naz Foundation came as a crushing defeat to the movement and LGBTQ individuals at large. The courtroom hearings[4] indicated a bench that lacked empathy toward the struggles faced by the LGBT community, reflected in the final judgment's language, which brushed away the community as having so-called rights. With these words, the highest appellate Court in the country had, in no uncertain terms, seemingly ended a litigation battle that had gone on for more than a decade. Furthermore, after four years of being subject to equal citizenship under the law, queer persons were now once again placed within the category of unapprehended felons. The Delhi High

Court's 2009 decision had opened the doors for a range of conversations around the future of queer rights in India: that would have to once again recede into the background as the focus reverted to battling criminalization.[5]

At the same time, it is also the case that the backlash to the decision revitalized the movement and instigated a renewed series of conversations that would ultimately lead to the expansiveness of the *Navtej Singh Johar* decision. Three elements of this period, I will argue, play out into the Court's reframing of the public-private divide. First, there was more public discourse on the issue than ever before, whether in terms of public gatherings, engagements in performance and popular culture, or direct engagement with the state. Second, the litigation changed gears in terms of finding different ways to approach the Court with a strategy that centered on bringing a set of personal faces front and center to the issue. Finally, the Supreme Court's own jurisprudence evolved in the intervening years, with two cases in particular knocking out the rational of Suresh Kumar Koushal while simultaneously pushing the discourse on privacy. This section will discuss each issue in turn.

i. Public discourse

Immediate public reaction to the judgment included a massive series of coordinated protests in 17 cities in India and 22 other cities across the world. Termed the Global Day of Rage Against Section 377, the protests featured large gatherings of individuals in each of the cities coming together to condemn the judgment and asking for the repeal of the section.[6] This energetic, public discourse also put pressure on the government to respond. Sonia Gandhi, the president of the Indian National Congress (the ruling party in India at the time) made a plea to Parliament to address the matter. Rahul Gandhi, the vice president of the Indian National Congress, noted that he agreed with the High Court verdict and that the question was one of personal freedom, to be left to individual choice. A number of political parties issued statements condemning the judgment and its effects.[7] Additionally, the National Human Rights Commission, which had, until then remained silent on the issue, released a statement noting, "All people regardless of their sexual orientation or gender identity should be able to enjoy their human rights."[8] Meanwhile, the discussion of LGBTQ issues received one of its biggest public platforms when the popular TV talk show, "Satyamev Jayate," hosted by Bollywood star Aamir Khan, ran an episode focusing on LGBTQ lives.

I would like to single out one strand of public discourse in particular to exemplify ways in which the conversation around queer sexuality was evolving. Spaces of theater and performance found an energetic set of vocabularies to creatively perform dissent against the Koushal decision. I will take two examples of productions from India in particular to touch upon how they imagine different frames of dissent in relation to the Suresh Kumar Koushal decision: *Queen Size*, conceived by Mandeep Raikhy and *Contempt*, a rendition of the Section 377 hearings that I have written.

Queen Size is a performance piece devised in response to an article by late gay filmmaker Nishit Saran on the need to remove Section 377, published in 2000. Titled "Why My Bedroom Habits Are Your Business," the piece begins with the following lines, a sentiment that Saran notes is articulated often before him:

> Of course it is completely fine if you are gay. What you do in your bedroom is none of my business. . . . But why do you need to talk about your sexuality? Why do you need to make a public issue of such a private matter?

In its early iterations, the audience were given this chapter to read prior to entering the performance space. It soon becomes clear that the piece is going to very affirmatively make a public issue of a private matter. The audience sits around the queen-size bed of the title, watching two fully clothed men seated at different points around it. As the performance begins, the two men begin to engage in choreographed foreplay. The music rises in intensity, the men begin to undress, and an intense, intimate encounter plays out. The performance takes place in three loops of 45 minutes each, with the men regularly shedding their performer avatars to interact with the audience moving in and out of the space. From its first performance in 2016, *Queen Size* has traveled across 25 cities in India for over 60 performances.

In a conversation with Ranjana Dave, Raikhy speaks of how the piece emerged for him as he moved away from an interest in art that served purely aesthetic purposes toward looking at how it could be served as a more political response: in this instance, to see how intimacy had to be played out to protest against Section 377. This meant, in part, that the piece had to be one that would provoke but at the same time make an argument about a body demanding its own rights.[9] As the process went along, the aesthetic and the political merged, even as some audience members would find difficulty in embracing the content of the performance. In response to the reality of some audience members taking offense at the work or finding it vulgar, Raikhy finds the political potential of the work emphasized. In his words,

> What I realized early on in the process was that this wasn't the kind of work where three or four performances would have any meaning. Did I make this work so that it could be watched by 300 or 400 people who were familiar with contemporary dance and at peace with homosexuality? There was no point to that. There is a whole lot of queer activism in the country and the joy of this work is to take it outside the theatre into different kinds of contexts. In Guwahati, we performed the work in a legal chamber. I want to open up discussions around section 377, about the discomfort of seeing two men on a bed, and the relationship between the political and the performative in the arts.[10]

The prospect of opening up discussions around Section 377 is also what prompted the writing and production of my own play, *Contempt*. The Suresh

Kumar Koushal decision prompted a massive backlash and criticism: there was less focus on the hearings that led to the decision. During the final arguments before the Supreme Court in 2012, there was a moment when the judges took pause in their constant excavation of what constituted carnal intercourse against the order of nature. It was a moment prompted by a story in a book titled *Same Sex Love in India: Readings from Literature and History*, edited by Ruth Vanita and Saleem Kidwai. The story was "Vijay Dan Detha's Dohri Zindagi." The Court had just resumed after lunch, when Justice Singhvi remarked that he had a chance to read the story over his break. What followed was one of the few truly reflective moments during the course of a six-week hearing where the judge spoke about the struggles he'd had with the case, while acknowledging the reality of the story he had read: that same-sex relationships had indeed formed a part of the country's past. This was a remarkable moment, all the more notable for its complete erasure from the text of the final decision.

For me, the moment seemed to reflect on the ways in which advocacy strategies might engage with the legal imagination. Could there be a manner of using literary narratives to break through the law's formalism, of engaging with an otherwise unyielding bench? Further, as far as public understanding of what had transpired in the courtroom went, could we use the medium of the theater to communicate the manner in which the judges had displayed a lack of empathy toward LGBTQ persons?

As I wrote *Contempt*, I attempted to grapple with these questions. The play is structured around four scenes based on the unofficial transcripts of the Suresh Kumar Koushal hearings. Each scene features a different line of argument employed by a lawyer before the two judges: the historical basis of the law, the law's impact on HIV/AIDS efforts, the law's legitimization of police violence, the law's effect on the dignity of LGBT persons. As each of these scenes progresses, the play shows how the judges constantly invoked the same question – what constitutes carnal intercourse against the order of nature – to avoid substantively engaging with the content of the lawyers' arguments. My vision of dissent within this play is in the form of the scenes that are juxtaposed with each narrative in the courtroom – monologues that feature the lived narratives of different queer persons. Where the courtroom space denies the experience of queer subjectivity, I attempt to place the voices of the very same persons in the courtroom space as an implicit denial of the Court's rhetoric.

In the climactic scene of the play, a man interrupts the space of the courtroom to recount the story of an intensely erotic encounter with his lover. As he proceeds to relay the story, other characters on stage join in the recounting, making the intimate act a shared experience. At its very conclusion, a kiss between the two men that was otherwise merely described by the characters is performed before the audience. From the opening of its run in February 2018, the play had a total of 30 performances at venues in Delhi, Sonipat, Bangalore, Hyderabad, London, and Oxford. Partly given my own connections within the legal academy, roughly half of these venues were law school auditoriums. The play's longest extended run was at a performance venue, however, the Oddbird

Theater in Delhi. The specific locations where the play was performed would often play a strong role in the post-show discussions we had. At law school campuses, these would shift in the direction of asking questions about legal advocacy and the strategies before the judiciary; in more traditional performance venues, there was a sense of surprise and outrage about the prejudice displayed by the judges in the courtroom. The kiss itself was treated as an emotional climax rather than a provocation.

What both these plays provide are public performances of a certain kind of act that was rendered a criminal offense. Performing these acts in the most public of spaces constituted a dissent to the law while also reframing the domain of what is possible.

ii. The Supreme Court

Merely six months after the *Koushal* decision, a different two-judge bench of the Indian Supreme Court delivered the *NALSA v. Union of India* decision, in every way a reverse of what the Court had stated in *Koushal*. "Moral failure lies in society's unwillingness to contain or embrace different gender identities and expressions" (National Legal Services Authority v. Union of India, 2014). With these words, in its opening paragraph, the Court went on to craft a deeply inclusive document that elaborated on a range of constitutional rights as they pertained to transgender persons.

At the heart of the decision was the idea of legal gender recognition. The Court defined transgender identity in the broadest manner possible, removing it from a restrictive medical model and locating it in the principle of self-identification. In keeping with this importance of recognizing self-expression, the Court embarked on an analysis of Article 19(1)(a) of the Constitution that is particularly significant. This provision of the Constitution recognizes the right to freedom of speech and expression. The Court found that this included the right to expression of self-identified gender. Importantly, the Court did not just look at this as a right that accrued within legal documents. Rather, it held that self-identified gender could be expressed through dress, words, action, or behavior, or any other form.

This was linked to the court's articulation of autonomy and privacy. Given that gender identity lies at the core of an individual's personal identity, the Court found that restriction or interference with the expression of such personality, whether it be in terms of behavior or presentation, would result in a restriction of the guaranteed rights of privacy, self-identity, autonomy, and personal integrity.

The Court also made a fleeting reference to Section 377 and, consequently, the *Koushal* decision. In tracing the history of discrimination and harassment suffered by transgender persons, the Court found that Section 377 was a particularly egregious source: "Though associated with specific sexual acts, (377) highlighted certain identities, including *Hijras*[11] and was used as an instrument of harassment and physical abuse against *Hijras* and transgender persons." The judges acknowledge the existence of the *Koushal* decision but decide to express no further opinion on it. Nevertheless, this constituted a strong judicial challenge to the underlying rationale of the earlier decision.

With the *NALSA* judgment in 2014, the Supreme Court all but overruled *Koushal*. The *Koushal* opinion was further rejected in a landmark judgment on privacy rights in India, *JK.S. Puttaswamy vs. Union of India*, issued on 24 August 2017. In the opinion, Justice Chandrachud features a section titled "Discordant Notes." The section discusses two Supreme Court decisions: the first being *ADM Jabalpur*, which infamously upheld the denial of basic fundamental rights during the imposition of emergency. The habeas corpus decision – as it is also referred to – is considered one of the most shameful passages in the Court's history. The second case featured in this section is *Suresh Kumar Koushal*. On a purely discursive level, this is a stinging repudiation of the decision by the Court: in placing it within this frame, it acknowledges the gravity of recriminalizing millions of queer persons in the country. The Court then goes on to reject the *Koushal* Court's rhetoric of the so-called rights of LGBT persons. Instead, Justice Chandrachud finds that sexual orientation is an essential attribute of the right to privacy.

The *Puttaswamy* decision also challenges *Koushal's* invisibilization of LGBT persons – the idea that since the community constituted a "miniscule minority" it was not a sound basis for striking down the law. The *Puttaswamy* Court notes that this *de minimis*[12] hypothesis is misplaced as the invasion of a fundamental right and is not rendered tolerable when a few as opposed to a large number of people are subjected to hostile treatment. It then goes on to explain that such acts of hostile discrimination as constitutionally impermissible because of the chilling effect that they have on the exercise of the fundamental right in the first place.

The conclusion of Justice Chandrachud's opinion presages *Navtej Johar* by going on to hold that privacy includes at its core the preservation of personal intimacies and sexual orientation. The Court further notes that the right to privacy recognizes personal choices governing a way of life – that it is not lost or surrendered merely because an individual is in a public space. Many possibilities were opened out by this rendering of the right to privacy, possibilities that the *Navtej Johar* decision brings to life.

iii. Legal strategy

The defeat in *Suresh Kumar Koushal* was a moment of reflection for the litigation team – or rather, given the diverse number of players involved in the process, litigation *teams*. In the first round of litigation before the Court, submissions were made by lawyers representing *Naz Foundation*, Voices against 377 (a group of nongovernmental organizations working on gender and sexuality rights issues) and Member of Parliament Shyam Benegal, along with briefs representing groups of parents of LGBT persons, mental health professionals, and academics. All of these groups kept the legal battle alive using the limited appellate process within the Supreme Court. A curative petition is a remedy through which the court acknowledges that a particular judgment might require reconsideration to set right a miscarriage of justice. On the 2 February 2016, the three senior-most judges of the Court agreed to hear the curative petition and listed it before a constitution bench.

Even as the hearing of the curative petition awaited an indefinite future, a set of lawyers who were already part of the litigation process decided to pursue a parallel strategy simultaneously. This team included Menaka Guruswamy, who had represented MP Shyam Benegal's brief in the *Suresh Kumar Koushal* case. In an interview, Menaka Guruswamy notes how a question that stayed with her after the 2013 decision was one that was posed by a judge on the bench to a law officer: "Do you know any gay people?"[13] The response was in the negative. As the judgment observes that LGBT persons constitute a miniscule minority, a fact which according to the judges requires extra caution before invalidating a statutory provision. One of the reasons for this apathy, Guruswamy notes, was the fact that the existing petitions before the Court took the form of a public interest litigation: organizations or groups that included or were speaking on behalf of LGBT persons. What was missing was an actual LGBT petitioner approaching the Court and telling his or her story. That, instead, was something that could be made possible under a petition under Article 32 of the Constitution, the provision that enshrines a fundamental right to approach the Supreme Court in case of rights violations. In Guruswamy's words,

> One of the things we realized was that in the absence of Article 32 writ petitions, and in the absence of LGBTQ Indians actually coming to Court themselves, the stories were harder to tell in Court. Courtrooms are set up to tell stories. And I think that is something I have learned during other cases as well. It is important to humanize the units before the Court. Thus, we decided that the strategy would be different and we would have to trigger, in Dr. Ambedkar's words, the soul of India's Constitution – Article 32. We decided that we should take the stories of LGBTQ Indians to the Supreme Court . . . in a 32 petition, the petitioner has to actually tell a story of loss to the Court. I also feel that petitioner who comes to the Court by way of a 32 litigation shares a very intimate relationship with his or her Constitutional court.

Guruswamy and her team went on to file a petition involving a group of five gay and lesbian Indians, arguing that they were directly affected by the reinstatement of Section 377. The approach of the *Navtej Johar* petition, as it was named, was subsequently followed by a group of three transgender persons. These individuals in turn claimed a detrimental impact of Section 377 on their lives, despite the existence of the NALSA judgment.

Additional Article 32 petitions challenging Section 377 filed by Keshav Suri, Avinash Pokkaluri, and others (Indian Institute of Technology students and alumni); Ashok Row Kavi and others; Arif Jafar and Dr. Akkai Padmashali and others (from transgender communities). Interventions were also filed by the lawyers representing groups that were awaiting a hearing under the Court's curative petition: Voices Against 377, Minna Saran (representing parents of LGBT persons), Alok Sarin (representing mental health professionals), Nivedita Menon and other academics (representing teachers), and Naz Foundation.

How does *Navtej Johar* perform publicness?

The hearings in *Navtej Johar* took place over a week in July 2018. There was intensive media scrutiny on the case: even as live broadcasts of the court proceedings were not permitted at the time, every exchange within the courtroom was documented through multiple Twitter feeds and live blogs.[14] It is not within the scope of this chapter to analyze the hearings themselves, though it is important to note that one can find ripples of the effect of this kind of public scrutiny in the text of the decision. The Court, at multiple points, acknowledges its role as a public institution and seems to speak directly to the communities affected by its decision. In keeping with the frames I have identified from Michael Warner's work, I will look at three ways in which the decision engages with notions of public and private space.

i. Privacy in public spaces

In his opinion, Justice Chandrachud draws on the notion of privacy from his own prior judgment in the *KS Puttaswamy v. Union of India*. In that nine-judge bench decision, the Court recognized the existence of a constitutional right to privacy. One of the key elements of the *Puttaswamy* decision rests on the idea that privacy includes at its core the preservation of personal intimacies and sexual orientation. The Court further noted that the right to privacy recognizes personal choices governing a way of life, that it is not lost or surrendered merely because an individual is in a public space.

Chief Justice Mishra in his opinion uses a metaphor borrowed from the traditional notion of privacy. "Within the compartment of privacy," he notes, "individual autonomy has significant space." Thus, if we are to insist on thinking of privacy as pertaining to spaces, then we must think of autonomy as creating a room of its own. Individuals may carry this compartment in public:

> Any display of affection amongst the members of the LGBT community toward their partners in public so long as it does not amount to indecency or has the potentiality to disturb public order cannot be bogged down by majority perception.

These notions of privacy were discernible in the Delhi High court back in 2009 as well. Where *Navtej Johar* largely differs from the Delhi High Court is in its holding. Four of the five judges write separate, concurring opinions. It is worth recounting the operative paragraphs of each pertaining to Section 377.

Justice Misra, in an opinion written for himself and Justice Khanwilkar, held: "Section 377 IPC, so far as it penalizes any consensual sexual relationship between two adults, be it homosexuals (man and a man), heterosexuals (man and a woman) or lesbians (woman and a woman), cannot be regarded as constitutional. Justice Rohinton Nariman's holding was a restatement of this position: Section 377 insofar as it criminalizes homosexual sex and transgender sex between consenting adults is unconstitutional." Similarly, Justice DY Chandrachud held: "Section 377 of the Penal Code, in so far as it criminalizes consensual sexual conduct between adults of the same sex, is unconstitutional."

If there was a significant difference in any of the final holdings, it was in the decision rendered by Justice Indu Malhotra, the sole female judge on the bench who held, "*Insofar as Section 377 criminalizes consensual sexual acts of adults (i.e., persons above the age of 18 years who are competent to consent) in private, is violative of Articles 14, 15, 19, and 21 of the Constitution. It is, however, clarified that such consent must be free consent, which is completely voluntary in nature, and*" devoid of any duress or coercion.

A crucial word missing from the first three of these four opinions is "privacy." The Delhi High Court's final holding, it may be recalled, had only decriminalized consensual sexual acts between adults "in private." By removing the "in private" rider that had limited the Delhi High Court decision back in 2009, a majority of the *Navtej Johar* Court decriminalizes sexual acts by LGBTQ individuals regardless of the space that they take place in. This does not mean that any sexual acts in public are legal – the public obscenity and indecency laws in the country see to that – but it does mean that LGBTQ persons are not specifically vulnerable to the violence of the law outside the four corners of a private space.

ii. The public power of a private act

Starting from the proposition that public places are heteronomative, Justice Chandrachud notes that relegating homosexual acts into the private sphere, would in effect reiterate the "ambient heterosexism of the public space." Public intimacy here is not a casual act – it has world-altering consequences. To perform queer intimacy in the public sphere then would challenge this "ambient heterosexism" in a way that a merely private exercise of the same intimacy may not.

From recognizing the importance of protecting the performance of the "homosexual act," Justice Chandrachud proceeds to frame it within the importance of protecting the individual's right to "engage in sexual relations on their own terms," identifying a broader right to intimacy. This enables "an exercise of the individual's sexual agency, and includes the individual's right to the choice of partner as well as the freedom to decide on the nature of the relationship that the individual wishes to pursue."

Parallel to this frame of the right to intimacy is Justice Mishra's articulation of the right to union:

> As a concept, union also means companionship in every sense of the word, be it physical, mental, sexual or emotional. The LGBT community is seeking realization of its basic right to companionship, so long as such a companionship is consensual, free from the vice of deceit, force, coercion and does not result in violation of the fundamental rights of others.

Across these instances, whether it is expressing intimacy, choosing a transient intimate partner, or engaging in a more stable union, the link that the judges make is between the exercise of a private choice and a concomitant transformation of the public sphere. The phrase which has so far restricted the exercise of this right – "the order of nature" – is identified by Justice Chandrachud to be a mere proxy for forms of intimacy that the social order finds disturbing. Within the Indian context, there are a range of other unions that are also met with societal unease – intimacy across caste and religion leading the charge. Justice Chandrachud's final move is to link the intimate relationships between LGBT persons to these other forms of intimate transgressions. Across these instances, individuals exercise a seemingly private right to love and in the process disrupt existing lines of social authority.

iii. Private speech in public documents

What is the role of a constitutional Court? Who does it speak for, who does it speak to? What does it mean for the Court to break past formal conventions of speech and address?

At multiple levels, *Navtej Johar* plays around with these boundaries. Justice Chandrachud's decision draws on the work of activists and academics working on LGBT rights over the past two decades and in turn speaks to that very work. The first few pages of Justice Mishra's opinion are devoted to an extended reflection on the very notion of identity and self-hood. Justice Nariman reaches back to the prosecution of Oscar Wilde in crafting his opinion, opening it with acknowledging "the love that dare not speak its name," from the poem "Two Loves" written by Wilde's lover Lord Alfred Douglas. And Justice Indu Malhotra gives us an apology.

This last point is perhaps the most significant. Justice Malhotra notes,

> History owes an apology to the members of this community and their families, for the delay in providing redressal for the ignominy and ostracism that they have suffered through the centuries. The members of this community were compelled to live a life full of fear of reprisal and persecution. This was on account of the ignorance of the majority.

In offering this apology, the Court takes a moment of private emotion and transforms it into a public duty. It doesn't stop here, either. As a primer on the decision by the Alternative Law Forum notes,

> An apology only has meaning if one wants to atone for the wrongdoing of the past. An apology is not only about the past but should really provide a pathway to the future. Navtej Singh Johar is rooted in a deep sense of responsibility for having been complicit in an egregious form of violation and then seeks to redress the wrong.[15]

Justice Chandrachud acknowledges the difficulty in setting right the wrongs of history: "But we can certainly set the course for the future." The Court does this through not only providing a charter of equality for LGBT persons but also by actively urging the government about the need for implementing the same. Justice Nariman's opinion ends with urging the Union of India to take all measures to ensure the judgment is disseminated, along with providing periodic sensitization and awareness training to government officials.

Conclusion

Angel Gonzalez's poem "Inventory of Places Propitious for Love" begins by simply noting, "There aren't many." Gonzalez uses the word "love" as a stand-in for varying acts of intimacy. When he goes on to detail the potential places, he finds they are not simply dictated by the confines of architecture and geography, but other factors such as the seasons and the weather; the ways in which spring calibrates intimacy differently from autumn. The other determinant of the "propitious places," according to Gonzalez,

> there are bylaws, too proscribing caresses
> (with exemptions made for particular epidermal areas – of no interest – in children, dogs and other animals)
> and "not touching, danger of ignominy" can be read on a thousand gazes.
> The question he finally comes to: "Where to flee then?"

As *Navtej Johar* shows us, perhaps we do not have to flee at all, perhaps there is a space we might carve out for the public within the private. It is a space that we create when we take love seriously as both a subject of jurisprudence as well as an act of social transformation. And yet what does it mean for the law to provide a sanction to love?

Three months after the Supreme Court's decision, I find myself standing next to an extremely public road crossing at the end of a date. People bustle around about us, but as this man leans in for a kiss, all I feel is a sense of abandon. I can't say this is because of the judgment: most crucially, we are on a street in London, not Delhi, in a city that has very different notions of public intimacy, in a country that decriminalized homosexuality more than 50 years ago.

And yet there is a space of freedom I feel within which I carry with me as I traverse the streets back home. The radical transformation of the public sphere is an ongoing process; if the "ambient heterosexism" we are surrounded with has been punctured, the shift is slight. It is, however, perceptible. Delhi's 11th Pride March, the first post-judgment, sees larger crowds and fewer masks. In the bubble of safety we create as we march in numbers, I see queer lovers and friends kiss and embrace.

Notes

1 For an examination of some of these issues through case law in the context of Singapore, see George B. Radics, "Decolonizing Singapore's Sex Laws: Tracing Section 377A of Singapore's Penal Code," *Columbia Human Rights Law Review*, 45, no. 1 (2013): 57–99.
2 Men Having Sex with Men, see, e.g., LGBT Section 377, Lawyers Collective, available at http:/ /www.lawyerscollective.org/vulnerable-cormmunities/1gbt/section-377.html, accessed 16 February 2018.
3 The specific question of HIV/AIDS prevention supplied the grounds with which Naz Foundation approached the Delhi High Court, represented in the petition by the argument that Section 377 was violative of the right to life, given that it drove homosexual activity underground, thus jeopardizing HIV/AIDS prevention efforts. However, the petition also argued against the constitutionality of Section 377 on a number of other contentions. It made a case for how the prohibition of certain private consensual sexual relations violated the right to privacy guaranteed within the ambit of the right to liberty under Article 21, that the criminalization of non-procreative sexual relations was unreasonable and arbitrary and therefore violative of Article 14, that it further violated the prohibition of sex discrimination under Article 15 and finally that the criminalization of predominantly homosexual conduct curtailed the enjoyment of liberties guaranteed under Article 19.
4 Unofficial Transcripts, available at http://orinam.net/content/wp-content/uploads/2012/04/Naz_SC_Transcript_2012_final.pdf; I discuss the hearings at length in another essay: Danish Sheikh, "The Road to Decriminalization: Litigating India's Anti-Sodomy Law," *Yale Human Rights and Development Journal*, 16, no. 1 (2013): 15–25.
5 See NUJS Law Review Special Edition on Naz Foundation v. Union of India, Volume 2, Issue 3, 2009.
6 See "Dignity First", available at http://altlawforum.org/campaigns/dignity-first-one-year-of-resistance-to-re-criminalisation-of-lgbt-lives/, accessed 17 February 2018.
7 The issue of decriminalization even made its way into the manifestos of the Aam Aadmi Party and the Communist Party of India (Marxist). Notably, the Bharatiya Janata Party, which is now the party in power in the country was silent on the matter.
8 National Human Rights Commission wants Section 377 Modified, available at www.dnaindia.com/india/report-national-human-rights-commission-wants-section-377-modified-1934603.
9 Deconstructing Intimacy: Ranjana Dave In Conversation with Mandeep Raikhy, available at www.ligament.in/interview-mandeep-raikhy.html.
10 Ibid.
11 The hijra community occupies a distinct sociocultural identity comprising transgender individuals who voluntarily seek initiation into the community, with members living in accordance with a set of customs and rituals that vary from region to region. Some have argued that the term "transgender" is problematic. Jain (2017, 45) argues that it is "imperative to understand that in the South Asian context, transgender does not accurately describe the diversity of this heterogeneous community. Transgender has multiple meanings depending on the region, culture, or nation in which it is used." Thus,

she prefers to use the more inclusive term "gender-variant people" to describe this community.

12 The *de minimis* hypothesis that the *Puttuswamy* case rejects is *Koushal's* argument that Section 377 only affects a small minority of individuals since there have been only 200 cases of prosecutions under it.

13 *Bar and Bench* interview with Menaka Guruswamy, available at https://barandbench.com/menaka-guruswamy-interview-section-377-lgbtq/.

14 See "Right to Love," available at http://altlawforum.org/publications/right-to-love-navtej-singh-johar-v-union-of-india-a-transformative-constitution-and-the-rights-of-lgbt-persons/.

15 "Right to Love: Navtej Singh Johar v. Union of India: A Transformative Constitution and the Rights of LGBT Persons," available at http://altlawforum.org/wp-content/uploads/2018/09/RightToLove_PDFVersion-1.pdf.

References

Cases

National Legal Services Authority v. Union of India [2014] 5 S.C.C. 438.
Naz Foundation v. Government of NCT of Delhi 160 [2009] DLT 277.
Suresh Kumar Koushal v. Naz Foundation [2014] 1 S.C.C. 1.

Books and articles

Bar and Bench Interview with Menaka Guruswamy. Available at: https://barandbench.com/menaka-guruswamy-interview-section-377-lgbtq/

Dave, N.N. (2012) *Queer Activism in India: A Story in the Anthropology of Ethics*. Durham, NC: Duke University Press.

"Dignity First." (2014) 'Dignity First: One Year of Resistance to Re-Criminalization of LGBT Lives,' *Coalition for Sex Workers and Sexuality Minority Rights (CSMR)*. Available at: http://altlawforum.org/campaigns/dignity-first-one-year-of-resistance-to-re-criminalization-of-lgbt-lives/ (Accessed on: 17 February 2018).

International Commission of Jurists. (2017). 'Unnatural Offences.' Available at: www.icj.org/wp-content/uploads/2017/02/India-SOGI-report-Publications-Reports-Thematic-report-2017-ENG.pdf

Jain, D. (2017) 'Shifting Subjects of State Legibility: Gender Minorities and the Law in India,' *Berkeley Journal Gender Law & Justice*, 32, p. 39.

Men Having Sex with Men, see, e.g., LGBT Section 377, Lawyers Collective. Available at: www.lawyerscollective.org/vulnerable-cornmunities/1gbt/section-377.html (Accessed on: 16 February, 2018).

Narrain, A. (2004) *Queer: Law, Despised Sexuality and Social Change*. Bangalore: Books for Change.

Radics, G.B. (2013) 'Decolonizing Singapore's Sex Laws: Tracing Section 377A of Singapore's Penal Code,' *Columbia Human Rights Law Review*, 45(1), pp. 57–99.

Warner, M. (2005) *Publics and Counterpublics*. New York: Zone Books.

Chapter 4

Gambling with criminal law

The legal paradox of "jogo do bicho" (animal lottery) criminalization in Brazil

João Araújo Monteiro Neto and Nestor Eduardo Araruna Santiago

Introduction

Brazil has one of the largest illegal gaming industries of the world (Guimarães, 2017; Freire, 2019). Recent studies suggest that the most popular illegal lottery in Brazil, "jogo do bicho" (animal lottery), alone generates between 1.3 to 2.8 Billion Brazilian Reais per year ($350 to $800 USD million), making it the largest illegal gaming activity in the world (Huff Post Brasil, 2015). The country's complex and anachronistic gaming regulatory framework is based on a rationale plagued with the contradiction that opposes the criminalization of gaming to protect social morality but at the same time uses state-controlled gaming operations to collect funding resources. The use of criminal law to regulate and restrict access to gaming practices also disregards the nationally widespread gaming habit. This enrooted gaming culture (Medeiros, Grant & Tavares, 2016; Tavares, 2014) that encourages more than 20 million people to play "jogo do bicho" everyday (José, 2016) also affects the enforcement of the existing regulatory framework, including the softening of criminal law provisions applied to illegal gaming. Investigating the operation of criminal law in an environment where regulatory elements based on criminal law are opposed to cultural values is crucial to understand some important socio-legal interactions that influences the day-to day practice of criminal law in Brazil. To shed light on these interactions, this chapter observes the particular role played by the *social adequacy theory* in the ambiguous criminalization of "bicho[1]" in Brazil and at the same time analyzes its potential to support the development of an alternative policy approach promoting the decriminalization of gaming practices like it. While this theoretical framework is considered by Brazilian scholars to be a crucial element to support and legitimize a democratic criminal law system focused on the protection of society's core values (Prado, 2010), the lack of clear judicial guidelines and the fragile judicial consensus around its operation create a blurry semi-legal area where criminal law enforcement is weakened. This ambivalent legal space contributes not only to the flourishing of a very particular criminal ecosystem associated with "jogo do bicho" (Chazkel, 2007; Freire, 2019; Coelho, 2018) but also to the instability and inefficacy of the constitutional framework to regulate crimes in Brazil.

Using a socio-legal approach the chapter presents the historical development and the legal framing of the criminalization of "jogo do bicho" in the country. The second section explores theoretical elements used to support the non-application of criminal provisions by law and enforcement actors in "jogo do bicho" cases and the third section explores the mafia-like ecosystem that emerges in the shadow of its criminalization. The last section discusses the effects of this ambiguous regulatory scenario on the criminalization of gaming activities and in the general structure of the Brazilian criminal law system. It is important to note that during this discussion, the social adequacy theory is used to explain the rationality underpinning the government's "soft" enforcement of a somewhat harsher legal regulatory framework of illegal gambling. At the same time, the social adequacy theory serves as a lens to analyze the phenomenon of continued gambling despite its criminalization and to propose an alternative policy approach, such as its de-criminalization.

Historical and legal contextualization of "jogo do bicho" in Brazil

"Jogo do bicho" embodies cultural elements that synthesize much of the evolution and contradictions found in Brazilian society and its relationship with the law. The game has been strongly connected to the romanticized culture of the "bom malandro carioca"[2] (Coelho, 2018) that flourished in Rio de Janeiro during the 1920s and 1930s. This association completely changed in the 1970s and 1980s when "jogo do bicho" became operated by large criminal organizations involved with serious criminal offenses, such as drug trafficking and bank robbery (Freire, 2019; Labronici & Da Silva, 2018). Even though this transformation deeply influenced the legal structure regulating gaming practices in Brazil, it had little effect on the cultural framework feeding the Brazilian interest in betting and in games such as "jogo do bicho." In a recent study, the Brazilian think tank Getulio Vargas Foundation suggested that the regulation of "jogo do bicho" could increase the government's tax collection by more than 30 billion Brazilian Reais or approximately 8 billion US dollars (Valor Econômico, 2017).

The game was created in the later years of the 19th century with the objective of generating funds to maintain a small zoo in the city of Rio de Janeiro (Mattos, 1991). Aiming to promote the study of zoology, Mr. João Batista Viana Drummond, the baron of Drummond, used one of his properties to establish in 1888 a small exhibition of animals found in the Brazilian fauna. Suffering from severe financial difficulties, particularly due to elevated feeding and maintenance costs, the Baron, who was a close friend of Emperor Dom Pedro II, considered closing the zoo when he was granted some support from the Brazilian imperial government. While the support was welcomed, the financial sustainability of the zoo was still in jeopardy, and the baron continued to work to secure funding arrangements able to guarantee the long-term maintenance of the first zoo to be opened in the country (Lucena, 2017; Chazkel, 2007).

Nonetheless, this stable source of funding would be very short due to historical changes in the government. On 15 November 1889, the Brazilian Empire was overthrown, and the Brazilian Republic was proclaimed. Under the influence of republican principles, the new regime canceled government funding for the zoo. In order to raise funds to maintain the project, with authorization of local authorities, the baron of Drummond decided to explore some gaming activities. Using the expertise of Manuel Ismael Zevada, a Mexican citizen with gaming experience, Drummond decided to explore a lottery game based on the animals exhibited in the zoo. He painted 25 pictures each representing a different animal. The picture was also associated with a group of four sequential numbers. These figures and numbers were printed randomly on the zoo's entrance tickets (Figure 4.1), and every day the baron picked one picture to be put in a secret box displayed at the zoo. At the end of the day, the figure was revealed, and all visitors holding tickets with the same animal would receive a prize (Magalhães, 2009, 2011)

After the first drawing, the game became very popular, "unleashing a new gambling market" (Freire, 2019). While gaming activities could only be explored under very restrictive licenses – for instance, playing games of chance were already illegal – the success of the game and its direct impact on the day-to-day life of the city called the attention of law enforcement authorities. Most of the city, including many unemployed people, came to visit the zoo just to play the game. Even the public transportation system was impacted; the number of people traveling to the zoo was much more than the trams could transport. This led the baron to start selling the game tickets in the city center and other local shops in order to allow people to play the game without attending the zoo (Chazkel, 2007). Analyzing this process, Magalhães (2009, 2011) pointed out that "official documents indicates that the number of persons attending the zoo only to bet was one of the main reasons leading to a public scandal and the decision to ban the game."

Figure 4.1 Ticket to the Rio de Janeiro Zoo allowing the holder to join the "jogo do bicho" draw

Source: Museu da Imagem e do Som, Rio de Janeiro. Reproduced in Chazkel (2011, pp. 35–36).

The "jogo do bicho" craze swept the whole city after independent sellers entered the marketplace (Magalhães, 2011; Soares, 1993). A network of street bookmakers, called "bicheiros," expanded the original game in innovative ways. Evading state regulations, "bicheiros" made the lottery available in every part of Rio by scalping tickets or promoting their own versions of the clandestine numbers game (Chazkel, 2007, 2011, p. 37). "Jogo do bicho" became so widespread that Olavo Bilac, a major literary figure in 19th-century Brazil, summarized the situation as follows: "Today [1895], in Rio de Janeiro, the game is everything. [. . .] Nobody works! Everybody plays" (Pacheco, 1957, p. 43). But this state of affairs did not last. As noted by Chazkel (2007, p. 536), the fragile legal consensus supporting the legal operation of the game and its initial treatment was reversed less than one decade after its first emergence. Civil servants and police officers criminalized "jogo do bicho" on the grounds of "public safety" and launched a countrywide campaign against the game (Benatte, 2002; Villar, 2008; Coelho, 2018; Freire, 2019, p. 2).

Although it was formally prohibited in order to protect the morality of Brazilian society, the game's basic rules had already spread throughout the city, and, consequently, gambling was almost impossible to control. Its popularity was based on the simplicity of the rules, which made it easy and seductive to play as the association of animals and numbers became culturally intertwined with the interpretation of dreams or day-to-day facts that could be translated to animals and, consequently, to numbers and ultimately bets. The subsequent association of the game with the Carnival (Brazil's most famous annual festival) and other elements of the cultural environment of Rio de Janeiro (Coelho, 2018), and the adoption of carefully designed reputation strategies (Freire, 2019, p. 4) made it even more difficult to create the social and political support necessary to repress the game.

"Jogo do bicho" is a popular game not only because of its simple rules: the game operation was also simple and based on two main pillars: hierarchy and trust. There are three different actors distributed throughout the hierarchical structure of the game: the "apontadores" (bookmakers), the "gerentes" (managers) and the "banqueiros" (bankers) (Chazkel, 2007, 2011; Freire, 2019). At the bottom of the hierarchy are the "apontadores." They occupy the lower operational structure of the game and oversee ticket distribution, collect the bets, and market the game. They normally work alone and are easily recognizable by their traditional "banca," a simple stand with annotation blocks containing the bets, prizes, and results (Chazkel, 2011). The "gerentes" are in charge of supervising the operation of all "apontadores" in a specific area. They manage the movement of money and information between "apontadores" and "banqueiros," which include the payment of all actors involved in the lower operation of the game (Chazkel, 2007; Coelho, 2018).

The "banqueiros" are at the top of the game structure. They provide the financial support to the game and benefit from its profits. Their main objectives are funding the game, controlling the game's financial operations, offering logistical support (including the payment of bribes to law enforcement officers), and providing legal representation for prosecuted employees (Freire, 2019; Labronici, 2012; Labronici & Da Silva, 2018). This simple and operative organizational design contributes to the game's widespread dissemination throughout the country and contributed to the "trust" players have in the game's fair operation. The well-established hierarchical regime contributes significantly to the game's high level of trust because each actor knows that any deviant behavior or cheating will be severely punished by the actor in the position above (Coelho, 2018). Despite its nonwritten rules, "bicho" is highly regulated, which increases trust in the organization (Vasconcelos, 2016).

Most of the players do not realize that when they win, their payment is paid out not only by the bookmaker but also by all involved in the game. One good example of this process is the practice of the "descarga" ("unloading"). It is a financial mechanism based on the game's hierarchical structure that guarantees the payment of higher winning bets (Magalhães, 2011). As illustrated by Freire (2019) and Lambronici (2012) small bankers and booking agents are sometimes due to honor very expensive bets as the animal game top prize can pays up to 4,000 times the amount invested; consequently the "bicheiros" have to create mechanisms to raise quickly thousands of Brazilian Reais to honor the bet, pay the winners and maintain the game's trust. To prevent the "quebra da banca" ("bust of the bank"), "bicheiros" and small bankers purchase insurance from wealthy financiers who offer this service for a fee that ranges from 20% to 25% of the total selling amount. This informal insurance mechanisms supports liquidity of small bookmakers and the continuity of the gaming operations (Labronici, 2012).

Such mechanisms and practices give the game a good reputation for consumers. Brazilians widely perceive the game as honest, as its popular motto exemplifies this: "Vale o escrito; ganhou, leva" ("What is written down is what counts; if you win it, you take it") (Magalhães, 2011; Freire, 2019; Santos, 1996). This way "jogo do bicho" becomes reliable because it is simple. One does not need to know how to read to play, and it is reliable as it only depends on the word of the banker who must honor the winning bet or might have his word discredited. Although informal, bettors, scorers, managers, and bankers must follow a number of unwritten rules that are seriously enforced (Santos, 1996; Misse, 2011).

Even though it is widely played and deeply associated with the cultural and political environment of almost all Brazilian big urban centers, the operation of "jogo do bicho" has faced legal obstacles since its early years (Coelho, 2018, Chazkel, 2007; Lambroncini & Da Silva, 2018). The criminalization of its operation and its practices was the first and only strategy adopted to regulate the game. Years later, this approach was reinforced with the enactment of the "Decreto-Lei n. 3.688/1941," the "Lei das Contravenções Penais" (Minor Criminal Offenses Law) that established that any action contributing to the promotion of "jogo do bicho" was considered a minor criminal offense (art. 58). This approach was reinforced in 1944 in the Decreto-Lei n. 6.269/44. The new law was produced particularly to regulate the newly established state-operated lottery system while it reinforced the criminalization of the operation of the animal lottery.[3] Later, this context was tightened with the Decreto-Lei n. 204/1967, establishing the need to fight against activities promoting illegal gambling while authorizing governmental institutions to exclusively run the lottery industry.

Despite numerous bills proposing the decriminalization and consequent regulation of the game, and changes in the administration or the law in other areas, there was little progress in regulating (or de-regulating) "jogo do bicho." The operation of the game is still formally considered a minor criminal offense. This characterization feeds an unstable and uncertain operational space where government actors do not agree with which criminal approach to adopt when regulating gambling in general and "bicho" in particular. The softening of law enforcement under the informal application of the social adequacy theory or the tightening of the enforcement through the application of provisions designed to punish more serious offenses that flourish in association with "jogo do bicho" destabilizes the constitutional framework supporting the operation of criminal law in Brazil. Moreover, this scenario limits not only the adoption of the social adequacy theory but also its contribution to the development of a more transparent and democratic criminal law system.

Thinking about "jogo do bicho" (de)criminalization through criminal law theory

Any legal analysis of the regulation of "jogo do bicho" in Brazil must take into account two elements. First, it is important to observe the socio-legal aspects supporting the criminalization of gaming activities in Brazil; second, it is crucial to understand the role played by the theoretical frameworks used to guide and legitimize criminal laws in Brazil, particularly taking into account the significant influence the Brazilian Constitution has in this arena (Prado, 2010). The protection of "legal goods" (also legally protected interests, legal values, or legal assets) and its theoretical structure is one core element guiding all stages of the criminalization process in Brazil. Essentially, this theory proposes that policy-making processes and the application of legal provisions by law enforcement authorities and courts should be consistent with legal assets found in the text of the Constitution (Tavares, 2002). While the "legal goods" theory has some currency in making sense of the complex phenomenon of "jogo do bicho," this section will review this theory in conjunction with competing theories that can be seen as influencing Brazilian criminal law to explain how and why "jogo do bicho" is criminalized. Starting with the legal interest theory, the section will then move on to discuss the competing theories of minimum interference and, finally, social adequacy – it is argued that the social adequacy theory can help understand "jogo do bicho's" operation in the shadows as well as propose for more equitable ways of dealing with it.

i. Legal interest theory

The "legally protected interest" rationale, an axiological theoretical framework developed by Claus Roxin (Roxin, 2013), associates the criminalization process with the protection of values necessary to provide society with the minimum conditions for a free and peaceful development. Widely embedded in criminal law theory, the concept of legal goods or "legally protected interests" is used to guide the criminalization process (Puig, 2008), mainly by indicating "what interests are or ought to be protected by criminal norms" (Santarelli, 2013, p. 408).

This theoretical framework can be seen as being applied not only in the process leading up to the establishment of the Brazilian criminal code in 1940 but also in the development of almost all Brazilian criminal laws after the code's promulgation. Nevertheless, it is important to note that in some cases, the criminalization process was dissociated from the constitutional frame of "legal protected interest" enshrined in the criminal code. Take, for example, the Brazilian Federal Law n. 8.137/1990, which criminalized acts against the tax system, the economic order, and the consumer relations: many criminal law scholars could not accept the fact that the tax criminal law was designed to protect the state activity of a collecting taxes (Prado, 2010) when normally this use of the criminal law system, in democratic conditions (Silveira, 2003), is intended to protect the public administration in its transindividual perspective as a collective right, not the government's capacity to collect taxes.

One of the key aspects that must be observed during the criminalization process under the protection of "legal protected interest" theoretical framework is the need to evaluate carefully which interests should be protected using criminal law, what should be the level of protection, and what values motivate and support the use of criminal law to establish its protective framework. These are key aspects backing not only the development of a balanced criminal law system but also to evaluate to what extent it is reasonable to use the full power of criminal law provisions to regulate the so-called dwarven offenses – minor criminal acts that carry a lower level of social reprobation, are punished with reduced penalties, and do not generate criminal records for offenders.

The operation of criminal law and the consequent protection of legal interests removes the protected value from its concrete form and elevates its meaning in the criminal law system to a more strategic position (Prado, 2002a). Moreover, since the Brazilian criminal law system uses the "legal good" framing as its main reference point, it also recognizes the theoretical framework role in the interpretation of the criminal offenses mainly by 1) conditioning the scope of application of the criminal norm to its need to protect the "legal interest's" core elements and 2) recognizing the noncriminal nature of acts that does not cause injury or exposes to danger the protected "legal interest." As noted by Szczucki (2016, p. 46), "In the axiological-teleological concept the central stage is occupied by a negative valuation of an action, one that refers to societal goods, as well as a statutory order to avoid such behavior." While actors conducting the criminalization process have a certain degree of freedom to select what goods should be protected by criminal law provisions and what punishments should be attributed, this selection process must primarily take account of the system of values established in the Brazilian constitution.

ii. Minimum intervention theory

The legal interest theory contrasts with one of the core elements informing the scholarship supporting the operation of criminal law in Brazil, "the Direito Penal Mínimo"[4] and the "principle of minimum intervention of criminal law." Based on Cesare Beccaria's landmark book *On Crimes and Punishment* (Beccaria, 1764 [2013]), and the need to avoid the criminalization of unnecessary acts in order to avoid criminal law's loss of efficacy, the "minimum interference of the criminal law" principle is understood to protect the criminal law effectiveness by only allowing the intervention of criminal law in situations where the "legal interest" can only be effectively protected by the use of criminal law. This protection must be used only in cases where other protective mechanisms established are considered insufficient to shelter the "legal good or interest."

With the enactment of the 1988 Brazilian Constitution, the constitutional framing of criminal law significantly changed the rationality behind the criminalization of "jogo do bicho." Built upon a democratic and human-centric approach, the Constitution established, mainly in Article 5, a group of principles guiding the criminalization process and the application of criminal law. While recognizing traditional criminal law principles like legality and anteriority, the constitutional order also recognized the principle of the minimum intervention of criminal law (Paschoal, 2003).

Recognizing the relevant role played by the "legal protected interest" theory, and to a certain extent the "minimum interference" theory, in the application of criminal law in Brazil, and the existence of relevant cultural practices in relation to gaming activities in Brazil, particularly in relation to "jogo do bicho," some key questions begin to resonate in the mind of scholars, practitioners, and law enforcement authorities, such as, What is the legal interest protected throughout the criminalization of gaming activities like "jogo do bicho"? Does the criminal protection sufficiently protect the legal interest set out in the Brazilian Constitution? To what extent is the protection of this legal interest perceived as necessary by the population? Does enrooted customary practices have the power to halt the application of criminal law provisions? While the Brazilian criminal law system does not authorize the use of customary practices to repeal the law, the day-to-day operation indicates a contrasting reality. The criminalization of established social practices like gaming create a blurred regulatory space where legal and nonlegal – or more precisely criminalization and the non-criminalization – coexist creating an "in between legal space" where uncertainty flourish. Out of the minimum interference theory, a theoretical development grounded the principle of *social adequacy* began to play a significative role in the operation of the contrasting rationales guiding the application of criminal law in Brazil. The next section will discuss the social adequacy theory and its potential to better understand the questions noted earlier.

iii. Social adequacy theory

The notion and the effects of the principle of social adequacy in the application of criminal law is largely attributed to the German criminal law scholar Hans Welzel (Bitencourt, 1999; Prado, 2002b; Szczucki, 2016). According to Stajnko (2017, p. 126), "The notion of socially adequate conduct was first mentioned and developed by Welzel in his contribution from 1939, titled 'Studien zum System des Strafrechts' (Studies on Criminal Law System)." It is in this particular article that Welzel began to construct the idea of social adequacy. He argues that if criminal law is considered a socio-ethical phenomenon, it is imperative to comprehend this system under the influence of contingent social rules historically developed, and

> this is where the doctrine of social adequacy becomes relevant. If a certain action or omission is, in the light of the so-called social integrity (Ger. 'das soziale Ganze'), deemed to be acceptable by society, the injustice of the conduct is not significant enough for it to be considered conduct subject to criminalization.
>
> (Stajnko, 2017, p. 127)

Following this rationale, Welzel (2011) develops his doctrine, indicating that only conducts that harm or endanger legally protected interests that are in line with established elements based on historically developed contingent social rules can be subject to criminal regulation. Consequently, under the influence of the social adequacy doctrine, an action can only be considered socially adequate if a certain behavior is accepted as necessary to promote a stable and safe level of coexistence in a given community. Therefore, it can be used as a mechanism to limit the power of legislators to criminalize behaviors by checking those purported criminal behaviors against the current morals of the community in which the criminal law is realized (Szczucki, 2016, p. 48). In other words, the text of the law must correspond with historically developed social rules.

As mentioned earlier in this chapter, the enactment of the 1988 Brazilian Constitution provided criminal law scholars a framework able to support the minimum interference theory. It can be argued that this framework also demonstrates the operation of the doctrine of social adequacy as well. The appropriation of its concept by influential academics and practitioners (Prado, 2002b; Lopes, 2000; Bitencourt, 1999) paved the way not only for the theoretical development of the doctrine but also to its application in very conflicting legal cases. Take, for example, the questioning of the criminalization of copyright violations and illegal gaming practices in cases ruled by the Brazilian Supreme Federal Court. Challenges in these types of cases have been dismissed on the principle of social adequacy, rejecting a more formal application of the law.[5]

While Brazilian academics and practitioners push forward the application of the social adequacy doctrine to decriminalize conducts accepted socially, this process leads to the adoption of some progressive criminal policies – for example, the softening of criminal laws on the possession of drugs for personal consumption (Federal Law n. 11.343/2006, article 28). However, it is important to note that this process has not yet touched the criminal regulation of gambling in Brazil. Looking carefully to the historical development of "jogo do bicho" and its criminalization process, it is important to note that all reforms to the Brazilian criminal law system in the last 30 years, including the most recent proposal,[6] never discussed any changes to "jogo do bicho's" criminal status. Instead, they suggest the continuity of the criminal rationality applied to gambling and support its transformation from minor to major criminal offense, which includes enhancing its punishment (Arguello, 2012).

The need to strengthen the criminal repression in criminal offenses related to gambling, particularly in the case of "jogo do bicho," is based on three distinct factors: a) moral order as the regulation of gambling and gaming can stimulate the addiction and moral degeneration; b) instrumentality to serious offenses as the "jogo do bicho" industry is deeply associated with criminal organizations that practice drug trafficking and corruption; c) procedural restrictions do not allow law and enforcement authorities to use more sophisticated and invasive investigative methods like electronic and telephone wiretapping.

This rationality of criminalization and enhanced punishment contrasts with the sociocultural environment informing the operation of criminal law in Brazil. While criminal law provisions are still enforceable, in the case of "jogo do bicho" there is a distinct intersection between crime and culture very similar to the one supporting the emergence of the samba music movement and the romantic view of the criminal associated to the jogo do bicho as the "bom malandro carioca" (the good vagabond from Rio de Janeiro). These cultural values are strong enough to affect the enforceability of criminal law provisions and weaken attempts to repress games like "jogo do bicho" (Arguello, 2012).

However, according to Brazilian positivistic approaches to criminal law and the conservative interpretation of the constitutional framework regulating criminal law application, cultural values or customary practices cannot repeal criminal law provisions, particularly the ones establishing crimes and its penalties. Nevertheless, recent theoretical developments, particularly the theory of the "teoria da tipicidade conglobante" (criminalization based on a normative system considered in its totality rather than in isolation), gained relevance in the operation of the principle of social adequacy as an instrument to repeal the criminalization of behaviors included in criminal law but is widely accepted and practiced in the social context (Zaffaroni & Pierangeli, 2004).

In this context the social adequacy of criminal law has two important functions. Initially, it works to restrict the scope of criminal law by imposing limits on its interpretation. Its other relevant role is to support the decriminalization process (Carvalho & Prado, 2006). The social adequacy principle supports lawmakers during the selection of the behaviors that should be considered criminal offenses by indicating that practices accepted by society should not be criminalized or conversely, behaviors that are criminalized but socially accepted must be decriminalized: "quando o Direito ignora a realidade, a realidade se vinga, ignorando o Direito" (when the Law disregards reality, reality avenges itself by disregarding the Law) (Ripert, 2000). In other words, the principle helps to construct a more solid, transparent, legitimate, and democratic system once two boundaries are established: 1) the legal protected interests established by the Brazilian Constitution and 2) the social acceptation of the law.

The Brazilian application of the social adequacy principle extends the original concept proposed by Hans Welzel, mainly in the judicial operation of criminal law. Connecting the theory with other constitutional values guiding the application of criminal law, Brazilian courts began to not consider crime actions that cause only minor damage to legal interests protected by the criminal law provision, or when harming the legal interest is accepted by the community. Using this legal rationale, courts acquit defendants when although the act fits perfectly in the abstract provision of the law, it does not damage or endanger the legal interest in the way required to trigger criminal law intervention. Nevertheless, there is no consensus among legal practitioners on this interpretation, which means that it will depend on which judge, police officer, or prosecutor handles the case to see if there will be a viable criminal suit or not. Of course, the absence of a consistent understanding of the application of the social adequacy principle by those who enforce the law produces a space of uncertainty that weakens the criminalization system, encouraging arbitrariness or introducing the potential for prejudice.

In the case of "jogo do bicho," this decriminalization rationality is reinforced by the particular nature of the "legal protected interest." Criminalization of gambling and gaming in the Brazilian context takes place when they are associated with moral depravity and vice, two interests in dissonance with the constitutional values guiding the operation of criminal law in Brazil. The use of criminal law to police "morality and good behavior," vague and blurry "legal interests," in cases such as a minor offense established in the Brazilian criminal law system, particularly "jogo do bicho," "vadiagem" (vagrancy), and "mendicância" (begging) contrast with the freedoms and rights guaranteed in the Brazilian Constitution. Moreover, all these acts could easily be regulated through less invasive mechanisms like administrative law or decriminalized under the social adequacy principle (Nucci, 2014). In response to its criminalization, however, "jogo do bicho" has developed a whole new set of issues that make its regulation even more complicated. The next section will look at the mafia-like manifestations in "jogo do bicho" that have emerged in the shadows of its criminalization.

Mafia behavior vs. elite moralization

Since the late 1980s, there has been a new approach toward law enforcement of "jogo do bicho." Misse (2011) argues that the structure of the "bicho" enterprise resembles a "mafia" organization. In 1993, some "banqueiros" from Rio de Janeiro were arrested and later convicted under the Criminal Organization Law. The background for this conviction was the fact that in 1980, the "banqueiros" ended their disputes by creating a mafia-like council due to the fall in profits from the daily lotteries offered by the official lottery. Some of the "consigliere" invested in legal activities and in small clandestine casinos; others preferred to continue a dispute over control of the distribution of slot machines in Rio de Janeiro. Similar prosecutions and convictions happened after 2000 in the Brazilian states Ceará and Pernambuco.

In this way, acting like a criminal organization made it easier for law enforcement to prosecute "banqueiros," with a slight consequence to "apontadores" and "gerentes." In spite of its regulation, the "bicho" structure and operation was left virtually intact. The appeal of the game remains strong despite criminalization: people do not understand why "bicho" is illegal and state lottery is not, considering that trust is the central nucleus of operation of both lotteries. The boundaries between the organization of the "bicho" and the society it serves are unclear, making the game so popular, attractive, and difficult to be understood as illegal (Santos, 1996).

It is important to note that despite not being the main objective of this chapter, the fragile legal consensus supporting the criminalization of "jogo do bicho" has been characterized by socio-legal scholarship as the result of a "moral passage" process (Huggins, 1985; Chazkel, 2007), implicating the use of criminal law to regulate aspects of Brazilian society other than solely its public morality. As noted by Aguirre and Salvatore (2001, p. 13), the operation of law in Latin America, not surprisingly, has generally reflected the continuous power exercised by state officials, members of the upper classes, and professional lawyers and jurists. Particularly in Brazil, the use of criminal law to protect the modernizing and aristocratic notion of public morality was the mechanism selected to regulate two emerging elements of the new republic: the urban poor and the private commercial entrepreneurship (Chazkel, 2007, 2011).

Analyzing the social and cultural elements grounding the construction of crime in cases resembling to "jogo do bicho" in Brazil, Piccato (2001), Borges (2001) and Rivera-Garza (2001) indicate some of the instrumental rationales underpinning the social elements guiding the moralization phenomenon that lead society to designate practices such as gambling, prostitution, drinking, vagrancy, and cultural manifestations like "capoeira" (an Afro-Carribean martial art) to be considered illegal. Particularly in relation to "jogo do bicho," Chazkel (2011) suggests that the criminalization of the game was mainly grounded in the need to regulate the emerging ecosystem of commercial enterprises and the uncontrolled competition and consumption arising from the game. At the same time, these regulations indirectly control the access of the lower classes to entertainment able to spur undesirable behaviors that threatened the "stability and progress of the new Brazilian Republic" (Chazkel, 2007, p. 536).

Criminalizing "jogo do bicho" contradicts the existing constitutional framework behind the Brazilian criminal law system that regulates only acts that are able to harm Brazilian society's main values and interests. Furthermore, criminalization only contributes to weaken the criminal law system and the development of semi-legal practices that undermines the maintenance of a transparent and democratic use of criminal law. As noted by Chazkel (2007, p. 564), the criminalization of "jogo do bicho" still reflects "an instrumental effect than a moral consensus;" or, in essence, allows law enforcement authorities and citizens to modulate the effects of criminal law according to their interests, even when the game culturally or constitutionally should not be considered illegal.

Some final considerations

The criminalization of gaming in Brazil and the application of criminal law provisions to "jogo do bicho" expose an inconsistency that causes legal uncertainty and undermines criminal law efficacy and enforceability. The informal decriminalized nature of "jogo do bicho" that occurs in the day-to-day operation of law enforcement conflicts directly with the refusal of Brazilian courts to accept and apply this principle to certain types of criminal offenses, including gaming. The uncertainty created by this unusual operational scenario not only affects the normativity of criminal law in Brazil but also promotes the development of unregulated performative spaces. In these gray areas, law enforcement authorities operate the application of criminal law and the concretization of the criminalization process through practices diverging from core values of the Brazilian criminal law system. This divergence between the formalized criminal law and the practiced one creates blurred areas where law and enforcement authorities promote arbitrariness, unregulated discretion, and corruption.

This unregulated and blurred governance also creates a continued suspicious aura over operators and players. This atmosphere stigmatizes the gaming activity, its practices, and growth. The lack of clarity associated with the operation of criminal law in the gaming regime creates an invisible but tangible legally inducted barrier that inhibits the ludic and commercial potentialities normally associated with the gaming industry developed in a stable and coordinated regulatory environment. At the same time, the criminalization of "jogo do bicho" as a minor offense provides criminal organizations or serious offenders a very tentative space to exercise criminal entrepreneurship. The lack of a more serious response to the criminal activity stimulates the use of the "jogo do bicho" as a mechanism to avoid a higher degree of criminal accountability mainly by preventing the application of stronger penalties or by enabling the application of procedural benefits used only for the investigation and trial of minor offenses.

Finally, the main consequence of this informal and unregulated use of criminal law by the Brazilian government and its law and enforcement bodies is the contrasting way they operate the social adequacy doctrine in policy-making and legal operation processes interconnecting gaming and criminal policy. In the criminalization of gambling, the Brazilian state promotes and supports a modulated application of the social adequacy of gaming activities exploited by government bodies but criminalizes and represses traditional and culturally accepted gaming practices of private actors. This incongruent position only strengthens the growing need to regulate gaming in Brazil more coherently, particularly promoting its decriminalization and the unnecessary use of criminal law to control society's morality.

Notes

1 Shorthand for "jogo do bicho."

2 The good vagabond from the city of Rio de Janeiro.

3 Art. 58. Realizar o denominado "jogo do bicho", em que um dos participantes, considerado comprador ou ponto, entrega certa quantia com a indicação de combinações de algarismos ou nome de animais, a que correspondem números, ao outro participante, considerado o vendedor ou banqueiro, que se obriga mediante qualquer sorteio ao pagamento de prêmios em dinheiro. Penas: de seis (6) meses a um (1) ano de prisão simples e multa de dez mil cruzeiros (Cr$ 10.000,00) a cinqüenta mil cruzeiros (Cr$ 50.000,00) ao vendedor ou banqueiro, e de quarenta (40) a trinta (30) dias de prisão celular ou multa de duzentos cruzeiros (Cr$ 200,00) a quinhentos cruzeiros (Cr$ 500,00) ao comprador ou ponto.

§ 1° Incorrerão nas penas estabelecidas para vendedores ou banqueiros:

a) os que servirem de intermediários na efetuação do jogo;
b) os que transportarem, conduzirem, possuírern, tiverem sob sua guarda ou poder, fabricarern, darem, cederem, trocarem, guardarem em qualquer parte, listas com indicações do jogo ou material próprio para a contravenção, bem como de qualquer forma contribuírem para a sua confecção, utilização, curso ou emprego, seja qual for a sua espécie ou quantidade;
c) os que procederem à apuração de listas ou à organização de mapas relativos ao movimento do jogo;
d) os que por qualquer modo promoverem ou facilitarem a realização do jogo

4 Among many, cf. Paschoal, Janaína Conceição. *Constituição, criminalização e direito penal mínimo*. São Paulo: Revista dos Tribunais, 2003.

5 STF – HC 118322 / MS – MATO GROSSO DO SUL, 22/10/2013. STF – RHC 115986 / ES – ESPÍRITO SANTO, 25/06/2013.

6 BRASIL. Senado Federal. *Anteprojeto de Reforma do Código Penal*, 2012. Available at www.conjur.com.br/dl/anteprojeto-codigo-penal.pdf. Acesso em 05 de agosto de 2018.

References

Aguirre, C.A. & Salvatore, R.D. (2001) Writing the History of Law, Crime, and Punishment in Latin America. In Salvatore, R.D., et al. (eds.), *Crime and Punishment in Latin America: Law and Society since Late Colonial Times*. Durham: Duke University Press, pp. 1–32.

Arguello, K. (2012) Criminalização dos jogos de azar: a contradição entre lei e realidade social. *Revista da EMERJ*, Rio de Janeiro, 15 (60), pp. 239–250.

Beccaria, C. (2013) *Dos delitos e das penas*. São Paulo: EDIPRO.

Benatte, A.P. (2002) *Dos Jogos que Especulam Com o Acaso: Contribuição À História do Jogo de Azar no Brasil (1890–1950)*. PhD thesis. Campinas: University of Campinas.

Bitencourt, C.R. (1999) *Manual de direito penal – Parte geral*. 5th ed. São Paulo: Revista dos Tribunais.

Borges, D. (2001) Healing and Mischief: Witchcraft in Brazilian Law and Literature, 1890–1922. In Salvatore, R.D., et al. (eds.), *Crime and Punishment in Latin America: Law and Society since Late Colonial Times*. Durham: Duke University Press, pp. 181–210.

Carvalho, E.M. & Prado, L.R. (2006) Adequação social e risco permitido: aspectos conceituais e delimitativos. *Revista dos Tribunais*, São Paulo, 844(2006), pp. 435–451.

Chazkel, A. (2007) Beyond Law and Order: The Origins of the Jogo do Bicho in Republican Rio de Janeiro. *Journal of Latin American Studies*, 39(3), pp. 535–565.

Chazkel, A. (2011) *Laws of Chance: Brazil's Clandestine Lottery and the Making of Urban Public Life*. Durham: Duke University Press.

Coelho, D.N. (2018) Territorial and Corrosive: The "jogo do bicho" (Animal Game) and Organized Crime in Brazil. *International Journal on Criminology*, 6(1), pp. 7–37. doi:10.18278/ijc.6.1.2

Freire, D. (2019). Beasts of Prey or Rational Animals? Private Governance in Brazil's Jogo Do Bicho. *Latin American Perspectives*, 46(4), 230–244. https://doi.org/10.1177/0094582X19846519

Guimarães, T. (2017) *Como o jogo do bicho se tornou a maior loteria ilegal do mundo*. BBC Brasil. Available at: www.bbc.com/portuguese/brasil-40140693

Huff Post Brasil. (2015) Caixa Estima que Legalização de Jogos de Azar Pode Quintuplicar Arrecadacão do Brasil. Available at: https://bit.ly/2SVrrf3

Huggins, M.K. (1985) *From Slavery to Vagrancy in Brazil: Crime and Social Control in the Third World*. New Brunswick: Rutgers University Press.

José, M. (2016) *Debate sobre jogos de azar deve fugir do moralismo e focar nos ganhos econômicos*. Consultor Juriidico. Available at: www.conjur.com.br/2016-jul-31/magnho-jose-debate-jogos-azar-focar-ganhos-sociais#author

Labronici, R.B. (2012) *Para Todos Vale o Escrito: Uma Etnografia do Jogo do Bicho*. Master's Thesis. Niterói: Universidade Federal Fluminense.

Labronici, R.B. & Da Silva, G.B. (2018) Uma contravenção controvertida: reflexões acerca da tutela penal do jogo do bicho. *Revista Interdisciplinar de Direito*, 14(1), 201–213. Available at: http://revistas.faa.edu.br/index.php/FDV/article/view/257

Lopes, M.A.R. (2000) *Princípio da insignificância no direito penal: análise à luz das leis 9.009/95 (juizados especiais criminais)*, 9.503/97 (código de trânsito brasileiro) e da jurisprudência atual. 2nd ed., rev. atual. e ampl. São Paulo: Revista dos Tribunais.

Lucena, F. (2017) *História do Jardim Zoológico de Vila Isabel, o primeiro do Brasil*. Available at: https://diariodorio.com/historia-do-jardim-zoologico-de-vila-isabel-o-primeiro-do-brasil/

Magalhães, F. (2009) *E o Rio não civiliza-se . . . O jardim zoológico e o jogo do bicho no Rio de Janeiro*. XX Simpósio Internacional Processo Civilizador, Recife, Brasil. Available at: https://jornalggn.com.br/sites/default/files/documentos/c_magalhaes.pdf

Magalhães, F. (2011) *Ganhou, leva! O jogo do bicho no Rio de Janeiro (1890–1960)*. Rio de Janeiro: Editora FGV.

Mattos, M.B. (1991). *Vadios, jogadores, mendigos e bêbados na cidade do Rio de Janeiro do inicio do século*. MA Thesis. Universidade Federal do Rio de Janeiro, Rio de Janeiro.

Medeiros, G., Grant, J. & Tavares, H. (2016) Gambling Disorder Due to Brazilian Animal Game ("Jogo do bicho"). *Gambling Behavior and Psychopathology*, 32: 231. https://doi.org/10.1007/s10899-015-9527-0

Misse, M. (2011) Crime organizado e crime comum no Rio de Janeiro: diferenças e afinidades. *Revista Sociologia e Política*, 19(40).

Nucci, G.S. (2014) *Leis penais e processuais comentadas*. 8th ed. rev. atual. e ampl. Rio de Janeiro: Forense.

Pacheco, R.J.C. (1957) *Antologia do Jôgo de Bicho*. Rio de Janeiro: Editora Organização Simões.

Paschoal, J.C. (2003) *Constituição, criminalização e direito penal mínimo*. São Paulo: Revista dos Tribunais.

Piccato, P. (2001) *City of Suspects: Crime in Mexico City, 1900–1931*. Durham, NC: Duke University Press.

Prado, L.R. (2002a) *Bem jurídico-penal e Constituição*. 4th ed. São Paulo: Revista dos Tribunais.

Prado, L.R. (2002b) Curso de direito penal brasileiro – Parte geral. *São Paulo: Revista dos Tribunais*, 1(3).

Prado, L.R. (2010) Curso de Direito Penal brasileiro. *Ed. São Paulo: Revista dos Tribunais*, 1(10).

Puig, S.M. (2008) Legal Goods Protected by the Law and Legal Goods Protected by the Criminal Law as Limits to the State's Power to Criminalize Conduct. *New Criminal Law Review*, 11.

Queiroz, P.S. (2001) *Direito penal – Introdução crítica*. São Paulo: Saraiva.

Ripert, G. (2000) *A Regra Moral nas Obrigações Civis*. Campinas: Bookseller.

Rivera-Garza, C. (2001) The Criminalization of the Syphilitic Body: Prostitutes, Health Crimes and Society in Mexico City, 1867–1930. In Salvatore, R.D., et al. (eds.), *Crime and Punishment in Latin America: Law and Society since Late Colonial Times*. Durham, Duke University Press, pp. 147–180.

Roxin, C. (2013) *A Proteção de Bens Jurídicos Como Função do Direito Penal*. André Luis Callegari & Nereu José Giacomolli (Translation). Porto Alegre: Livraria do Advogado.

Santarelli, N.C. (2013) The Protection of Global Legal Goods. *Anuario Mexicano de Derecho Internacional*, 13, pp. 405–450, México, D. F., ISSN 1870-4654.

Santos, J.N. (1996) Paratodos Bahia: uma organização no jogo do bicho. *Organização & Sociedade*, 3(6).

Silveira, R.M.J. (2003) *Direito penal transindividual: direitos difusos*. São Paulo: Revista dos Tribunais.

Soares, S.S. (1993) *O jogo do bicho: a saga de um fato social brasileiro*. São Paulo: Bertrand.

Stajnko, J. (2017) Criminal Law and Criminology. *Юридичний вісник*, 4(45), pp. 124–130.

Szczucki, K. (2016) *Proconstitutional Interpretation of Criminal Law*. Lanhan: Lexington Books.

Tavares, H. (2014) Gambling in Brazil: A Call for an Open Debate. *Addiction*, 109(12), pp. 1972–1976.

Tavares, J. (2002) *Teoria do injusto penal*. 3rd ed. Belo Horizonte: Del Rey.

Valor Econômico. (2017) *Jogo do bicho pode elevar arrecadação em R$ 30 bi por ano*. Available at: https://www.valor.com.br/valor-investe/casa-das-caldeiras/5088828/jogo-do-bicho-pode-elevar-arrecadacao-em-r-30-bi-por-ano

Vasconcelos, A. (2016) *Teoria da norma jurídica*. 7th ed. Florianópolis: Conceito Editorial.
Villar, J.L.M. (2008) *Contravenção e a Cultura da Ascensão Social*. São Paulo: Blucher Acadêmico.
Welzel, H. (2011) *O novo sistema jurídico penal: uma introdução à doutrina da ação finalista*. São Paulo: Revista dos Tribunais.
Zaffaroni, E.R. & Pierangeli, J.H. (2004) *Manual de direito penal brasileiro: parte geral*. São Paulo: Revista dos Tribunais, p. 172.

Part II

Political tensions

Chapter 5

(Cr)immigration in the Dominican Republic? Decolonizing the human rights of vulnerable Haitian migrants

Carolina Yoko Furusho

Introduction

In June of 2000, Nadege Dorzema and a group of Haitian nationals crossed the border illegally in a truck. Dominican soldiers pursued the vehicle and ended up shooting and killing seven undocumented migrants, including Nadege. Seeking justice, the next of kin of Nadege and the other victims filed an application before the Inter-American Commission on Human Rights, which identified undocumented migrants or those in an irregular situation as a vulnerable group due to their susceptibility to suffering potential or actual violation of rights.[1] The case was referred to the Inter-American Court of Human Rights (IACtHR) and in 2012, the Court held the Dominican state accountable for violating the human rights of the applicants.[2] In 2014, another ruling acknowledging the victimization of Haitian migrants was issued by the (IACtHR).[3] The case concerned the arbitrary detention and expulsion of hundreds of people to Haiti, including documented and undocumented Dominicans and foreigners, some of which held permanent residence documents in the Dominican Republic. Several other judgments have been issued by the IACtHR, which attest to the serious and systematic human rights violations committed by the Dominican state against people of Haitian descent.

Indeed, the appalling situation of structural discrimination, racism, and violence in the Dominican Republic against people of Haitian descent is well documented. This infamous scenario is not an out-of-the-curve aberration or a tale of a failed and evil state. In fact, the Caribbean island's scenario seems to mirror in many ways the strict legal and political migratory apparatus built in the Global North, particularly in the United States, which is targeted at migrants coming from the Global South. More than an abstract comparison between case studies from two different countries in the globe, I attempt to show herein that the situation in the Dominican Republic is intrinsically interwoven with the situation in the United States. In examining the evolution of US laws and policies concerning migration, Juliet Stumpf (2006, 2013) coined the term "crimmigration." The concept denotes the encroachment of criminal law into immigration law, both in terms of substance and procedures – e.g., detention centers for asylum-seekers. Although making use of a conceptual tool devised in a North-South context, particularly in reference to the migratory scenario of the United States, I suggest applying crimmigration to the Caribbean context reveals similarities in power dynamics and, more importantly, a ratchet effect in harmful and oppressive relations that trickles down between, on the one hand, states and societies, and on the other hand, racialized and poor migrants. In this chapter, these harmful relationships are examined through crimmigration practices, such as detention, accelerated deportation, mass deportation, and other forms of punitive measure against migrants. These relations materialize in socioeconomically exclusionary and punitive legal practices in relation to migrants from the Global South, disproportionately disadvantaging Haitians.

International systems of human rights protection can turn diffuse structures of harm into more intelligible situations by analyzing concrete cases. However, their punitive focus on accountability and shaming states has limitations. Rather than circumscribing the issue through a narrow lens of state sovereignty, I suggest that we shift our focus to how the crimmigratory chain reaction works, unveiling opportunities to promote inclusion and foster resistance by vulnerable groups. This entails an examination of interstate and state-migrant relations. Moreover, it implies a more nuanced understanding of economic exploitation, political subordination, and racially driven forms of violence, which have been normalized in the Caribbean from colonization to contemporary forms of neo-imperial hegemony. Bearing this in mind, my main argument in this chapter is threefold. First, I propose that Stumpf's (2006) explanation about the crimmigration crisis in the United States through membership theory can to a great extent be applied to the Dominican legal framework of exclusion and othering of migrants, particularly those of Haitian origin. Second, I argue that another perverse layer of the postcolonial migration dynamics is evidenced by the production of victimization and vulnerability in South-South crimmigration to an extent such that membership exclusion by the state paves the way to state-sponsored crimes against humanity (Zaffaroni, 2009). Third, while crimmigration is a useful concept to ascertain the boundaries of the relationship of victim-perpetrator, I suggest that the international community depart from a narrow lens of individual state accountability and blame. By opening up the examination to how relationships of subordination, subjugation, and harm are systematically reproduced according to postcolonial geopolitical relations among states, other avenues can be explored to better prevent systematic exclusions that can ultimately bring about crimes against humanity.

North-South and South-South crimmigration: from the United States to Hispaniola

Globalization's interdependence is anything but a fair game that is based on equality of arms, being rather a dynamic framework that reproduces the familiar colonial logic of imposition of hegemonic interests and economic and racial subalternity. Globalization has taken place alongside the strengthening of border controls and securitization of migration (Bosworth & Guild, 2008; Brotherton & Kretsedemas, 2008). Several aspects of international migration are being dealt with by criminal policies and actions, as is evidenced by criminologists who unveil the ways migration controls and criminal justice systems work to perpetuate racial subordination (Bosworth et al., 2017). Furthermore, the boundaries of sovereign states' discretionary powers under international law are largely designed and decided by the Global North, with vested interests in maintaining the geopolitical power balance in their favor. Racist migratory controls restrict the ascension of historically marginalized and thus socioeconomically disadvantaged groups to power. The political economy underlying migration and race works as a mechanism to perpetuate the status quo to the detriment of those at the end of the food chain, which in this case are individuals of Haitian descent or nationality. South-South relations are deeply affected by inequality-breeding globalized neoliberal logic and profit-seeking transnational corporate and financial interests. Moreover, they seem to replicate and mirror socioeconomic, racial, and ethnic conflicts that can be traced back to remnants of imperial and neo-imperial dynamics and which are imbricated in the current geopolitical and economic balance of power.

Regarding the punitive tendency of states against migrants, crimmigration law is the depiction of a phenomenon that blurs the boundaries between criminal justice and immigration policy, with increasing reliance on immigration procedures in criminal law and crime control through immigration practices (Stumpf, 2006). Immigration detention illustrates how the lines between immigration and criminal punitiveness have gradually become increasingly blurred (Bosworth, 2017). Bosworth also warns about detention and expulsion abiding by a criminal punitive logic. Citizens who belong to ethnic minorities and foreigners have constituted an increasing part of the prison populations in European countries since the 1990s (Melossi, 2003). This stigmatizing depiction of migrants as dangerous others leads to increased forms of lawful violence and coercion aiming at detaining, excluding, imprisoning, and marginalizing migrants. Stumpf (2006) posits that the lines between criminal law and immigration law have merged and offers an explanation for such confluence rooted in membership theory. Insofar as criminal and immigration law converge by means of the expansion of the state's discretionary power, Stumpf argues that criminally convicted citizens and foreigners alike are excluded from membership in a collectivity stemming from a social contract. In other words, "it marks out the boundaries of who is an accepted member of society" by restricting membership-deriving rights and privileges, such as the right to vote or to remain in US territory (Stumpf, 2006, pp. 377–378). In both criminal law and immigration law, the state is able to exercise its exclusionary power by morally condemning and stigmatizing, as well as administering punishment, which creates both precarious forms of membership and "bordered penality" (Aas, 2014, p. 534).

In the case of the United States, the significant percentage of incarcerated Latinos[4] is only part of the story. Amanda Armenta (2017) posits that American proactive policing practices tend to lead to the "disproportionate arrest of black and Latino men" (p. 129). In her case study of Nashville, she reports how this leads to a "feeling of omnipresent surveillance" among Latinos in which overwhelming police presence in Latino neighborhoods is felt more like patrolling than a commitment to protect inhabitants (p. 127). Armenta argues that "the immigration enforcement regime, which is unprecedented in size and scope, ensures that living in the United States with the ever-present possibility of deportation becomes its own form of punishment," a burden which falls to a disproportionate degree on Latinos (p. 148). Moreover, Armenta posits that "race is central to understanding the crimmigration system's devastating effects on Latino communities." Given that nearly 80% of unauthorized migrants in the United States are of Mexican or Central American origin, empirical findings suggest that "a system of state laws and local law enforcement practices converge to reinforce Latinos' subordinate status in the racial hierarchy" (Armenta, 2016, p. 2). "Racialized crimmigration" and its harmful effects on Dominican immigrants in the United States is a topic of growing concern. Similarly, racialized crimmigration seems to occur in the Dominican Republic against people of Haitian descent, particularly migrants.

i. (Cr)immigration in the Caribbean?

Against this backdrop, let us shift the geopolitical focus to the South, zooming in on the Caribbean island of Hispaniola, which harbors the infamous bad-blood relationship between neighbors Haiti and Dominican Republic. Both countries in 2018 had a population of approximately ten million people each. In the Dominican Republic, of those 10 million, more than 500,000 are Haitian migrants, not to mention additional hundreds of thousands Dominican-born individuals of Haitian descent.[5] Haiti is the poorest country in the Americas,[6] and its demographic makeup is predominantly of African origin, historically explained by being the only nation in the American continent whose independence was led by African slaves in 1804. French Haiti was the richest colony of the West Indies during the 18th century. Half a million slaves lived there by 1800, compared to 40,000 in the Spanish settlement in the territory that is now the Dominican Republic (Martin et al., 2002, p. 572).

After conquering their independence from French colonizers, Haitians took over the entire territory of Hispaniola. The Dominican Republic declared its independence from Haiti in 1844. Dictatorships ensued in which large amounts of debt were contracted to US lenders and even a brief period of Spanish imperial domination, until independence was regained in 1865. Nonetheless, between 1916 and 1924, US intervention in the country was carried out to ensure debts were paid. In 1930, military dictator Rafael Trujillo came into power. Influenced by fascist and nationalist ideals, Trujillo planned to bolster national manufacturing and replace importations by heavily investing in Dominican infrastructure. Similar to other fascist regimes at the time, censorship and violent episodes of repression were an integral part of the regime.

In 1937, the so-called Parsley Massacre took place: although sources vary about the death toll, between 12,000 to 25,000 Haitian sugarcane workers ("braceros") were massacred over the course of one week. The incident was only reported by local media two months after it happened, and although blame was placed on Dominican vigilantes, popular wisdom reveals that it might have been premeditated as part of Trujillo's "Dominicanization program" (Strongman, 2006). In fact, historian Eric Paul Roorda (1996) ascribes the blame to the Dominican army, depicting the massacre as "a kind of genocide with 'ruthless efficiency,' apparently at the personal instigation of Rafael Trujillo" (p. 301). Roorda adds that when Trujillo worked in the national guard, he was actually trained by US Marines during the period of US intervention in the country. When comparisons of Trujillo to Hitler or Mussolini started flooding the news, US president Franklin Delano Roosevelt, committed to his Good Neighborhood Policy, which entailed supporting many Latin American dictators, called the symbolic indemnification amount paid to Haiti by the Dominican Republic a successful resolution to the case. "In the case of the Haitian massacre, Good Neighbor diplomacy meant not protesting the destruction of what one Dominican diplomat labeled a 'miserable proletariat' of dark-skinned 'pariahs'" (Roorda, 1996, p. 314).

In the aftermath of the Haitian genocide, Trujillo offered to accept 100,000 Jewish refugees in the country, an offer he later reneged, taking in only a couple hundred refugees in the city of Sosua. This was nonetheless part of his plan to attract light-skinned immigrants as replacements for Haitian and West Indian workers. The United States sent a team of immigration experts to help draft racist legislation promoting "neo-white" immigration. A *New York Times* article a couple of years later[7] discussed the Sosua Jewish settlement while portraying an account of the massacre that supported the official Dominican version. It highlighted that "olive-skinned" Dominicans were outnumbered by black and mulatto Haitians three million to one-and-a-half million, and the tension between neighbors "flared up" in 1937 when "Haitian squatters were killed and driven out of the Dominican Republic." This version of events, "which hinged on racial fears and claimed self-defense, seems to have found considerable acceptance in the United States" (Roorda, 1996, p. 319).

According to Roberto Strongman (2006), "the racist Trujillista discourse" still lives on in the 21st century (p. 43). David Howard (2007) argues that "racialized violence" still underpins "acts of state violence that have been perpetrated as pre-emptive attempts to defend racialized national spaces or boundaries" (pp. 726–727). After the assassination of Trujillo in 1961, a left-wing president, Juan Bosch, was elected president, but ousted by the military; attempts to restore him to power were curbed by US intervention. Joaquin Balaguer was in office for a considerable part of the period between 1960 and 1990, implementing policies to foster sugarcane production and rural enterprises and, in the 1980s, promoting zones with incentives for foreign companies to set up factories and manufacture products to export ("maquiladoras") (Martin et al., 2002, p. 572). In 2002, the Free Trade Zone of Pedro de Macoris alone harbored 100 factories owned by 50 foreign companies. Despite the unacknowledged genocide of 1937, Haitian migratory flows to the Dominican Republic continued throughout the 20th century. Haitian migrants in the Dominican Republic have been traditionally recruited or smuggled to work in sugarcane plantations, as well as in rice and coffee fields. In 2002, the Dominican Republic reported 2,000 lawful residents and 2,000 refugees of Haitian origin living in its territory, which means that between 500,000 and 800,000 lived in illegality (Martin et al., 2002, p. 586).

ii. Crimmigration and postcolonial harms: exclusion, racism, slavery

The interstate dynamics among Haiti, Dominican Republic, and the United States rely on American hegemony and Caribbean dependency on US economy. In the United States, exclusionary crimmigration policies affect the lives of Dominican and Haitian economic migrants. Moreover, those who are most vulnerable often live in illegality or are detained and deported. In Hispaniola, the economic migratory flux in the island occurs from Haiti to the Dominican Republic. The Dominican Republic thus holds sway in the lives of many Haitian migrants. Both crimmigratory frameworks in the United States and the Dominican Republic have the following elements: first, exclusionary structural mechanisms that entail legal and material vulnerability of Global South migrants; second, a racist aspect embedded in state institutional practices; and third, a concern in appearing to be human-rights-respecting states in the eyes of their peers. More importantly, exclusion and racism are not only common features but also deeply intertwined intersectional axes that should be understood within a postcolonial framework of dependency and subordination.

Within a perverse value gradation consonant to darkness of skin, a parallel can be made to racism against Haitians in Dominican territory. Infringement of their rights in the present-day represents a visible continuity with the treatment received by slaves during the forced African diaspora to the Americas. For centuries, white masters literally had property entitlements over black slaves (Nellis, 2013), meaning that human rights violations against African individuals were not seen as such since their humanity was not recognized. Crimmigratory racist practices in Hispaniola can thus be construed as remnants of local habit, continued social practice, and persistent disavowal of humanity according to categorizations of people on the basis of race and ethnicity. Through this historical socioeconomic lens of exploitation, we can move from the 19th century to more recent temporalities and find analogous patterns: Haitian braceros, who work as cheap laborers in sugarcane plantations, are the weaker link in the economic relationship. Placed on the losing end of the balance, these migrants from Haiti, the poorest country in the Western hemisphere, arrive at the Dominican Republic with no bargaining power and often struggling to survive. They then face crimmigration-deriving exclusions that take on perverse shapes and features. Far from being a novel phenomenon, as identified by Stumpf and other scholars in the North-South realities of the United States and Europe, mass deportations, incarceration, and even extrajudicial killings of migrants by state officials illustrate how stakes are higher in South-South crimmigration in Hispaniola and part of a long history of discrimination, othering, and exploitation.

iii. State sovereignty, national security, and racist exclusion of migrants

As different as North-South crimmigration in the United States may be from South-South crimmigration in the Dominican Republic, in international law, both provoke invocations of the old ironclad argument of state sovereignty in response to external criticism. In fact, it is not a mere coincidence that this argument holds for both, as it held when Trujillo used it in the aftermath of the genocide committed against Haitian migrants in 1937 (Langley, 2016). Recognizing parallel systems of institutional racism, exclusion, and othering in which the higher degree of melanin in your skin, the better you fare, can be used to critique and restructure the ways we conceive of international law and its standard-setting function to domestic jurisdictions. In Garland's (2001) "criminology of the other," those who commit offenses, such as illegal immigrants, are considered as another "kind" of human, intrinsically different from law-abiding citizens and presenting threats to the existing social order. Aas (2010) argues that this is a relevant notion to understanding how the public eye interprets and expresses concern over the prejudiced perception of foreigners "contaminating the local," especially when concerning issues of human trafficking, terrorism, and transnational organized crime. On a related note, Melossi (2003) discusses the notion of the "deviant immigrant" as the result of negative perceptions and feelings of danger and insecurity arising from global transformations.

As Stumpf (2006) posits, crimmigration has to do with the sovereign's state power to punish and morally condemn individuals, and with the aftereffects of stigmatization and membership exclusion. The conservative discourse on migration relies on the ascription of the status of "folk devils" (Cohen, 2002), a collectively ascribed stigma of deviance to asylum-seekers, refugees, and undocumented migrants (O'Neill & Seal, 2012). This negative image that links migration and the stigma of illegality often propels audiences to feelings of anxiety and fear, paving the way for misrecognition, exclusion, othering, and even racism (ibid.). Aas (2010) reminds us that irregular immigrants might be considered the "global others." Moreover, Aas contends that the critical debate concerning the divides of West-Rest and Us-Others has to be engaged, questioning whether we should be concerned with human security or with secure states. If the response is the latter rather than the former, an ensuing query rests upon whose security is implied in the attempt to guarantee the security of states and, by the same token, at the expense of whose human rights this feat will be achieved.

Relying upon the abstract idea of a nation-state being threatened by external enemies encroaching upon its borders is set out as the moral justification for translating this discourse into the practice of criminal and immigration law. This happens to the detriment of perceiving how vulnerable migratory contexts can render individuals who are seeking socioeconomic opportunities, fleeing from violence and persecution or simply struggling to survive alongside their families. An important difference that must be stressed is how the Dominican state has gotten away with genocide while the international community stood idly by, as exemplified by the United States' Good Neighbor policy. It is virtually impossible to formulate a theory from the Global South without positioning the South in relation to the North. Developed and underdeveloped world are so intricately intertwined and geopolitical blindness entails ignoring relevant factors that lie beneath the surface and mark the construction of racialized criminalities and illegalities. In this case study, I suggest these factors can only be seen through the lens of economic, political, and human relationships that link Haiti, Dominican Republic, and the United states, relations that are imbued on the one hand with dependence, migratory and business opportunities, desire, fluxes, and exchanges, and on the other hand, fear, othering, precarity, violence, power, and control. Dominican and Haitian societies were forcefully acquainted to modes of relationality introduced by European colonizers for centuries, of which the most infamous and paradigmatic example consists of the slavery of members of the forced African diaspora.

It stands to reason that power relations that organically ensued were tainted by the white slave-owner legacy, whereby black subalternity was shaped according to evolving socioeconomic relationships. Although this assertion can to some extent apply to both US and Dominican contexts, the latter unfolded in such a way that it consolidated the ethnic and national group of Haitians of African descent as a vulnerable group. Their vulnerability is infamously instantiated by the 1937 genocide, which, as historical sources corroborate, was instigated and promoted by the Dominican state and condoned by the US government at the time (Roorda, 1996). US support was such that in the aftermath of the massacre, a partnership was established for the purposes of a racist crusade disguised as demographic planning. From an international human rights standpoint, there is a missing link between the harms of crimmigration and a sovereign state perspective – that is, a narrow approach that is consonant to the Westphalian rationale. Digging deep into what these harms mean, one has to pay close attention to underlying structures of vulnerability that shape criminal legalities and illegalities, addressing the cross-border effects of enduring issues of race and class in migration and punishment (Bosworth et al., 2018).

Immigration law and other branches borrow mechanisms and procedures contaminated by criminal law's punitive spirit, conflating aims and interests in such a way that harmful human rights violations become embedded as institutionally accepted and legally supported, pushing those at the borders of the territory to the margins of society. Haitians are vulnerable to increasing harms from crimmigration laws and policies in both Dominican Republic and the US. In their home country, Haitians are deprived of dignity-ensuring infrastructural conditions. Since colonial times up until the present day, Haiti's geopolitical position has been strikingly underprivileged, with extreme poverty, environmental catastrophes, and political instability as important markers. Unsurprisingly, there has always been significant economic emigration from Haiti – though environmental and political factors have also been relevant in different periods – (Lennox, 1993). A hierarchy of migrant vulnerability is visible in the United States according to racial gradation where Haitians are placed lower than Dominicans by virtue of the color of their skin and at the margins other intersectional structures of oppression such as gender.[8] Social injustice has to be assessed through this lens of postcolonial domination and scales or intensities of vulnerability in the geopolitical distribution of power. Haitians are detained, deported, excluded, beaten, and even killed through legal mechanisms that render violations to their human rights invisible by making access to justice extremely difficult. Although in the United States, there are more resources and organizations that can help make these invisible harms visible, South-South relations in Hispaniola are sometimes harder to see, as there are fewer international actors capable of bringing this to the attention of the international community. As illustrated by the Parsley Massacre, this lack of visibility globally can lead to alarming scenarios that might deteriorate to genocide or crimes against humanity.[9]

Human rights law: from individual accountability to resistance in vulnerability

Moral boundaries are presently drawn not only through discourse but also through exclusionary practices against migrants. When analyzed through the lens of vulnerability, I argue that these harmful relations evidenced by crimmigration – interstate relations and states vis-à-vis migrants – shift the focus from defining who can be blamed for the harm to assessing how power relationships can be revisited in terms of capacity to bring about change. More than assigning blame, unequal power imbalances among states and states vis-à-vis individuals should be dissected to rethink how powerful actors, regardless of having contributed or not to causing harm, can be called upon to mitigate and prevent patterns of victimization. In this section, I examine Haitians' vulnerability and human rights in the context of contemporary migration. Vulnerability and victimization in international human rights law are well-suited concepts to dissect the harmful effects brought about by state human rights violations. A framework of state crime (Rothe & Kauzlarich, 2014) brings to the fore state accountability on a par with the gravity of harms inflicted upon victims in scenarios of vulnerability.

The Inter-American Commission on Human Rights released a report in 2015 concluding, "(. . .) notwithstanding the measures the State is taking, the violence and discrimination against Haitian migrants in the Dominican Republic is extremely worrisome."[10] Repeated condemnation of the Dominican state by the IACtHR was not well received by Dominican authorities. In the Niñas Yean y Bosico judgment,[11] the Court recognized the vulnerable situation of people of Haitian origin in Dominican territory.[12] Similarly, in Nadege Dorzema,[13] it recognized the situation of special vulnerability of Haitian migrants, noting that violations against the rights of migrants often remain in impunity due to cultural factors, power structures, and legal arrangements that hinder access to justice.[14] Following the condemnation of the Dominican state for its racist and exclusionary migratory practices, the Dominican Constitutional Court issued a decision on the case of Deguis (TC-168–13, "Sentencia 168/13"), placing yet another legal piece in the exclusionary crimmigration-based legal puzzle. The Dominican tribunal declared that children of undocumented parents fell into an exception to the jus soli principle of citizenship[15] – that is, Dominican citizens of foreign descent could have their citizenships taken away. The harmful impact of this decision was significant, as the decision was crafted to have retroactive effects reaching as far back as 1929. Accordingly, the Dominican court ordered the executive branch of the government to review birth certificates and implement the decision. Mounting pressure followed this decision issued by the highest court in the country, especially considering that it went in a diametrically opposite direction from the IACtHR's rulings, which imposed legally binding duties upon the Dominican state to modify the legal and political framework to minimally ensure the human rights of Haitian migrants and Dominicans of Haitian descent.

According to a 2013 report issued by Dominican nongovernmental organization Centro Bonó,[16] the Haina detention center, where migrants await deportation, has been the epicenter of complaints about situations of extortion, physical aggression, and human rights violations against Haitian migrants. The report emphasizes the strategically discreet and almost invisible location of the center, built on the structural remnants of a converted prison and virtually unknown by the general population. Despite consistent reports from reputable international organizations, as well as IACtHR condemnations of the Dominican state for systematically infringing upon the human rights of the Haitian population within its jurisdiction, the legislative framework had been amended in such a way as to formally appear in synch with international human rights law, though blatantly allowing for human rights breaches to continually be carried out by the state. To exemplify, the Dominican Republic enacted laws and statutes, such as a law on the Illegal Trafficking of Migrants and Persons (2003)[17] and a General Migration Act (2004)[18]. More illustratively, in consonance with international human rights treaties the Dominican state has entered into in the recent past, the 2014 Criminal Code (Código Penal) incorporates crimes that are well-known in the realm of international criminal law. Having previously ratified the Rome Statute, the Dominican state's Criminal Code establishes, for example, genocide (Art 89) and crimes against humanity (Art 91).[19]

In the aforementioned article 91, "infracciones de lesa humanidad" is defined as acts perpetrated on purpose and as part of a generalized or systematic attack against a civil population.[20] I place my focus on deportation or forced removal of population (item 12), which is accompanied by a corresponding reservation in the article's sole paragraph: "For the application of this article, it shall not be considered as forced removal or deportation of population the exercise of migratory control over people who enter or remain illegally in national territory." Although this exception might seem prima facie reasonable, it is actually an important legal cog in the bellicose Haitian-targeted machinery of the Dominican state. Despite its overspilling effects reaching not only those of Haitian nationality, as recent trends (e.g., Venezuelan influx) show, in the larger framework, this exception enables the perpetuation of a system that excludes, marginalizes, and kills Haitian migrants at the borders without holding those responsible accountable. Moreover, this system remains complicit and allows for exploitation and abuse of people of Haitian descent by private parties under their jurisdiction, given that those labeled as "illegal" are afraid to report even the most serious crimes committed against them to the authorities. This virtually creates an environment that becomes breeding ground for systematic, generalized, and concatenated actions against this racial, ethnic, and national group.

As Eugenio Zaffaroni (2009) explains, the most serious mass crimes are committed by agencies in charge of enforcing the state's punitive power when they operate without containment (pp. 8–9). He also argues that punitive power first, "with its structural selectivity, criminalizes a few persons and uses them to project itself as neutralizer of social evil", and second, "always tends to mass homicide" by creating an enemy that is seen as a threat to humanity (ibid., p. 11). He further explains that enemies have always been created by agencies who assume a moral role and have the monopoly over punitive and vindictive speeches that are politically effective. These enemies are "invented and sacrificed; (. . .) afterwards a new enemy is invented and a new sacrifice occurs" (ibid., p. 18). The abhorrent human rights violations that comprise detention, mass deportation, and extrajudicial killings of people of Haitian descent can be better understood as the production of enemies whose bodies are visibly marked by a distinct cultural and racial ancestry, compared to Dominicans. Antonio Cançado Trindade further adds that crimes against humanity

> are perpetrated by individuals who . . . follow State policies, with the institutions, human and other resources of the State at their disposal, and who

> are favored by the impotence or tolerance or connivance or indifference of the social body that does nothing to stop them.[21]

With globalized societies, the meaning of "social body" increasingly transcends the borders of the national state, implying that we all share responsibility for responding ethically and resisting whenever there is a risk that such crimes might be committed.

In addition to crimmigration and physical exclusion by deportation (and killing), many people of Haitian descent who had been born in Dominican territory were legally excluded from the system by having their Dominican nationality stripped by Sentencia 168/13. As illustrated earlier, the Dominican legal framework and law enforcement practices allow for systematic human rights breaches against persons of Haitian descent. Although the Dominican state criminalizes crimes against humanity, legal exceptions and de facto behavior of state agents in concrete cases show that the Dominican state seemingly falls dangerously close to the scope of the crime it proscribes: condoning acts as part of a systematic attack against a civil population, in that case, crimmigration legislation, policy, and practices targeted at Haitian migrants and their descendants. Vincent Chetail (2016) poses the question: is there blood on our hands? This disturbing question touches on our responsibility as world citizens and part of an international community that set out to live by certain principles embedded in international law in the post-Holocaust world. Standing idly when we have knowledge of a systematic pattern of racism, violence, and marginalization that has once in history led to a genocide – albeit underplayed by the politics of the time – seems like the only response we can say with certainty is ethically wrong.

The exclusion process entailed by crimmigration comprises myriad acts, and its most harmful outcome is arguably the constitution of a scenario where crimes against humanity are enabled. Cançado Trindade asserts that "crimes against humanity (. . .) is yet another expression of the universal juridical conscience, of its immediate reaction against crimes that affect humanity as a whole." International human rights law reflects this universal juridical conscience and efforts to hold the Dominican State accountable by the Inter-American system of human rights protection are an example of how this legal framework presently unfolds. Furthermore, international criminal law also has the potential to "domesticate" the state's discretionary scope regarding deportation of migrants (Chetail, 2016). However, given the aforementioned, if human rights law can be instrumentalized to defeat the very purposes for which it was built, will a punitive stance from the international community, shaming criminal states into acknowledging their morally condemnable actions, be enough to prevent another genocide or crimes against humanity? The Dominican legal framework, which on the surface appears to be in synch with international human rights law by continuing to engage with accountability mechanisms albeit enacting little change, is a disguise. This does not seem to affect the state's international position vis-à-vis its peers. Although grave concern may be expressed by regional and multilateral institutions of human rights protection, momentum for change is hardly gained with scarce international mobilization. Systematic membership exclusion of migrants in this context signifies deportation, detention, precarious illegal labor, exploitation, vulnerability to suffering violence, and even extrajudicial killings by state officials with impunity. The main target of these policies are undoubtedly black Haitians.

Zaffaroni argues that "[i]nternational punitive power does not prevent state mass homicides" (2009, p. 10). I thus propose we rethink avenues other than international criminal law and international human rights law. By transcending the boundaries of sovereignty, other solutions can be explored. In that way, I propose disrupting political and economic relationships that are not wholeheartedly committed to human rights and tackling scenarios of vulnerability, which are rather conveniently shaped by economic and political interests of powerful and arguably white(r) elites. In the case of the Dominican Republic, it seems clear that a coalition of local and international groups with a common racist agenda made it easier to avert the gaze from the massacred Haitian victims, disavowing the use of the victim label and propping up moral panics (Cohen, 2002) against racialized migrant bodies. My proposal for further avenues of critical research is threefold. First, we have to examine the ways the racialized migrant is shaped under a logic of illegality – i.e., how the legal architecture is built to frame and punish this particular type of subjectivity. Second, we should analyze how a globalized political economy feeds into local contexts of vulnerability by investigating, for example, the relationship between the prison-industrial complex and economic forces underlying global value chains. Third, we cannot shy away from acknowledging that the human rights framework is problematic, given that its neutral language of universality often hides how historical power struggles have artificially normalized unequal power relations in contemporary geopolitics. Mindful that advocates of the right to security have insidiously coopted human rights discourse, we must resist and contest dominant narratives by underscoring how migration is situated within deep-rooted genealogies of colonialism, racism, and criminal law.

Conclusion: the path from crimmigration to decolonizing resistance

In light of the exclusions and risks of state-sponsored crimes against humanity entailed by crimmigration in the Dominican Republic and the United States, I suggest we turn our attention to insidious racism and pervasive vulnerability and victimization for people of Haitian descent. These relations are permeated by postcolonial interstate dynamics and legal and political structures across the North-South global divide. A systemic analysis should be undertaken beyond individual state sovereignty as a unit of analysis. In this context, the international community can explore global modes of socioeconomic dependency and geopolitical responsibility, which are intricately imbricated in globalized networks of relations involving states and powerful non-state actors – such as corporations and individuals. A sharper focus on victims of human rights violations and ensuing contexts of vulnerability is imperative, as well as to find less punitive and more constructive solutions to crimmigration-related harms.

Rather than allowing states to frame economic migration as a threat to national security, which buttresses crimmigration practices, the unparalleled vulnerability of people of Haitian descent should be regarded as a matter of achieving better redistribution of resources and prioritizing the inalienable human dignity for all globally. Focusing on state responsibility not as "paying for what I did," but as "doing whatever I can do" could normalize a more humane migratory system that considers the human rights of migrants as valuable as the human rights of citizens. Racially motivated prejudice and violence would then be tackled through networks of empowerment and united agendas. This could ultimately prevent the materialization of crimes against humanity against specific groups, for example, impoverished black Haitians.

Notes

1 I/A Court H.R., Case of Nadege Dorzema et al. v. Dominican Republic (Merits, Reparations and Costs, Judgement of 24 October 2012 Series C No. 251).
2 Ibid.
3 I/A Court H. R., Case of Expelled Dominicans and Haitians v. Dominican Republic (Preliminary Objections, Merits, Reparations and Costs, Judgment of 28 August 2014 Series C No. 282)
4 According to Armenta, "The term Latino is a pan-ethnic label that describes culturally and geographically heterogeneous groups of Latin American ancestry" (2016, p. 12).
5 International Organization for Migration, "Perfil migratorio en Republica Dominicana" (2017). Available at: www.iom.int/es/news/republica-dominicana-presenta-su-primer-perfil-migratorio-con-apoyo-de-la-oim (last access 24 February 2019).
6 According to a World Bank Report, "Haiti remains the poorest country of the Americas: based on the most recent household survey (2012), over 6 million of Haiti's population of 10.4 million (or 59 percent) live below the national poverty line of US$2.41 per day, and more than 2.5 million (24 percent) fall below the national extreme poverty line (US$1.23 per day)" Available at: www.worldbank.org/en/country/haiti/overview (last access 18 October 2018).
7 *New York Times*, edition of 11 February 1940.
8 For example, Nadjhia N. Skakavac (2016), in a comparative quantitative analysis, concluded that Dominican, Cuban, and Jamaican had better employment status than women Haitian women. Skakavac also argued that the biggest gap between immigrant groups was between Cubans and Haitians, suggesting racial and ethnic discrimination as an explanation: "It is possible that the growing acceptance of Hispanics in the country helps to explain the Cubans and Dominicans' higher employment status; whereas Haitians and Jamaicans' association with blackness and marginalization may have contributed to some challenges in their employment statuses" (2016, p. 87).
9 For a different example of evaluating systematic state violence as crimes against humanity, see Emilio Peluso Neder Meyer's chapter in this collection.
10 OEA/Ser.L/V/II. Doc. 45/15, 31 December 2015, Para 644.
11 I/A Court H.R., Case of the Girls Yean and Bosico v. Dominican Republic (Preliminary Objections, Merits, Reparations and Costs, Judgment of September 8, 2005. Series C No. 130).
12 Ibid., paragraph 168.
13 I/A Court H.R., Case of Nadege Dorzema et al. v. Dominican Republic (Merits, Reparations and Costs, Judgement of 24 October 2012 Series C No. 251).

14 A caveat to be noted is that although the Inter-American Commission on Human Rights and victims' representatives alleged that the reason underlying the conduct of the Dominican state had been xenophobia and racism, the Court refrained from ruling on structural discrimination, indicating what she described as "a sign of hesitation" (Peroni, 2015, p. 487).

15 Interpretation of art. 18, item 3 of the Dominican Constitution (2010), which established a list of exceptions to ascription of nationality and citizenship for those born in Dominican soil, inter alia children whose parents were in transit or residing illegally in Dominican territory.

16 Boletín Observatorio de Derechos Humanos "Qué es el centro de detención de Haina". Available at: http://bono.org.do/publicaciones/boletines-odh/ (last access 15 August 2018).

17 Ley No. 137-03 sobre Trafico Ilicito de Migrantes y Trata de Personas. Available at: https://www.oas.org/dil/esp/Ley%20N%C2%B0%20137-03%20Sobre%20Tr%C3%A1fico%20Il%C3%ADcito%20de%20Migrantes%20y%20Trata%20de%20Personas%20Republica%20Dominicana.pdf (last access 13 June 2019).

18 "Ley 285 (2004) sobre Migración. Available at: https://www.oas.org/dil/Migrants/Republica%20Dominicana/1.Ley%20sobre%20migraci%C3%B3n%20N%C2%B0%20285%20del%2015%20de%20agosto%20de%202004%20%28reemplaza%20la%20Ley%2095%20de%201939%29.pdf (last access 13 June 2019).

19 In addition to that, the punitive spirit of the new Criminal Code can also be seen, e.g., in the increase of the maximum incarceration period for one crime, from 30 to 40 years. Consistent with a more punitive state is the maintenance of legal restrictions to the human rights of minorities, as exemplified by the Dominican Constitution of 2010, which proscribes abortion and bans all kinds of recognition for same-sex partnership.

20 Article 91 sets out a list of "infracciones lesa humanidad," which includes inter alia murder, torture, extermination, slavery, detention, or grave deprivation of liberty, persecution of a group or collectivity with particular identity for political, racial, national, ethnic, cultural, religious, sexist discrimination, disability, or other universally recognized motives in international law as unacceptable, racial segregation, other inhuman acts of similar character that cause great suffering or gravely breach the physical integrity or mental or physical health of victims.

21 Separate Opinion of Judge Antonio Cançado Trindade in the Judgment of *Case of Goiburú et al. v. Paraguay*.

References

Aas, K.F. (2014) "Bordered Penality: Precarious Membership and Abnormal Justice," *Punishment & Society*, 16 (5), pp. 520–541.

Aas, K.F. (2010) "Global Criminology," in McLaughlin, E. and Newburn, T. (eds.), *The SAGE Handbook of Criminological Theory*, London: Sage Publications Ltd., pp. 427–446.

Armenta, A. (2017) *Protect, Serve and Deport*, Berkeley: University of California Press, pp. 129–140.

Armenta, A. (2016) "Racializing Crimmigration: Structural Racism, Colorblindness, and the Institutional Production of Immigrant Criminality," in *Sociology of Race and Ethnicity, American Sociological Association*, Thousand Oaks, CA: Sage Publications, pp. 1–14.

Bosworth, M. (2017) "Immigration Detention, Punishment and the Transformation of Justice," *Social & Legal Studies*, 28 (1), pp. 81–99.

Bosworth, M., Aas, K.F., and Pickering, S. (2018) "Punishment, Globalization and Migration Control: 'Get Them the Hell Out of Here'," *Punishment and Society*, 20 (2), pp. 34–53.

Bosworth, M. and Guild, M. (2008) "Governing through Migration Control: Security and Citizenship in Britain," *The British Journal of Criminology*, 48 (6), pp. 703–719.

Bosworth, M., Parmar, A., and Vasquez, Y. (2017) *Race, Criminal Justice, and Migration Control: Enforcing the Boundaries of Belonging*, Oxford: Oxford University Press.

Brotherton, D.C. and Kretsedemas, P. (eds.). (2008) *Keeping Out the Other: A Critical Introduction to Immigration Enforcement Today*, New York: Columbia University Press.

Chetail, V. (2016) "Is There Any Blood on My Hands? Deportation as a Crime of International Law," *Leiden Journal of International Law*, 29 (3), pp. 917–943.

Cohen, S. (2002) *Folk Devils and Moral Panics: The Creation of Mods and Rockers*, 3rd ed., London: Paladin.

Garland, D. (2001) *The Culture of Control: Crime and Social Order in Contemporary Society*, Chicago: University of Chicago Press.

Howard, D. (2007) "Development, Racism, and Discrimination in the Dominican Republic," *Development in Practice*, 17 (6), pp. 725–738.

Langley, E. (2016) "Performing Postmemory: Remembering the Parsley Massacre in 'Nineteen Thirty-Seven' and Song of the Water Saints," *The Latin Americanist*, 60 (1), pp. 63–77.

Lennox, M. (1993) "Refugees, Racism, and Reparations: A Critique of the United States' Haitian Immigration Policy," *Stanford Law Review*, 45 (3), pp. 687–724.

Martin, P., Midgley, E., and Teitelbaum, M.S. (2002) "Migration and Development: Whither the Dominican Republic and Haiti?," *The International Migration Review*, 36 (2), pp. 572–590.

Melossi, D. (2003) "'In a Peaceful Life': Migration and the Crime of Modernity in Europe/Italy," *Punishment & Society*, 5 (4), pp. 371–397.

Nellis, E. (2013) *Shaping the New World: African Slavery in the Americas, 1500–1888*, North York: University of Toronto Press.

O'Neill, M. and Seal, L. (2012) *Transgressive Imaginations: Crime, Deviance and Culture*, London: Palgrave Macmillan UK.

Peroni, L. (2015) *On the Road to Substantive Equality: Due Process and Non-Discrimination at San José in DEMBOUR, Marie-Benedicte. When Migrants Become Humans*, Oxford: Oxford University Press.

Roorda, E.P. (1996) "Genocide Next Door: The Good Neighbor Policy, the Trujillo Regime, and the Haitian Massacre of 1937," *Diplomatic History*, 20 (3), pp. 301–319.

Rothe, D. and Kauzlarich, D. (eds.). (2014) *Towards a Victimology of State Crime*, Abingdon, UK: Routledge.

Skakavac, N. (2016) "The Impact of Human and Social Capital on the Employment of Haitian Immigrant Women in the U.S. Labor Force: A Comparative Analysis," *International Journal of Social Science Studies*, 4 (4), pp. 78–90.

Strongman, R. (2006) "Reading through the Bloody Borderlands of Hispanio Fictionalizing the 1937 Massacre of Haitian Sugarcane Workers in the Dominican Republic," *Journal of Haitian Studies*, 12 (2), pp. 22–46.

Stumpf, J. (2013) "The Process Is the Punishment in Crimmigration Law," in Aas, K.F. and Bosworth, M. (eds.), *The Borders of Punishment: Migration, Citizenship, and Social Exclusion*, Oxford: Oxford University Press.

Stumpf, J. (2006) "The Crimmigration Crisis: Immigrants, Crime, and Sovereign Power," *American University Law Review*, 56 (2), pp. 367–418.

Zaffaroni, E.R. (2009) "Is an Efficient Criminal Contribution Possible to Prevent Crimes against Humanity?," *Rivista di Criminologia, Vittimologia e Sicurezza*, 3 (2), pp. 6–30.

Chapter 6

Cosmologies of federal criminal procedural reform

Democratizing and humanizing criminal justice in Argentina

Julieta Mira

Introduction

This chapter will present the arduous process of federal criminal procedural reform[1] pursued by a group of Argentine legal experts whose work has impacted the transformation of criminal codes, not only in Argentina but also across Latin America.[2] This reform is highly significant because it concerns the rules governing proceedings for judging federal crimes, such as crimes against humanity, counterfeiting of money, trafficking in human beings, drug dealing, terrorism, and corruption. For this purpose, the views of the agents committed to federal criminal procedural reform in Argentina will be presented. Starting from the end of the military dictatorship in 1983, this reformative movement becomes very influential and persists along successive democratic governments to the present. In this chapter, I will focus on the "reformers" – a group of self-nominated legal experts who have fought for justice reform for decades. The chapter explores how justice reform was constructed as a *cause* (Israël, 2001; Gaïti and Israël, 2003), the system of interests underpinning it, and the political and historical role that the "reformers" have played in these campaigns.

Still in progress, the reform of the federal criminal procedure code in Argentina is a complex and laborious enterprise undertaken by law experts, though much of its development has been plagued with disputes (see Table 6.1). The first legislative work regarding the criminal procedural law codification in Argentina began with the *Código de Procedimientos en Materia Penal* or the Code of Procedures in Criminal Matters (Law 2.372) of 1888 known as "Obarrio's Code" in homage to its author Manuel Obarrio (1836–1918). The second regulation was passed as the *Código Procesal Penal de la Nación* or the Federal Criminal Procedural Code for Argentina (Law 23.984) of 1991, also called "Levene's Code," in recognition of Ricardo Levene II (1914–2000), the jurist who spearheaded the initiative. This change of the criminal procedural code took over more than a century to complete. One of the factors leading to this drawn-out reform was conflict between the "Peronista"-connected "Levene Project" (elaborated in 1975 and revised in 1989) and the "Maier Project" (1986), first elaborated on by Julio Maier (1939) during the presidency of Raúl Ricardo Alfonsín (1983–1989) from the *Unión Cívica Radical* political party.

The former, "Levene's Code," can be considered a partially oral proceeding, while the latter, "Maier's Project," was to be a fully oral proceeding. "Levene's Code" is still in force today because the third *Código Procesal Penal de la Nación* or the Federal Criminal Procedural Code (Law 27.063) passed by the Congress in 2014 was suspended by the 257 "Necessity and Urgency Decree" issued by the president Mauricio Macri in 2015.

The "reformers" assert, with determination and forcefulness, that Argentina has been experiencing a "crisis" of the national criminal procedural system due to its "inquisitorial configuration." The agents understand the problems of the "inquisitorial system" (see Table 6.2) as the nontransparent and purely written nature of procedural acts (case file) synthesized as a long-term and "secret" proceeding (as opposed to oral and public hearings), the judge's conflicting investigative and adjudicative roles, and the weaknesses of rights of the victims and defendants throughout the judicial process (Maier, 1987, 1989, 1996; Binder, 1993; Bovino, 1993; Córdoba, 1993). They further link this system to tradition and the "inquisitive culture," one which they have identified as a "crisis" and that serves as the flag of republican[3] thought (Binder, 1993). The "reformers" consider that a democratic and respectful of human rights justice system requires legislative changes to implement more "accusatorial" or "adversarial" elements (see Table 6.2) that centrally promote oral proceedings (audiences), the role of the prosecutor with persecutorial functions, and trial by jury (Maier, 1993, 2000; Bovino, 1993).[4]

Out of these debates, Antoine Vauchez and Laurent Willemez argued that in these legislative changes, process emerged a *raison réformatrice* or reform rationale (Vauchez and Willemez, 2007, pp. 2, 4, 5 and 20), which can be understood as a way of criticizing the functioning of the legal order and then proposing solutions with normative reforms. At the same time, these agents were gestating the *cause* in which they committed and deployed their *activism* (Agrikoliansky, 2001; Fillieule, 2001; Siméant, 2002). These elements contributed to the "struggle" of the "reformers" against the "inquisitorial" system, generating a series of legislative initiatives to enact the reforms necessary to achieve their ideal "accusatorial" system.

In the face of this dispute between the "inquisitorial" and the "accusatorial" paradigms, the theoretical-methodological focus facilitates an understanding of the actors' *cosmologies*, or ideal representations of the social order (Douglas, 1966, 1986, 1988). This chapter will identify and describe the diverse *cosmologies* that the "reformers" have used in their public positions to criticize "Levene's Code" for its "inquisitorial system remnants" and to promote a code reform to achieve their solution for the legal system though their version of an "accusatorial system" (see Table 6.2).

With this purpose in mind, the following pages will first discuss the ethnographic methodology that was central to this research. Second, the main "reformers" of the "Obarrio's Code" in Argentina history will be addressed. Third, the chapter will explore the four main *cosmologies* expressed by the legal experts around the federal criminal procedural reform promoted in Argentina. Lastly, the text will conclude by discussing how the demands of the "reformers" for the "change of the inquisitorial system" have cultural dimensions,[5] which have led to transformations in the legal field.

Methodology: ethnographic research perspective

This chapter is based on fieldwork in Buenos Aires, Argentina, from 2009 to 2014 while reform of the "Levene's Code" was being discussed. At that time, "reformers" were promoting a new federal criminal procedure known as "Albrieu's Project" (2010). Although, Albrieu's Project did not become law, it did inform much of the debates on the need to reform the criminal procedure. For this research, I participated in events related to the criminal procedural reform, which allowed me to *follow the actors* (Guber, 1991; Latour, 2008) in a multiplicity of public places where they were frequented and were active participants in. Specifically, the events were held in spaces where the "reformers" deployed their *cosmologies* in favor of the national criminal procedural reform. The reconstruction of the "reformers'" *cosmologies* around this reform is possible by means of the adoption of the theoretical-methodological scaffolding of the *sociology of law* (Treves, 1987) and an ethnographic research perspective (Guber, 2001).

This research project was inspired by John Cunha Comerford (1999) who in *Fazendo a Luta. Sociabilidades, Fales e Rituais na Construção de Organizações Camponesas* (Making Struggle: Sociability, Speeches and Rituals in the Construction of Peasant Organizations) studied the social and political organization of Brazilian agricultural rural workers by attending their association meetings. From this perspective, I attended events, such as public hearings, that constituted a socialization arena in which the academic world and political world converge. Furthermore, the events allowed me to get to know the actors, their speeches, positions, and trajectories, as well as their agreements, disagreements, and alliances. This ethnography reminded me that these events, besides just an observation space for the researcher, constituted a tactic in themselves, generated by the legal experts to promote their reforms and their values in relationship with justice. These qualities transformed such events into *ritual events* (Vecchioli, 2014, p. 71) worthy of study in themselves.

My methodological design required that I also attend as many conferences, congresses, seminars, symposia, and public audiences in the National Congress as possible. These events, besides providing me with entrée into the field, allowed me to generate contacts and build a reputation as a researcher in front of the *natives*,[6] especially since I consider myself an outsider from the legal world. This methodological decision was originated as a strategy to circumvent the first difficulties founded in the search of beginning bonds with some legal professionals who can be considered *important people* (Thomas, 1993), or those who handle important tasks and work in multiple occupations.

The diversity of interaction spaces visited is closely related with the multisite character of these agents' work and the complexity of relationships among intimately linked arenas: university, professional associations, nongovernmental organizations, law firms, national parliaments, and state institutions. Having achieved access to the "reformers" by participating in the events that they organized, this research centers strong methodological effort in *participant observation*. Rosana Guber has outlined the benefits of engaging in participation as a research methodology:

> If a game is learned by playing it, a culture is learned by living it. For that reason participation is the condition *sine qua non* of sociocultural knowledge. The tools are direct experience, sensory organs, and affectivity that far from tarnish your results, bring you closer to the object of study.
> (2001, p. 60)[7]

Furthermore, the description of the trajectories contained in this chapter is also based on the consultation both of secondary sources and primary sources. In particular, the works and the curriculum vitae (CV) of the "reformers" were reviewed, and the collection of files found in the Faculty of Law at the University of Buenos Aires and other various archives throughout the country were consulted. Information was also collected through interviews. For this project, some of the most important criminal justice "reformers," such as Julio Maier and Alberto Binder were interviewed. In the case of Levene (II), his son Ricardo Levene (III) was interviewed. This was only feasible by virtue of the deliberate construction of personal ties acquired through fieldwork – namely, personal encounters in events in the field of law – or "referral." These personal ties also allowed me to establish a chain of links through *snowball sampling* (Guber, 1991).

Finally, this research was done inside my own culture and city. Roberto Da Matta points out that "the problem is, then, to remove the layer of a member of a class and of a specific social group in order to be able – as an ethnologist – to miss some familiar social rule." Upon doing so, he adds that there lies the possibility of "discovering (. . .) what is exotic in what is petrified inside ourselves due reification and mechanisms of legitimatization" (1974, p. 267). With these considerations in mind, I proceeded to conduct my research into the *cosmologies* of the "reformers."

The Argentine criminal justice "reformers": Ricardo Levene (II) and Julio Maier

Ricardo Levene (II) and Julio Maier stand out among the criminal law experts in Argentina since a) they fought for the federal criminal procedural reform which they defined, with differences, as "accusatorial," and b) they sought to replace the "Obarrio's Code." Both experts considered this code "inquisitive," "colonial," "old," and "obsolete," and for these reasons searched for legal remedies oriented to "modernize" the criminal procedural law according to "republican" ideas. Moreover, they argued that they followed relevant law precedents from abroad and from the Argentine law in order to "modernize" the federal criminal law.

The analysis of the professional trajectories of these jurists, Levene (II) and Maier, and indeed the historical context when they were asked to promote these reforms in the criminal justice, demonstrate the *social capital* in special *symbolic capital* (Bourdieu, 1987, 1991, 2009; Fillieule and Pudal, 2010) belonging to the "reformers" and their intervention logics. Using data from their personal and professional biographies, a comparative study of the "reformers" trajectories is presented with the purpose of highlighting both common issues and heterodox elements. This approach facilitates the appreciation of strong similarities between the professional paths of both Argentine law personalities who are renowned at the national and international level. Thanks to this kind of analysis, it is possible to show that in spite of Levene (II) and Maier being presented as simply "reformers" of the legal field, they can be seen as forerunners who share similar properties.

First, both Levene (II) and Maier invested a great part of their professional career critiquing "Obarrio's Code" for its "inquisitorial" link to the Spanish legal system and its lack of modernity. Their critique involved laborious methods, such as studying criminal procedural codes from other countries in different languages, writing manuals about the topic, teaching activities at the university level, participating in professional congress and academic meetings both in the country and abroad, engaging in alternative code projects for the federal and local courts in many provinces in Argentina, and participating in criminal justice reform processes in other countries, especially in Latin America and Central America.

Besides these common elements, Levene (II) and Maier also asserted and exchanged a strong criticism of each other. Despite the shared criticism of Obarrio, Levene (II) exposed the weakness of "Maier's Project" when it had been under debate in the National Congress after being issued by the executive power. Similarly, Maier coordinated a research seminar in the Faculty of Law in the University of Buenos Aires for discussing critically the "Levene's Code" after it was enacted. As a key result of this seminar, the book entitled *El Nuevo Código Procesal Penal de la Nación: Análisis Crítico* (The New Federal Procedural Criminal Code: Critical Review) was published by Editorial El Puerto in 1993. This book will be analyzed in the following pages.

In summary, the distinguished trajectories of the "fathers of the reform" of the *Código de Procedimientos en Materia Penal para la Justicia Nacional* are supported in the following shared attributes in their careers: top positions in the main important tribunals in the country, professors in criminal law subjects and continued as emeritus professors, jurists with relevant publications and treaties in criminal procedural law, fellowships in relevant institutions around the world, homages and prizes for their contribution to the law, prestigious labor at international level, and founders of institutions dedicated to comparative criminal law. In relation to the last point, it is worthy of note that the creation of the *Instituto de Estudios Comparados en Ciencias Penales y Sociales* (Institute of Comparative Studies in Criminal and Social Sciences, or "INECIP")[8] by Maier among other lawyers and disciples, plays a key role in the criminal justice reform processes since 1989 as it will be showed in the next section. Finally, indeed, it is possible to identify shared ideas and visions between them in relation to the criminal law and the function of justice – for example, the need to limit the punitive power of state, the importance of oral ways of developing the proceeding, the protection of the rights of defendants, and the rights of victims to claim compensation for the harm suffered.

The tools for this reform competition include legal knowledge, diversification of positions in the professional field, and political connections. While the reform proposed by Maier was rejected in Congress, "Levene's Project" was passed in 1991 and is the current federal procedural criminal legislation in Argentina. Although the different political alliances of each of them play a role in the approval of "Levene's Project," it was the moderate tone – a compromise between the radical changes that Maier proposed and the old traditions from Obarrio – that made the difference. However, the approval of "Levene's Code" did not end the "struggle" over reform. This dispute continues into the present with a new generation of "reformers" who are critical of "Levene's Code," which they regard to be a continuation of the "inquisitorial" tradition. These "reformers" are mostly associated with Maier, who has come to be recognized as the "father" of the "accusatorial" reform movement in Argentina and Latin America. Their "struggle" will be explored through their cosmological arguments in the following section.

Four cosmological arguments regarding the federal criminal procedure reforms

Mary Douglas (1966, 1986, 1988) argues that the concept of a *cosmology* can be useful as a tool that agents use to discern, analyze, and or valorize reality. She maintains that *cosmologies* are exposed in classifications, theodicies, analogies, arguments, and conventions. The use of *cosmologies* becomes especially necessary when anomalies are presented – that is to say, in the moments that agents identify as out of the natural order. Since the "reformers" in this case operate under a belief that the criminal justice system in Argentina is inherently broken, unjust, and out of synch with an ideal legal order, Douglas's *cosmology* concept is especially useful to explore and frame the "reformers" motivations and actions.

This section will present the four key cosmological arguments that emerge from the speeches, interviews, and documents prepared by "reformers" engaged in the federal criminal procedural reform movement. These cosmological arguments form the basis of their critique of the "inquisitorial system" and serve as justification behind their proposals for the "accusatorial system." In particular, this chapter will outline the four most significant cosmologies identified in this research which are i) the strengthening of human rights and democratization, ii) "humanization of criminal justice," iii) "pursuit of the great crime," and iv) modernization and the overcoming of "old and obsolete." The notion of *cosmology* is manifested as revealing of the positions of the legal experts in relation to the *cause* that they promote.

i. Strengthening of human rights and democratization

A fundamental pillar of the reformers' speech is anchored in the respect for human rights, particularly the rights enunciated in the Argentine Constitution and in international treaties. This narrative reproduces the ideological position that justice should be central in a democratic nation. Justice, in this regard, revolves around the idea that procedural guarantees for both the victim and the defendant are provided. From there, another core criticism emerges to "inquisitorial type" legal codes: both "Obarrio's Code" and "Levene's Code" demonstrate disorder and discord with the normative harmony that is necessary to ensure that one's fundamental rights are respected.

Maier, in his cornerstone draft law, asserts that a modern procedural system "should perform the double function of providing enough power to the state to discover the truth and to assure the administration of justice" and to guarantee to the individual "the respect of his or her human dignity and the preservation of its fundamental rights" (1987, p. 653). According to Maier, "Obarrio's Code" does not satisfy this burden. For the advocates of the "accusatorial system," the main problem of the "inquisitorial system" is found in the "non-respect of the concrete and singular human being" (Maier, 1987, p. 654). In the case of "Obarrio's Code," Maier outlines that the judicial system currently suffers from "the arbitrary use of the preventive detention, lack of control regarding the judicial acts . . . [and the] enormous delegation of functions, etcetera" (1987, 654). Furthermore, Maier points out that the use of the preventive detention procedure "works in a way contrary to universal practice: it is suitable to solve those cases of smaller importance and, on the contrary, it is impotent to solve serious social conflicts" (Maier, 1987, p. 654).

With these arguments, Maier highlights what he considers to be the need to carry out judicial reforms once democratic institutions were reestablished after the last military dictatorship (1976–1983) in Argentina. To reinforce this position, Maier emphasizes the relevance of the legal transformation and justifies it as a social demand, indeed even a historical necessity, in the rebuilding of the country. In this line of thought, he expresses that

> recent examples demonstrate this statement: any honest person who knows how the national procedures work, knows that some current trials of great public importance, will never be resolved under the procedure of the Code

> in force and a decision will be delayed indefinitely . . . a situation which Argentine society should not tolerate.
>
> (Maier, 1987, p. 654)

It is clear that Maier's allusion to a "current trial of great public importance" is in reference to "Case 13" of the year 1984, known as the "Trial of the Military Juntas." The verdict[9] that sentenced the commanders was read on 9 December 1985 by the president of the tribunal *Cámara Nacional de Apelaciones en lo Criminal y Correccional Federal de la Capital Federal* (National Criminal and Correctional Appeals Court of Capital Federal) Judge León Arslanián in the Courtroom of the Palace of Justice. It should be stressed that this criminal trial served as a landmark case in the fight against impunity in cases of massive violations to human rights and has been taken as a model of justice in the transition processes to democracy elsewhere.

The "Trial to the Military Juntas" was the first oral trial to take place for a federal criminal crime in Argentina, notwithstanding the written procedural system in force during that time for the civilian courts. Having an oral trial despite the written procedural system in force could be explained in two ways. First, the oral trial was possible only because the procedure had already been allowed under the Code of the Military Justice. Second, the trial had initially been intended for the prosecution of the military members by their own cooperation, but this did not happen. Due to the delay and the unwillingness of the military justice to proceed, the civilian court decided to take over the case. Maier considered this oral trial indispensable for the transparency of the judicial process, which in turn was important, as Argentines sought justice for the massive crimes of the recent past and the reconstruction of the democratic system.

The recognition and promotion of human rights is linked with the ideology of the democratizing Argentina's criminal justice system and the necessity of legislative change after an authoritarian regime. Law, in this regard, serves as a social safeguard. This conception of the law is particularly pronounced in the *transitional justice* literature, which argues that such institutional reforms are necessary to guarantee nonrepetition of the past atrocities as a way of integral reparation (Novak, 2005; Galván, 2009; Heylen, Parmentier and Weitekamp, 2010; Fernando, 2014; Roth-Arriaza, 2016; Shala, 2018). This *cosmology* has also been central to the significant efforts of experts at an international level to find legal mechanisms to stabilize political scenarios, such as those found in the past, and to promote democratic governance in countries that have experienced violence and gross human rights violations.

ii. "Humanization of criminal justice"

Another *cosmology* proposes that criminal justice is missing humanity and connection with human beings, and for that reason requires a return to the mandate of serving the people. This *cosmology* is one of the most mentioned in the speech of "reformers" when they outline the crisis of the "inquisitorial system." Reforming to allow the "accusatorial system" into the criminal proceeding will alter the current state of affairs in which citizens are alienated from justice. This change, "reformers" argue, will offer society a more humane and understanding justice (Maier, 1987; Binder, 1993). Carmen Argibay, who after spending time in the international justice arena and was promoted to the *Corte Suprema de Justicia de la Nación* (National Supreme Court of Justice) from 2005 to 2014, states that Julio Maier "showed the people to us [when] we only saw files, writings, records, decisions" (2005, p. 7). Argibay highlights that Maier's promotion of transparency in the judicial system "argued with eloquence the necessity to eliminate secrets; the inquisitorial tradition trapped us in a Kafkaesque spider web that affected not only the accused, but also the victims and witnesses" (2005, pp. 7–9).

In this regard, Alberto Binder, who was a disciple of Maier, was one of the founders of the INECIP and was serving by that time as vice president of this institute. He stated that 1992 was a significant year in the promotion of the criminal procedural reform in Chile.[10] He remarked that the aim of this transformation was to "humanize criminal justice" (Binder, 1993, p. 88). Binder holds that "humanization" means "to not affect the person's dignity, respecting those protective shields that are the guarantees" and to understand that the so-called "'object of the process' is not a thing of social conflict, but a social relationship which is determinate, produced, and lived by human beings" (Binder, 1993, p. 88). His speech makes visible the appeal to the social dimension, a distinctive characteristic found in many of the "reformers'" speeches, one that points out the necessity to repair the bond between law and society.

With this purpose in mind, "reformers" intended to turn "the 'file' into a symbol of the inquisitorial method," as expressed by Carlos Chiara Díaz, former member of the *Superior Tribunal de Justicia* (a provincial appellate court), from Entre Ríos Province, in the Second Public Audience in the Deputies Chamber of the National Congress when they were promoting the "Albrieu's Project," which was developed with the INECIP's and Binder's support, 2 November 2010. "Reformers" argued that the "case file kills the person," a saying coined by Professor José Cafferata Nores and reiterated by district attorney and law professor Luis Cevasco (Public Audience, November 2010). From this antagonistic position, "Levene's Code" represents a system of criminal persecution "with inquisitorial remnants," since judges make adjudicatory decisions during the pretrial phase. This bureaucratic process generates a massive paper trail that accumulates into a file that is placed in several units and denominated bodies, with changes ultimately being made, and with both victims and accused being subjected to a non-transparent process that happens behind closed doors. "Reformers" affirm that the process is inhumane because these files are neither accessible to either party nor are the parties present during the judicial investigation.

On this basis, "reformers" argue that the "accusatorial system" would allow for the humanization of the criminal justice system, thanks to their public and oral processes. This change, the "reformers" argued, could overcome the obsolescence, over bureaucratization, and nontransparency of Argentina's criminal justice system. Under the "accusatorial system," they considered that oral trials and public audiences take place in a courtroom in front of a judge, allowing each party to confront each other. More than this, "reformers" recognize that beyond a change in the procedures, a transformation of criminal justice system must take place.

iii. "To prosecute the great crime"

A third important *cosmology* relates "to prosecuting the great crime" – that is, "crimes linked to power" that require an "integral" reform, as put forth by Carlos Chiara Díaz (Public Audience, November 2010). This *cosmology* attacks the problem that the "reformers" claim the "Levene's Code" generates because the code is incapable of rendering justice for power and political crimes. Juan Carlos Vega, former president of the Commission of Criminal Legislation of the Chamber of Deputies, argues that on the one hand, "it is necessary to shift from [the criminal persecution] of the poverty crimes towards to the power crimes," although "no law can solve cultural endemics as corruption," and on the other hand, there is a need to affirm the following sentiment that emerged during "Albrieu's Project":

> We wish that the crimes of power be punished in Argentina; something that up to now has not been the case. On this point we all agreed – surprisingly – all the political parties of this commission.
>
> (Public Audience, November 2010)

The "reformers" emphasized "*mafias*" are the targets of the reform promoted by "Albrieu's Project." The *Coalición de ONG's por la Reforma Procesal Penal Federal* (Coalition of NGO's for the Federal Criminal Procedural Reform)[11] made a public pronouncement on the 29 of July 2011 in favor of the criminal justice reform, mainly pointing out the limitations of "Levene's Code" particularly on the topic of corruption. The criticism is central to their argument especially as it applied to relevant cases of public interest, involving high-profile actors, such as LAPA airlines, Carlos Menem (former president of Argentina), and IBM-ANSES (bribery case between IBM and an Argentine Government social insurance agency) (Coalición de ONG's para la Reforma Procesal Penal Federal, 2011).

Moreover, the "reformers" see their proposals as an opportunity to change the focus of criminal prosecution through the prosecutor's new functions laid out in "Albrieu's Project" and other reform initiatives since it would have the ability to select the cases to prosecute according to social relevance and available resources.[12] In other words, the reformative process transforms prosecution of a crime into a process of defining what crimes are of social importance and worthwhile to pursue through the public apparatus of the criminal justice system.

This same logic drives the arguments of the project, which proposed the modification of the Federal Criminal Procedure Code passed on in 2014 (Law 27.063). In 2015, a lawyer with strong links with the nongovernmental organizations *Unidos por la Justicia* (United for Justice) and *Centro de Estudios de Justicia de las Américas* (Justice Study Center for the Americas, also known as "CEJA") of the Organization of American States, Germán Garavano, became minister of justice and human rights. Garavano presented before the Chamber of Senators a project of 47 articles with the intent to reform the Code in 2016, presenting among other arguments that the existing articles needed to be reformed since "they were imposed with the purpose of guaranteeing impunity" (Diario La Nación, 2016). He pointed out that the reform aims to match international standards with regards to the persecution of complex and organized crimes since "the Criminal Procedural Code approved by Law 27.063 is not able to address the complexity that emerges when pursuing crimes such as drug trafficking and terrorism" (Federal Criminal Procedural Reform Proyect, 2016, p. 3). Thus "the proposed reform comes to provide the National Justice with effective tools to such an end" (Federal Criminal Procedural Reform Proyect, 2016, p. 3). This speech once again articulates the struggle against impunity and complex crimes, and how these reforms provide necessary legal tools for effective criminal prosecution.

iv. Modernization and overcoming the "old and obsolete"

A significant *cosmology* emerges to argue that the codes currently in existence are obsolete legal creations that do not respond to the demands of the modern era, from Obarrio's time to the present. The reasons argued were that the codes were only "copies" of revoked legislation in other countries or that these laws could not respond to the challenges of the time in which they were formed, much less the challenges of today. This is particularly the case with "Levene's Code," which was open to debates and parliamentary initiatives to reform it because the law "was born old and obsolete" (Pastor, 1992, p. 64). The followers of Maier spotlighted different various key aspects that went unchanged between "Obarrio's Code" and the 1991 "Levene's Code," as follows: preventive detention, victim participation, trial by jury; and pretrial judge.

Daniel Pastor, one of the youngest founders of the INECIP, during the Maier's seminar previously mentioned, expressed strong criticism against the "Levene's Code." He argued that with regards to preventive detention, "The new Criminal Procedural Code provides nothing new regarding this problem: the preventive detention is still mandatory in the same cases in which was in the old code" (1993, p. 63). Pastor goes further and claims that the "Levene Code" "was born old and obsolete," taking into account that "these are rules concerning preventive detention which demonstrate how authoritarian and arbitrary the power of the State could be and how respectful it is of fundamental human rights" (1993, pp. 62 and 64). In the same collective book, Fernando Córdoba discusses victims' participation in the "Levene's Code" and considers that "the reform has demonstrated a small vocation for change." Moreover, Córdoba thinks that, "practically nothing changed" in comparison with the former code (1993, p. 101). Córdoba finalizes his analysis, affirming that "the reform is not committed to giving back to the victims their agency" (1993, p. 101).

Mirna Goransky, also one of the few females' founders of the INECIP, introduces the issue of the trial by jury in "Levene's Code" under the title "A Trial Without Jury." She begins by defining the jury "as the main missing element in the new Criminal Procedural Code," considering that "the jury is the filter for the utilization of the state power" (Goransky 1993, pp. 103 and 113). Nora Cherñavsky and Mirta López González argue, "The faculties of the pretrial judge, are not constricted at all, making one more inquisitorial figure in this stage of gathering of evidence for the accusation" (1993, p. 142). This approach allows them to conclude that "the new Federal Criminal Procedural Code is not following in this point the modern codes," considering that the modern legislation establishes "the function of the pre-trial judge is limited to guaranteeing the legality of the proceedings acts to be accomplished in this stage" (Cherñavsky and López González, 1993, p. 142).

However, the issue was never resolved, and debates continued until a new code was proposed by the executive power in 2014. Starting from Mauricio Macri's presidential victory and his electoral alliance with *Cambiemos* in 2015, the Law 27.063 (2014) was suspended by Decree 257/15, and for this reason, the "Levene's Code" continued to be in force. In this vein, Garavano created the "Program Justice 2020" focusing on innovation and modernization in the judiciary. Introduced in September 2016, the program intends to reform the third Federal Criminal Procedural Code (Law 27.063) "after meetings with judicial actors, institutions and members of civil society to establish a dialogue on redesigning and modernizing the mechanisms of criminal persecution of the federal crimes" (Programa Justicia 2020, 2016). Garavano described the proposal as "advanced legislation" in contrast to previous initiatives that were "born old" (Diario La Nación, 2016). This law project implies "a reform before a reform" in which legislative processes are still running their course and pending definition. In short, the dispute still emphasizes the demands of "modernizing" the law and overcoming the "obsolete" and inefficient.

Conclusion: federal criminal procedural reforms beyond the law

The *cosmologies* noted earlier demonstrate that disputes concerning the reform of the federal criminal procedural system go beyond the law. The "struggle" is not only to replace the "inquisitorial system" but directed against the "inquisitorial culture" that it generates. Through this lens, disputes and controversies proceed from the assumption that there is an intense need for "cultural change." "Reformers" speeches underscored that culture is a key factor for true transformation in the criminal justice system, which, in turn, will restore respect of human rights and the true democratization of the country. It is not a coincidence that references of "reformers" to culture is consistent over the time since it translates into the necessity for permanent reforms and requiring these legal experts to continue to pursue this *cause* across the generations. Moreover, these same legal experts affirm that the real reforms will only be successful when it promotes a "cultural change" in both the code and in the legal practice.

The question remains whether legal research on justice reforms takes into account that studies on the practice of law needs to go beyond the law and could find support in other social sciences. This research affirms that criminal justice reforms, in particular, could benefit from this type of analysis, especially because it concerns a dispute for power and affects society in a meaningful way. Furthermore, it is a field in which lawyers construct a broad and thick web of meanings to explain and justify their proposal of transforming the criminal system – especially in a Global South nation in Latin America that has over the past several decades aimed to reform what many consider "old and obsolete" and "inhumane" laws that contravene "modern" notions of human rights. *Cosmologies*, therefore, provide great explanatory potential in this field concerning criminal legal transformations in democratic nations with regard to its disputes and foundations of legitimacy.

Notes

1 Argentina is organized as a federal republic in which every local government (provinces) has its own criminal procedure legislation. In addition, there is a federal jurisdiction, which its own criminal procedure law. This chapter focuses on the debates regarding the reform of the latter.

2 This chapter is based on the research done for my PhD thesis entitled *Una promesa de democratización. Activismo, política y expertise jurídica en el proceso de reforma de la justicia penal en la Argentina* (A Promise of Democratization. Activism, Politics, and Legal Expertise in the Process of Criminal Justice Reform in Argentina), supervised by Prof. Dra. Virginia Vecchioli (Faculty of Social Sciences, University of Buenos Aires). I would like to express my gratitude to Prof. Dr. Stephan Parmentier (KU Leuven, Belgium) for his valuable comments and suggestions regarding a previous version of this chapter. The thesis has won the 2019 Argentinean National Prize for PhD Thesis on Social Sciences.

3 "Republican" refers to the liberal ideal of the state's organization being linked to civil rights and freedoms.

4 It is appropriate to mention that nowadays Belgium, France, and other continental European countries still adhere to the inquisitorial model, while the United Kingdom and the United States of America among others countries adopt the accusatorial model; this distinction is also relevant for international criminal justice, which is often a combination of both models. For more details concerning the legal dispute around the inquisitive and accusatorial system in Argentina, see Langer (2007, 2014).

5 This notion that assumes a homogeneous definition of culture has been used – and deeply reworded – by anthropologists. This model of cultural interpretation derives

from the theories regarding the cultural change proper of the decade of the '60s of the 20th century and relies on notions as *culture of poverty* that they were in use in the social sciences of that times for explaining why the adoption of political and economic reforms were not sufficient to accelerate the growth of Latin America (Lewis, 1972).

6 It is relevant to clarify that the *native* term is taken from the anthropologic classic literature in reference to the distinction among the ethnographer and those who belong to the locality that was an object of observation. In this research, the term is applied to the legal professionals and, more specifically, to the justice "reformers." This distinction among native statements (highlighted with quotation marks) and analytical perspectives or theoretical concepts (emphasized in the text in italics) is crucial as an heuristic tool since it allows us to distinguish the native speeches and their interested point of view from the distant approach proper from the social sciences that look for not to reproduce these normative perspective but to understand them sociologically (Vecchioli, 2011).

7 My own translation as well as the rest of the text when quotations are submitted.

8 INECIP was founded in Buenos Aires in 1989 "with the mission of contributing to the consolidation and progressive strengthening of the rule of law in the Latin America and Central America countries," and which "it was working on the specific field of reform processes of judicial systems and criminal systems linked to the democratic transition, promoting – from a scientific perspective- the defence of fundamental human rights" (website, INECIP, 2009). Available at: www.inecip.org/institucional/institucional.php.

9 It is available in the following link: www.derechos.org/nizkor/arg/causa13/.

10 In the frame of a communication presented in the International Seminar called *"Reformas procesales penales en América Latina y su impacto en la modernización de la gestión de los tribunales: la oralidad de los procesos"* (Criminal Procedural Reforms in Latin America and Its Impact in the Modernization in the Court Management: Oral Proceedings), Viña del Mar (Chile), 1992.

11 Integrated by the following social organizations: INECIP, *Asociación Civiles por la Igualdad y la Justicia* (ACIJ), *Observatorio Judicial, Asociación por los Derechos Civiles* (ADC), *Centro de Estudios Legales y Sociales* (CELS), *Asociación Pensamiento Penal (*APP), *Poder Ciudadano, Centro de Implementación de Políticas Públicas para la Equidad y el Crecimiento* (CIPPEC) and *Unidos por la Justicia.*

12 Similar logics are discussed in greater depth, albeit in the context of Brazil, in Neto and Santiago's chapter in this volume.

References

Agrikoliansky, É. (2001) "Carrières militantes et vocation à la morale: les militants de la Ligue des droits de l'homme dans les années 1980," *Revue française de science politique*, Paris, SciencesPo Les Presses, 52 (1–2), pp. 27–46.

Argibay, C. (2005) "El moderno proceso penal," AAVV, *Estudios sobre justicia penal. Homenaje al Profesor Julio B. J. Maier*, Buenos Aires, Editores del Puerto, pp. 7–9.

Binder, A. (1993) "Crisis y transformación de la justicia penal en Latinoamérica," Binder, A., et al., *Reformas procesales en América Latina. La oralidad de los procesos*, Santiago de Chile, La Corporación de Promoción Universitaria, pp. 67–88.

Bourdieu, P. (2009) *Intelectuales, política y poder*, Buenos Aires, EUDEBA.

Bourdieu, P. (1996) *A economia das trocas lingüísticas. O que falar quer dizer*, San Pablo, EDUSP.

Bourdieu, P. (1991) "Les juristes les gardiens de l´hypocrisie collective," Chazel, F. and Commaille, J. (dir.), *Normas juridiques et régulation sociale. Collection Droit et société*, Paris, Libraire Générale de Droit et de Jurisprudence, pp. 65–99.

Bourdieu, P. (1987) "The Force of Law: Toward a Sociology of the Juridical Field," *The Hastings Law Journal*, 38 (5), pp. 805–853.

Bovino, A. (1993) "El debate," AAVV, *El nuevo Código Procesal Penal de la Nación. Análisis crítico*, Buenos Aires, Editores del Puerto, pp. 167–195.

Cherñavsky, N., and López González, M. (1993) "La instrucción," AAVV, *El nuevo Código Procesal Penal de la Nación. Análisis crítico*, Buenos Aires, Editores del Puerto, pp. 141–152.

Comerford, J.C. (1999) *Fazendo a Luta. Sociabilidades, Fales e Rituais na Construção de Organizações Camponesas*, Rio de Janeiro, Relume Dumará.

Córdoba, F. (1993) "La posición de la víctima," AAVV, *El nuevo Código Procesal Penal de la Nación: Análisis Crítico*, Buenos Aires, Editores del Puerto, pp. 81–101.

Da Matta, R. (1998) [1974] "El oficio del etnólogo o cómo tener 'Anthropological Blues'," Boivin, M., Rosato, A., and Arribas, V. (eds.), *Constructores de otredad*, Buenos Aires, EUDEBA, pp. 263–272.

Douglas, M. (2007) [1966] *Pureza y peligro. Un análisis de los conceptos de contaminación y tabú*, Buenos Aires, Nueva Visión.

Douglas, M. (1988) *Símbolos naturales. Exploraciones en cosmología*, Madrid, Alianza Editorial.

Douglas, M. (1986) *How Institutions Think*, Nueva York, University of Syracuse Press.

Fernando, B. (2014) "Institutional Reforms as an Integral Part of a Comprehensive Approach to Transitional Justice," *International Journal of Transitional Justice*, 8 (2), 1 July 2014, pp. 187–193.

Fillieule, O. (2001) "Prepositions pour une analyse processuelle de l´engagements individuel," *Revue française de science politique*, Paris, SciencesPo Les Presses, 51 (1–2), pp. 199–215.

Fillieule, O., and Pudal, B. (2010) "8. Sociologie du militantisme. Problématisations et déplecement des méthodes d´enquête," Agrikoliansky, É. (comp.), *Penser les mouvements sociaux*, Paris, Le Découverte "Recherches," pp. 163–184.

Gaïti, B., and Israël, L. (2003) "Sur l´engagement du droit dans la construction des causes," *Politix.Revue des sciences sociales du politique*, Paris, Persée, 16 (62), pp. 17–30.

Galván, P. (2009) "Legislative Measures as Guarantees of Non-Repetition: A Reality in the Inter-American Court, and a Possible Solution for the European Court," *Revista IIDH*, 49, pp. 69–108.

Goransky, M. (1993) "Un juicio sin jurados," AAVV, *El nuevo Código Procesal Penal de la Nación. Análisis crítico*, Buenos Aires, Editores del Puerto, pp. 103–136.

Guber, R. (2001) *La etnografía. Método, campo y reflexividad*, Buenos Aires, Norma.

Guber, R. (1991) *El salvaje metropolitano. A la vuelta de la antropología postmoderna. Reconstrucción del conocimiento social en el trabajo de campo*, Buenos Aires, Legasa.

Heylen, B., Parmentier, S., and Weitekamp, E. (2010) The Emergence of 'Holistic Reconciliation': Lessons Learned from Victims and Offenders Inside the South African Truth and Reconcilitation Commision, *Int'L Perspectives in Victimology*, 5 (1), pp. 1–12.

Israël, L. (2001) "Usages militants du droit dans l´arène judiciare: le *cause lawyering*," *Droit et societè*, Cachan, Editions juridiques associées, 49, pp. 793–824.

Langer, M. (2014) "La larga sombra de las categorías acusatorio-inquisitivo," *Revista de Derecho Público*, Bogotá, Facultad de Derecho – Universidad de Los Andes, 32, pp. 1–34.

Langer, M. (2007) "Revolution in Latin American Criminal Procedure: Diffusion of Legal Ideas from the Peripheria," *American Journal of Comparative Law*, Oxford, Oxford University Press, 55 (4), pp. 617–677.

Latour, B. (2008) [2007] *Reensamblar lo social: una introducción a la teoría del actor-red*, Buenos Aires, Manantial.

Levene (II), R. (1989) *Proyecto de Código Procesal Penal para la Capital Federal y Justicia Federal*, Buenos Aires, Ediciones Depalma.

Lewis, O. (1972) *La cultura de la pobreza*, Barcelona, Editorial Anagrama.

Maier, J. (1996) *Derecho Procesal Penal. Fundamentos*, Tomo 1, Buenos Aires, Editores del Puerto.

Maier, J. (1993) "Democracia y administración de Justicia Penal en Iberoamérica: los proyectos para la reforma del sistema penal," Binder, A., Maier, J., Riego, C., et al., *Reformas procesales en América Latina. La oralidad de los procesos*, Santiago de Chile, La Corporación de Promoción Universitaria, pp. 67–88.

Maier, J. (1989) *Derecho Procesal Penal argentino*, Buenos Aires, Hammurabi.

Maier, J. (1987) "Presentación (Proyecto de Código Procesal Penal de la Nación)," *Cuadernos de la Revista Doctrina Penal. Teoría y Práctica en las Ciencias Penales*, Buenos Aires, Argent Consult, 1, pp. 645–670.

Maier, J., et al. (2000) *Juicio por Jurados en el Proceso Penal*, Buenos Aires, Ad-Hoc.

Novak, M. (2005) "Reparations by the Human Rights Chamber of Bosnia and Herzegovina," Feyter, K. de, Parmentier, S., Bossuyt, M., and Lemmes, P. (eds.), *Out of the Ashes: Reparations for Victims of Gross and Systematic Human Rights Violations*, Antwerpen and Oxford, Intersentia, pp. 245–288.

Pastor, D. (1993) "El encarcelamiento preventivo," AAVV, *El nuevo Código Procesal Penal de la Nación. Análisis crítico*, Buenos Aires, Editores del Puerto, pp. 43–63.

Pastor, D. (1992) "El Código Levene ¿nacerá viejo y caduco?," *No hay derecho*, 6.

Roth-Arriaza, N. (2016) "Measures of Non-Repetition in Transitional Justice: The Missing Link?", Gready, P. and Robins, S., *From Transitional to Transformative Justice (CUP), Forthcoming*; UC Hastings Research Paper No. 171.

Shala, N. (2018) "Guarantees of Non-Repetition for Violation of Human Rights," PhD thesis, Graduate Institute of International and Development Studies, Geneva.

Siméant, J. (2002) "Friches, hybrides et contrebandes: sur la circulation et a puissance militantes des discours savants," Hamman, P., Méon, J.-M., and Verrier, B. V. (dirs), *Discours savants, discours militants: Mélange des genres*, Paris, L´Harmattan, pp. 17–53.

Thomas, R. (1993) "Interviewing Important People in Big Companies," *Journal of Contemporary Ethnography*, Thousand Oaks, Sage Journals, 22 (1), pp. 80–96.

Treves, R. (2010) [1987] *Sociologia dil diritto. Origini, richerche, problema*, Torino, Einaudi Editori.

Vauchez, A., and Willemez, L. (2007) *La justice face à ses réformateurs (1980–2006). Enterprises de modernisation et logiques de résistances*, Paris, Presses Universitaries de France.

Vecchioli, V. (2014) "La recreación de una comunidad moral y la institución de un relato legítimo sobre los derechos humanos en la Argentina," *Publicar en Antropología y Ciencias Sociales*, Buenos Aires, Colegio de Graduados en Antropología de la República Argentina, Año VXII, N° XVII, pp. 1–27.

Vecchioli, V. (2011) "Presentación: Profesionales del derecho, activismo jurídico y creación de nuevos derechos. Hacia una mirada comprensiva del derecho desde las ciencias sociales," *Revista Política, Santiago de Chile, Universidad de Chile*, 49 (1), pp. 5–18.

Websites

Coalición de ONGs por la Reforma Procesal Federal (2011) "Coalición de ONG's se pronuncian a favor de la reforma del Código Procesal Penal de la Nación", Blog, http://reformaprocesal federal.blogspot.com/2011/07/coalicion-de-ongs-se-pronuncian-favor.html.

Diario La Nación (2016) "El Gobierno llevó al Senado el nuevo Código Procesal Penal", www.lanacion.com.ar/1944850-el-gobierno-llevo-al-senado-el-nuevo-codigo-procesal-penal.www.lanacion.com.ar/

Infoleg. Información legislativa y documental, http://servicios.infoleg.gob.ar/
Instituto de Estudios Comparados en Ciencias Penales y Sociales (INECIP), http://inecip.org/tag/inecip/
Federal Criminal Procedural Reform Proyect (2016) https://www.justicia2020.gob.ar/wp-content/uploads/2016/09/texto-final-del-proyecto-reforma-CPP.pdf
Programa de Justicia 2020 (2016) www.justicia2020.gob.ar/proyecto-reforma-al-codigo-procesal-penal-federal-ingreso-al-senado-la-nacion/

Annex

Table 6.1 Federal criminal procedural codes enacted in Argentina

Passed on	*Law*	*Code/Project*	*Called*	*Articles*	*Presidency*
4 October 1888	2.372	*Código de Procedimientos en Materia Penal* (CPMP) or the Code of Procedures in Criminal Matters/Project elaborated by Manuel Obarrio, 1882	"Obarrio's Code"	701 (modify version)	Miguel Ángel Juárez Celman, Autonomista Nacional Party (PAN)
21 August 1991	23.984	*Código Procesal Penal de la Nación* (CPPN) or the Federal Criminal Procedural Code for Argentina/ Project elaborated by Ricardo Levene (II), its first version in 1975 presented in the Chamber of Senators by José H. Martiarena and Alfredo L. Benitez and revised in 1989	"Levene's Code"	530 (revised version)	Carlos Saúl Menem, Justicialista Party(PJ)
4 December 2014	27.063	*CPPN* or the Federal Criminal Procedural Code for Argentina/ Project presented in the Congress by the Executive Power, suspended by presidential Decree 257 in 2015		349	Cristina Fernández de Kirchner, Frente por la Victoria Party (FPV)

Source: Own elaboration in base of official web sites: www.infojus.gov.ar and www.infoleg.gov.ar.

Table 6.2 Comparative attributes regarding the "inquisitorial system" and the "accusatorial system" according to "reformers" speech

System/Attribute	*"Inquisitorial System"*	*"Accusatorial System"*
Procedure acts, way of developing	Written	Oral
Way of disposal	Procedure	Litigation
Technology	Case file	Audience
Protagonism during the research before the debate	Judge inquisitor	Prosecutor (persecutorial functions)
Who is accused?	Judge	Prosecutor
Who makes the decision?	Judge	Judge (decision functions)
Accused	Object of the judicial investigation	Subject of rights
Victim	Reduced place, expropriated of the conflict	With chance of hearing, is protagonist, have a place
Duration time	Long-term	Limited time due to oral proceedings
Type of judging tribunal	Professional	Trial by jury (citizen participation in justice)

Source: Own elaboration in base of legal experts theories: Maier (1987, 1989, 1993, 1996), Binder (1993), Bovino (1993), and Córdoba (1993).

Chapter 7

Of punishment, protest, and press conferences

Contentious politics amid despotic decision in contemporary Burmese courtrooms

Elliott Prasse-Freeman

Introduction

On 12 September 2018, after an eight-month trial roundly condemned by domestic and international observers for its partiality against the accused, two Reuters reporters were convicted of violating Myanmar's State Secrets Act and sentenced to seven years in prison. Although the reporters, Wa Lone and Kyaw Swa Oo, maintained that they had been framed in retribution for reporting on specific atrocities the Myanmar military committed as part of its ethnic cleansing of the Rohingya minority in September 2017, *and* while a police officer testified confirming the entrapment plot, the judge conjured a scenario in which the reporters were consorting with terrorists to whom they intended to pass sensitive materials. When pressed about this gross violation of press freedom, the country's leader Aung San Suu Kyi objected to the characterization, insisting that the reporters had violated the law and that their sentencing was hence consistent with the overarching "rule of law" (Amnesty International, 2018).

Seven years into the country's much-lauded "transition" from military rule, international observers found the conviction bracing (see Reuters, 2018), marking a death knell of sorts to hopes for a tidy transition to liberal democracy. Suu Kyi, the former political prisoner and Nobel Peace Prize laureate, now not only defended the military's genocidal campaign[1] but also presented the machinations of a kangaroo court as emblematic of the "rule of law." In so doing, she distilled the emergence of an elite "democratic" authoritarianism embodied by a hybrid military/liberal pact (Prasse-Freeman and Phyo Win Latt, 2018). In this vein, the courts seemed to continue to act as they had in the past: as machines for despotic decision and social control.

And yet the events of September 12 were also noteworthy in other ways. First, in a significant break from the past, the gross miscarriage of justice was *observable*. Rather than occurring under a shroud of secrecy (Cheesman, 2015, pp. 117–120), the court was open for diplomats, reporters, family members of the accused, and normal citizens alike. Moreover, after the sentence was bestowed, the accused were not immediately whisked away; instead, "they were allowed a few minutes to address reporters," at which time "they spoke with the same defiance expressed over more than two-dozen court appearances" (Dunant, 2018), indicating how the entire trial process provided them a platform for riposte. Finally, when police eventually took them away, their police van "was instantly surrounded by angry Myanmar reporters and activists, who hammered the bonnet and shouted, 'let them speak!'" [ibid] Videos and images of this brazen act of defiance circulated across Burmese social media, generating endorsement from thousands of supporters.

Hence while the trial was exemplary of antidemocratic retrenchment in Myanmar's transition, it also stood as indicative of the remarkable ways in which Burma's courts are changing. Indeed, the trial stands as another token of Burma's courts becoming an increasingly ambiguous space: producing despotic decisions even as they stand as sites of highly mediatized political performances.

The following considers these changes for how they afford new opportunities for political action and for what they reveal about certain Burmese conceptions of political power, in particular, sovereignty. As a point of departure, it asks, "During the military dictatorship years, why did Burma bother to have courts, particularly for the political cases it construed as threats to the nation?" In initial response, academic work has in recent decades provided many potential answers, demonstrating that authoritarian legality facilitates the pursuit of a number of regime objectives: from suppressing opponents, outsourcing controversial policies, facilitating trade and investment, to coordinating competing factions within the regime (Ginsburg and Moustafa, 2008; Moustafa, 2014). Authoritarian courts even, perhaps unexpectedly, provide space for "contention both among the ruling elite and between regimes and their citizens" (Ginsburg and Moustafa, 2008). Given this latter finding, it is perhaps not surprising that Burmese courts today are beginning to operate as sites for contestation of systems of control.

And yet the chapter will dig more deeply into the contours and dynamics of those forms of control, showing how courts protected themselves from the kind of citizen capture identified in the literature, while still delivering indexical messages about normative citizenship. Specifically, the chapter will contest standard scholarly assumptions that Burmese governments – in this case Burma's military dictatorships – sought "legitimation" from "external" sources (e.g., support from either the populace or from the community of monks) as a central strategy for maintaining power. Against such dualism, I argue that Burmese political regimes have long been monist: focusing only on the perpetuation of their rule, taking maintenance of power itself as a sign of continuing maintenance of power. They have normalized the state of exception, collapsing any separation between "standard" and "exceptional" practices. This has had the effect of indirectly subjectivizing many Burmese citizens as nonparticipants in formal political processes. Such subjectivization has been accomplished, *inter alia*, through court practices, in which courts have conveyed through the effects of punitive decisions the extreme consequences of participation. The chapter will then focus on what the transformation from one mode of court practice (and the broader authoritarian complex in which it nested) to the new hybrid democratic-authoritarian court extant today can tell us about both the construction of Burmese political subjectivity and the revealed political ontology of the regimes in power.

Citizenship as a gift

During Burma's years of military dictatorship, the few researchers of the country's legal system able (and willing) to navigate the compounding challenges of limited access, reticent informants, and scattered archival materials found a legal system evacuated of legal content, given over to the administrative processes of prefigured political dictates. As Nick Cheesman describes this era, "The court's purpose was not to try the accused, not to establish any kind of guilt or innocence"; rather, it was an "administrative activity on which the law-and-order project depend[ed]" (2015, p. 216).

Here the "law-and-order" imperative, where law was used as a tool to suppress dissent and enforce a general quietude on the Burmese populace, could be reasonably construed as reflecting a disinterest on the part of ruling elites with governance's subjectivizing effects on that populace. To use Foucault's famous schema, Burma's state seemed to effect a blunt force "sovereign" type of power unconcerned with "disciplinary" effects (Foucault, 1995): people could do what they wanted and think what they wanted about the rulers, provided they obeyed and remained silent. Evidence supporting such an interpretation can be adduced from the negligent efforts on the part of Myanmar's rulers to build an infrastructurally sophisticated state (Mann, 1984) able to know, order, regulate, and hence hegemonize subjects through various "ideological state apparatuses" (Althusser, 1971), such as schools, courts, and cultural institutions. Instead, the military acted as a desultory quasi-imperial power, greedily hoarding and securing scarce resources for self-aggrandizement rather than pursuing ambitious "modernist" state building (Prasse-Freeman, 2012). As Guha (1997) put it about a different colonial project, this produced "dominance without hegemony."

However, while such an analytic might adequately describe the way the junta approached the problem of its masses, Burmese who made it into courts for cases deemed political were categorized and engaged differently. Those recalcitrant subjects who (momentarily) shattered the prevailing quietude were perceived as dangerously infectious, containing the potential to imbue those silent masses with rebellious fervor. Hence the military-state deployed significant resources to contain and punish such actors. Indeed, political activism was policed with extreme prejudice, with activists virtually always ending up in either exile or prison, the latter acting as a site of double-immurement, given that political inmates were quarantined in their own blocks so as not to radicalize "normal" prisoners. I argue that excessively long prison terms imposed on these political activists were meant less to discipline so much as to punish, or rather to discipline only through punishment. In other words, rather than using the prison term to regulate behavior (expanding or contracting the length of imprisonment in response to changes in prisoner conduct, thereby rewarding acquiescence), the juridical-incarceration complex somewhat abdicated that ability, communicating instead the sovereign prerogative to be unreasonable. When I conducted long-term participant observation with members of activist groups in Myanmar from 2014 to 2016, most of these individuals, who had spent years in prison, conveyed to me how disproportionate the punishments were. Prisoners, facing half-century-long terms, thus had little incentive to submit to any "rehabilitation." Further, the daily abuses suffered by prisoners (Ma Thida, 1994; Win Tin, 2012; Connelly, 2011) seemed mostly disconnected from state officials' instrumental objectives: violence was an outcome of the environment, of sadism, or of quotidian economies (prison guards exploiting prisoners). Military intelligence or special branch officials, responsible for maintaining quietude and discerning threats *outside* of the prison, were not ever-present inside: they were not working to "turn" political prisoners through inflicted pain. As Cheesman comments about an earlier political prison, the "detained . . . were not punished or rehabilitated"; the prison did "nothing other than isolate and terrify" (Cheesman forthcoming).

Moreover, the long prison terms were not merely for pacification through immurement because the punished often enjoyed early amnesties, decades before their full sentences had been served. I interpret these conditional pardons as sovereign *gifts* for which the recipients were meant to have been grateful. Cheesman (2015, p. 213) has located a pledge given to detainees from protests in 2007 that outlines how the state imagined amnesty as a largesse conveyed to apologetic subjects:

> I am aware that if I commit the same type of offence in the future, I will be subject to action in accordance with the law. I was arrested because of an offence. I am being released because the state has leniency. I pledge that if summoned, I will come at all times.

The pledge reminds the signer that the threat of violation has not been evacuated but remains vivified, potent – looming as a sepulchral presence. Moreover, in installing this phantom, the state calls attention to its own magnanimity – its own leniency is to thank for freedom.[2]

Beyond personhood and legitimacy

Cheesman invokes philosopher Giorgio Agamben to argue that Burmese

> courts functioned not to interrogate the work of the police and other personnel, not to determine the guilt or innocence of accused protest leaders

> brought before them, but to pull the accused back into the formal legal realm, to restore to them the juridical personhood withdrawn from them in the zone of anomie.
>
> (193)

Yet Cheesman also finds that "[m]any detainees left the [detention] camp in a manner as ambiguous as the way they went in, by signing imprecise assurances that they would obey the law in the future" (2015, p. 213). If court decisions were about restoring juridical personality, what explains the exclusion of these subjects and the retention of this ambiguity? I instead contend that the fact that many activists did not receive trials suggests that the regime did not care for such a rehabilitative project. In fact, a look at the released activists reveals the nondistinction between the subject sequestered in the camp and the one liberated back into society. They stand, I argue, as the same kind of juridical persons – that is to say, as objects fully subjected to sovereign will.

Here it is worth considering Agamben's study of the sovereign exception in Western jurisprudence (2004) and comparing it to the Burmese authoritarian version. Agamben finds that while there is an element of sovereign authority ultimately "founded not on a preexisting order but on a personal charisma" (2004, p. 84) whose violence is unbounded, that charismatic element is *co-constituted* by an aspect that is "normative and juridical in the strict sense" (p. 86). The state of exception acts as a way to "ultimately articulate and hold together the two aspects of the juridico-political machine by instituting a threshold of undecidability between" them (ibid.). This model depends on inoculation, separation, and quarantine between the two poles, so they are held in protective tension such that "their dialectic – though founded in friction – can nevertheless function in some way" (ibid.). Critical here is a suppression and disavowal of the presence of that unaccountable authority lurking behind the law. As Slavoj Žižek points out, "Discourse operate[s] on two levels; that the level of explicit statements [is] supplemented by an obscene unacknowledged underside" (2002, p. 106). The two are mutually parasitic: the pure violence sustains the order on which the law operates; that violence can exist because it relies on the symbolic trappings of the law to shroud it. This elision lubricates the system, allowing the belief in the explicit discourse (law) to remain and order to persist.

While Agamben demonstrates how that dialectic ultimately dissolves as the state of exception collapses the distance between law and figure of authority into regimes of monistic force (Rudy, 2010), the ideology of dualistic separation persists even today. In a world of Guantanamo and the War on Terror, in which law has been weaponized without constraint (Butler, 2006), the faith in "rule of law" grows only stronger (Rudy forthcoming). Burma's system, however, never purported to establish a distance or balance between authority and law. Authority always made its supremacy above the law more or less explicit, even codifying it legally. Its legacies persisted in the colonial era, and Soe Lin

Aung and Stephen Campbell (2016) draw continuities between that diarchic state and the present version. In a recent edited volume on present political possibilities under Burma's 2008 Constitution (Harding, 2017), no fewer than five separate contributions wrestle with the threat or reality of constitutionally inscribed exceptions. But, more critically, in discussions elsewhere (Crouch, 2017; Cheesman, D'Costa, and Haberkorn, 2016) of the existence of "everyday emergency" and "everyday impunity," respectively, we can observe how the state of exception has long been the norm in Myanmar. Returning to Žižek's observation, we do not apprehend a bifurcation between explicit and implicit discourse in Burma: the exception is advanced openly. In Jennifer Leehey's commentary on military-state era propaganda, the authoritarian state betrays a metapragmatic recognition of its own sovereign will:

> The ubiquitous red billboards asserting the 'People's Desires,' the poems and cartoons in the state-owned media, and the mass rallies with obligatory attendance where citizens are assembled to chant slogans on cue are not particularly persuasive and, in large measure, I argue, not really intended to persuade. Yet they do serve as concrete demonstrations of the regime's ability to command a public performance of a particular state-sanctioned reality. They display the regime's control of the symbolic realm, a control that need not produce legitimacy to be valued politically.
>
> (Leehey, 2010, pp. 52–53)

Although Leehey attempts to displace the centrality of legitimacy, most Burma scholars, nonetheless, *presuppose* that the problematic of "legitimacy" animates Burmese rulers' actions.[3] In doing so, they follow Weber (1978, p. 214)[4] in identifying the *source* of legitimacy as residing in an *external* entity's assessment of how the ruler fulfils a set of external standards.[5] This external entity is society, or even "the people," which would reference a set of transcendent common values and norms with which to assess the ruler. By doing so, these scholars de-emphasize the importance of the *maintenance* of power as the ultimate sign, ignoring the way that its perpetuation may implicate the interpretation of other signs. This logic is antithetical to the idea of legitimacy promoted by classic social contract theory, as a contemporary example will help illustrate.

Burma scholar Julianne Schober argues that that during the long period of military dictatorship, "Ruling in the absence of a national constitution, military leaders increasingly sought to legitimate their power by sponsoring large Buddhist rituals that ensured better rebirths for all citizens of the state" (2017, p. 168). Moreover, in the opening paragraph of her book *Modern Buddhist Conjunctures in Myanmar*, Schober describes September 2007's "Saffron Revolution," in which monks participated in a mass uprising in downtown Yangon as "a populist uprising led by monks, [that] contested the legitimacy of the state" (2011, p. 1). Benedicte Brac de la Perrière (2017), citing Schober, adduces that the "ritual link" conjoining Burma's military rulers and the country's monastic institutions was severed, adding that because the regime had used the national economy of merit as the cornerstone for its legitimacy and control over the monks, the break resounded with an astounding strength (Brac de la Perrière, 2017, pp. 54–55).

Both scholars rely upon a political model in which rulers *instrumentally* cultivate certain relations (here with monks) in order to justify and legitimate their rule as assessed by their subjects. These subjects are here granted power to *evaluate* the rulers' actions and cast judgment upon them: are they legitimate or not? We are told that when "*the* monks" (note the definite article) severed the link – and became objects of violent repression – the consequent appraisal by the people was an emphatic rejection of the military.

But installing the people into the role of judge – an imaginary in which they act as a co-sovereign with the ruler – misdescribes the relationship between governors and the governed. How those in power may assess their own actions – particularly in how those actions relate to the way they imagine Buddhist institutions – could be significantly different when viewed through the model introduced earlier. Meaning that rather than military leaders cultivating patronage relationships with monastic institutions as an instrumental maneuver to appeal to "the people," they instead could have been simply performing relations of both patron and client, thereby emulating centuries of kingly practice and producing better chances that their rule would perpetuate. "The people" are not the critical audience to which these rituals are performed as judges of the actions. Instead, rulers could continue perceiving the masses as material that is attracted to a strong, or repelled by a weak, ruler's aura (Lieberman, 1978, p. 477).[6] As Geertz (1980, p. 122) reminds us in his critique of various Western instrumentalist conceptions of the state, Weberian (monopoly of violence), Marxist ("executive committee of the ruling class"), and Millian ("pragmatic device for conciliating interests") models alike neglect a fundamental aspect of state power: its ability to install the state as "the axis round which the public life of society revolved" (ibid., p. 123). This ignored aspect of state power is its ability to *attract* and *order* subjects – something well illustrated, according to Geertz, by Southeast Asian dynastic states. By presenting the theatricalities, Geertz showed how Balinese kings projected themselves as "the numinous center of the world" (ibid., p. 126) and their kingdoms its "stationary axis" (ibid., p. 130),

Returning then to the discussion of the Saffron Revolution with this in mind, while it was possible that *certain* monks and *certain* people appeared to reject the rulers, the sign constituted by the rejection had to be assessed for its effects: *did the regime fall? Did the people flee? Did the monastic institutions dissolve?* When none of these outcomes materialized, the rulers could *reassess* "revolution" itself: those people who rioted in the streets were not *true* representatives of "the people," but were unruly subjects trying to corrupt the body politic; the *specific* monks in rebellion were not synecdoches of "*the* monks," but were in fact not even monks at all (and "bogus monks" was indeed the label the regime – and some academics (Aung-Thwin, 2013, pp. 303–312) – attached to the activist abbots; see Elgee, 2010)).

Law-and-order and indirect subjectivation

If the military dictators did not care about legitimacy, then why have trials at all? Indeed, the military regime's law-and-order imperative could have been served effectively by simply disappearing activists. Yet while the trace left by the suddenly absent body adequately indexes sovereign prerogative, it remains silent about a number of things, particularly the explicit reasons for the absence. The court, on the other hand, contains an element of the social control function (Shapiro, 1981, pp. 24–26), and delivers messages about the nature of that social control to the populace through various *indexical* semiotic devices. As Foucault stressed, for instance, trials under a regime of sovereign power can constitute a spectacle in which masses are meant to observe the state's libidinous and excessive violence. Liberal legal theorist Mark Osiel, who would endorse the spectacular nature of the juridical process if not the same kind of violence, has argued for the importance of "liberal show trials" to edify jaundiced or traumatized publics (Osiel, 1995, pp. 511–512; see Peterson, 2007 for another defense of "show trials"). In this latter sense, the trial is imagined as a Durkheimian totem in which the collective values of society, difficult to perceive in everyday life (not least because they may exist only in the ideal), are rendered in stark and clear terms for society to perceive.

Researchers of authoritarian states have contrasted those that use courts for political "crimes" with those that favor disappearances, noting how some mix strategies (Pereira, 2008). Burma's military regime for its part kept its courts sealed – already fully incorporated into the penitentiary, as Cheesman puts it (2015, p. 117) – and often took additional precautions with political cases. This meant that "in contrast to the 1950s and even most of the 1960s, when trials were reported by the state and private media alike, by the 1980s news about the work of the courts in Myanmar had practically ceased" (Cheesman, 2015, p. 119); moreover, family members were prevented from attending trials or even knowing about them. My informants relayed how they had to use informal networks to inform their kin of their own arrests and imprisonments. Ko Taw, who will be introduced more below, said prisoners sent word to their families sometimes through "jailors and sometimes [through] criminal prisoners and sometimes [through] political prisoners who were also sentenced before us" or by "writing letters, by calling on the phone." This inefficient process "could take three, four months, even a year." "For me," he added, "it took nearly four months" to inform his family.[7]

But even as the regime cordoned off the "courts,"[8] foreclosing them as sites for resistance, it also circulated *information* about the "criminals" tried in them. State-run newspapers often summarized violations, while then-head of military intelligence General Khin Nyunt gave press conferences to foreign and local media elaborating on them. Further still, Khin Nyunt in at least six occasions repackaged those press conferences and articles into books,[9] supplementing the original texts with visuals such as organograms, photos, and headshots of "the destructive elements" (Khin Nyunt, 1990) so as to best describe "the grand treachery of the traitors from inside Myanmar and the ax handles from outside" (Khin Nyunt, 1989b).

The amount of attention the texts give these "traitors" is remarkable. In the two texts (Khin Nyunt, 1989a, 1989c) that present the Burma Communist Party (BCP) as the architect of the 1988 mass uprising, BCP internal party memos and meeting minutes are presented in full, allowing the BCP to describe the military dictatorship in unflattering terms. In one (1989c), no fewer than 73 BCP members and associates have their political biographies outlined, complete with headshots and demographic information, beginning with place of birth, parental occupation, and early life, and continuing with political agitation that is then linked with arrest and period of incarceration. For those who had just been arrested at the time of publication, that link often remains implicit; one Thet Kaing, for instance, had in September 1986 come "down to Yangon and controlled the UG activities" and in 1988 "ignited the 1988 March [at] Yangon Institute of Technology" and had "even drawn up a blue print for forming an interim government" (p. 78). The last line of his entry – "He was arrested on 11 July 1989" – is given without explicit link to those events, presented as self-evident. For a Khin Nyo Lwin, we are told that she sold jewelry to support the BCP and tried to pass on a letter from a general in the jungle. This presumably justifies the final line: "She was detained on 21 July 1989" (p. 81).

In all these texts, the identities are anything but occluded: they are shared perhaps as a mode of social shame. It is noteworthy that former political prisoners such as Ko Taw were aware of those press conferences in which the generals "mentioned why they arrested us [activists] and what we did to destroy the country unilaterally." The Assistance Association for Political Prisoners of Burma (AAPPB), a nongovernmental organization (NGO) set up by former political prisoners, had knowledge of the existence of three of these books.[10]

Curiously, however, the duration of imprisonment was *not* conveyed in these texts, with the regime abdicating the opportunity to convey its conception of the severity of the violation through years of incarceration. But while the ambiguity of the form of communication is apparent, when combined with the conditional pardons given later, in which the state granted freedom as a gift and recirculated the body back into society, the despotic decision had the derivative effect of indexing the state's desired standard of behavior on the part of its subjects. Courts, hence, remained insulated, while still allowing incarcerations to stand as "exemplary punishments" (Cheesman, 2009/2010, p. 609) meant to deter others and affect all.

Post-"transition" political court cases

That courts indirectly convey political values becomes clear when the current struggles occurring within courts are analyzed. While Burmese courts today remain spaces for despotic *decision* for political "crimes," the processes that lead to those decisions are now represented to observing (and ultimately even participating) publics. During the military era, jurisprudence was pedagogical but not dialogical: the state did not have to consider any response. Although activists often voiced their opposition, in a sense, these incorrigible resisters shouted into an abyss, creating signs that did not signify (Cheesman, 2015, p. 221).[11] In contrast, the law is now becoming a dramaturgical space where conflicts over the meaning of citizenship and legal "rights" become visible and contestable. This is because these same courtrooms that host bestowals of unforgiving punishment also act – somewhat paradoxically – as spaces for the substantive *rehabilitation* of political subjects. Accused activists engage in various actions that in their contentious aspects perform an uncontained citizenship that is anathema to Burma's ruling elites' conceptions. Moreover, by being able to extend and continue the forms of resistance – street protests – that landed the accused in court in the first place, activists effectively occupy a "state space" (the court compound), intensifying the violation of aesthetic conceptions of normative political subjecthood, and hence deepening the contestation. Indeed, by drawing judges into conflicts over proper expressions of citizenship, the state's injunctions are recodified and thrown into relief as contestable. To illustrate, the following discusses a key court conflagration, with supplementary information from fieldwork in other courts.

"Illegally" protesting at a court trial about "illegal" protests

In April 2015, Thein Aung Myint, a Mandalay-based activist, was standing trial for allegedly leading an illegal protest opposing the military's extrajudicial murder of freelance journalist Par Gyi. Thein Aung Myint had recently been convicted for violating the same Peaceful Protest Law in a different case, that time leading a protest against the lack of municipal services, and so on the morning of 21 April, he had to be delivered to the court compound by a prison transport vehicle. Thein Aung Myint's supporters, activist colleagues, and lawyers hence waited for his arrival at the teashop across the street from the compound. There his lawyer reviewed the details of the case and relayed the rumor that Thein Aung Myint would be sentenced that day to six months in prison.

The gate to the courthouse was closed, but after 20 minutes, a dilapidated 1970s-era squad car rounded the corner and stopped at the entrance, at which point people started to assemble around the gate. The fact that they were gathering and preparing to enter was itself a change worth remarking on, given how courts in general, and trials on political prisoners in particular, were often long closed to even family members. Justice Base, a legal aid NGO, has conducted a study exploring the extent to which courts today have complied in practice with formal legal reforms that have opened courts (Justice Base, 2017), finding that while staff were questioned and even intimidated by court officials and judges for attempting to observe trials (despite this right being guaranteed by the 2008 Constitution), they were able to access courts in most cases. Particularly in high-profile political cases in which actors with social influence could invoke formal law to gain access to courts, authorities assented to public pressure.

Hence, when several minutes later the paddy wagon pulled into the lane and slowly reversed in, the assembled crowd flowed into the compound through the open gates. A voice emerged from an open window near the front: "There is no rule of law!"[12] A young police officer walked with purpose to the voice's source and forcefully closed the window. Thein Aung Myint's fingers tried to hold the pane open, but he retracted them as they were smashed against the side. The stream of injunctions was silenced.

The crowd redirected its focus to the back of the vehicle where "normal" prisoners were exiting, tied to each other two-by-two. Thein Aung Myint descended last, unadorned by companion. He recommenced his speech while being forcibly dragged by the police officers. At this point, his 9-year-old daughter rushed to him and grabbed his waist, which silenced him and suspended the grabbing and pulling. They held each other for a noiseless 15 seconds that felt interminable in front of the assembled audience.

After she released him, Thein Aung Myint continued yelling, and the guards continued to usher him back to the holding cell for those who would soon face trial. As he was pulled toward the holding cell, Thein Aung Myint's inner circle (four activist colleagues and the lawyers) talked with a man who appeared to be the coordinating policeman. Ko Taw soon returned from that conversation, reporting that Thein Aung Myint would be permitted to hold a press conference five minutes after his trial's conclusion. Ko Taw added that this was not normal: the authorities believed that Thein Aung Myint would continue to yell and were concerned about this in front of the crowd.

> If they didn't get him to stop, there might be a riot. And they said to me, "After the trial we will give him the opportunity to give a speech to the media." And then I said to Thein Aung Myint, please agree with the policeman, it will be better for you.

This was a strange situation – the more notorious the behavior, the more opportunities proffered.

After a trial in which the judge read his decision and delivered a sentence of six months imprisonment, Thein Aung Myint emerged from the room, with he and his coterie ushering reporters to the center of the court compound. He began to speak:[13]

> Today I don't believe at all in the legal jurisprudence. The legal decision being made by the dictatorship's hand, I see its decision perfectly. Since the time when Ko Par Gyi who was killed unjustly without his case ever being revealed, and those who demanded that the truth of Ko Par Gyi's case be revealed were ordered [to stop], the jurisprudence in this country has been

> quite off the mark. If I have to talk about it again, I have to talk about the dictatorship's handiwork. . . . These things that are wrong now must be immediately reformed. We must demand our rights as citizens. Today Ko Par Gyi was murdered unlawfully. We all know that. But why can't they still solve the case? Since the time when it has not been resolved, in our country the government itself is itself creating the tumult. I want to say that the government is causing the problems.

After his statement, journalists asked questions, but the policemen were pulling him toward the truck. As Thein Aung Myint approached the jaws of the wagon, Ko Taw, his head low, cupped his hands and bellowed, "May Thein Aung Myint be in good health." The crowd responded by echoing his call. Thein Aung Myint lifted his fist as he was pulled from behind into the car. The door closed. The truck lumbered over the bump at the entrance, and people followed it out, clapping and cheering as it drove off.

Later when Ko Taw eventually began to discuss what had just transpired, he fumed about the judge in particular:

> In his decision the judge mentioned Bogyoke Aung San's speech, a speech to the people about obeying discipline. And so he said that Thein Aung Myint is against the speech of Aung San. This is the first time we heard this kind of saying from a judge. So he wants to make it seem that Thein Aung Myint is going against the spirit of Bogyoke.

Ko Taw here conveyed that it was highly insulting for the judge to invoke Bogyoke Aung San, the father of the country, to censure the activists. The conviction had been expected; the moral righteousness, by contrast, was an insult that the activists "could not accept."

The next day, we returned to the courthouse to see if the judge's decision was ready. It was not, but the case did make it in the news. Critically, the court's information officer was quoted linking the moral critique with the actual judicial decision:

> During his protest, [Thein Aung Myint] stated the name of president and army commander-in-chief as just "Thein Sein" and "Min Aung Hlaing" [i.e., without titles], which is impolite. And he also said: "Get out you power-hungry lunatics." That's why the court found him guilty; his unauthorized protest was not only demanding justice for Ko Par Gyi, but also insulting the country's leaders.
>
> (Zarni Mann, 2015)

Even in the official decision, a copy of which I finally secured and translated two weeks later, the judge elevates moral condemnation above jurisprudence. For instance, he presents giving the state five days advanced notice to assess an application for a demonstration as follows: "If it is truly necessary to do a real protest, citizens or organizations who truly love and cherish the country would not encounter even a single difficulty" to grant the advanced notice. Further, the judge construes following the law as a duty and as worthy of the Buddha's praise. Finally, he includes, in the concluding paragraph motivating his ultimate decision, the lines about leaving out honorifics when speaking about the country's rulers and saying they are power-crazed, writing that, "because of the behaviors like these, I make the following decision."

As these passages and others from the seven-page judgment indicate, the judge is employing an explicitly pedagogical method, reflecting at length on the duties of citizens and warning of the chaos lurking, the "barbarity" waiting to be unleashed by disrespect of the law.[14] This marks a serious departure from early eras, when even "a one-page opinion" would be "lengthy when compared to those of other criminal cases in Myanmar decisions" (Cheesman, 2009/2010, p. 609). The judge indicates that the violation of the law was less important than the violation of his idea of a docile and obedient subject.

And yet, while his decision attempts to convey that objective, the contentious interactions that occur in the court compound itself before and after the decision act as a continuation of that debate over the proper role for citizens in the changing country. Indeed, in another court case I attended, activists who had just been sentenced to four years in prison for holding an illegal protest led the assembled crowd in an impassioned rendition of the national anthem as they exited the courtroom after their decision and sentencing. When one attempted to unfurl a banner condemning the decision, a policeman tried to snatch it away, leading to a five-minute mini-riot in which dozens of people – police, defendants, and supporters – wrestled and screamed. Rather than resulting in a violent crackdown, the incident resolved itself quietly – the police even permitted the defendants to loiter in the compound, giving interviews to the press and talking with their families. At this point, one activist took off her shawl, on which she had written "Rule of Law," and set it on fire.

How were these acts possible? When I asked Zeya, another activist present in Mandalay, how Thein Aung Myint was able to respond to the judge – to insult him and his court from within the court compound – he pointed out that, "the judge only has authority inside the room, and once he makes his decision, the rest of the compound belongs to the police, and their need to prevent a riot."[15] Yet this is not, strictly legally speaking, true: judges have de jure control over the entire court compound.[16] The judges in these situations could have reasserted control, but that they did not may reflect a subtle schism in the law-and-order apparatus in which the police (order) and juridical (law) are no longer perfectly aligned.

Further still, Ko Taw reflected that although "the policeman warned me repeatedly not to cry out, I really wanted to cry out about the injustice and the terrible system," and so "I still needed to yell out – so I only yelled that he should have a long life." The policeman's injunction, and the corresponding lack of consequences for Ko Taw's direct violation of it indicates that the police are now *managing* "tolerated illegalities" (Foucault, 1995, p. 87) rather than imposing despotic sovereign will, suggesting that in this new context, the law-and-order imperative has been relaxed or reinterpreted such that the protester is no longer a priori prohibited from acting. Law and order now *permits* certain outbursts – Thein Aung Myint's yelling, the Yangon activist's shirt burning, Ko Taw's calling for responses – as officials are concerned with containing these effects.

The question is whether the permission of outbursts in the court complex itself works *against*, or instead buttresses, the judge's pedagogy about the disciplined and silent citizen. It seems that at the least, law and order and its associated message about desirable political conduct no longer work in concert, indeed revealing that they had been only laminated together and are now being peeled apart: law versus order, with order being reinterpreted. Now that activists are no longer secluded in courts, now that their enunciations act as signs again, the judges' (and state's) law becomes that which disrupts order. Judges compensate by engaging in proclamations that correct citizen comportment – but by deigning to make such extralegal declarations, a judge risks becoming enrolled in debate and dialogue, making contestable both the judge/law and the contours of that asserted comportment.

Recall here the momentary embrace between Thein Aung Myint and his daughter. The state officials and the accused alike were both undone by the singular moment of human connection. But even as it created a rupture in the text of the political play, the moment was effectively staged for others to observe. They saw the human consequences of Myanmar's "justice" system, observing not only continuity with the previous era but also witnessing, participating in, its painful perpetuation. When juxtaposed with the judge's putative justifications for the incarceration – that Thein Aung Myint was not sufficiently obeisant to the powerful – the instant of reconnection and corresponding separation became a commentary on the risibility of Burma's current legal justice, rendering the judge's censure not as an attempt to manufacture consent but as an attempt to shame. As such, the caesura was reinscribed into the broader performance, one now available for public consumption.

Conclusion

Revisiting the discussion about legitimacy and citizenship as a gift introduced in the discussion of the military era's jurisprudence, we can assess Aung San Suu Kyi's version of democracy being enacted today. On one hand, it seems consistent with Myanmar's dictatorial period: while people are no longer being sent to prison for half centuries, her version of democracy is a reduction in degree, not a qualitative change, in that she asserts that the state is permitted to do what it wants and the citizen's role is to vote for those who will then make decisions (RFA, 2015). Protest is particularly objectionable because it calls attention not simply to the inadequacy of a specific policy but the inadequacy of the model: it is a *violation* of the process of democracy. An active citizenry, taking part in protest and advocacy to help inform the government and to redirect it toward ends more in keeping with local realities, is denied a role. During my fieldwork in 2016, after the National League for Democracy (NLD) had come to power, activists expressed to me how Suu Kyi conveyed contempt for their work and their esteem in society, slandered their ethics, and effectively insisted that they were irrelevant to the suddenly "democratic" Burma (Prasse-Freeman, 2016b). It is hence ultimately unsurprising that in early 2018, her party pushed through – with little respect for democratic process and no consultation with civil society – a public assembly law far more repressive than that of the Union Solidary and Development Pary (USDP), the military-linked party in power from 2011–2015 (Aye Thein, 2018).

Read in this way, Aung San Suu Kyi's first actions as head of the new government take on new meaning. First, just days after the election, she led a massive litter picking campaign – a humble symbolic gesture performing a set of essential social aspirations: cleanliness as producing order, made possible through an ethics of personally disciplined conduct. The NLD also launched a ban on betel nut chewing, in an attempt to clean public places of the red streaks of expectorate. Such discipline was meant to transpose onto society, such that when a number of journalists published an expose suggesting Yangon division prime minister Phyo Min Thein's fiduciary malfeasance, the PM's office responded by jailing them for defamation, given that the journalists showed "disrespect toward the Yangon regional government" (RSF, 2018). As this article went to press, the Reuters journalists discussed in the introduction, who had been convicted for, effectively, embarrassing the state, had just had their appeals denied. When such aesthetic projects are delivered by decree without discussion with Burmese subjects, they serve as a reminder to the latter's subservient role in democracy.

And yet the court cases described earlier demonstrate how activists are now able to take situations that appear the quintessence of defeat – the state declaring their guilt and exercising its prerogative to deny their liberty – and create new political sites, producing conflagrations that expose the state as executing rule *the wrong way*. Returning to the discussion of sovereignty and power from earlier, while those in authority still reject "external" sources of legitimation, and law continues to be a vehicle for the delivery of state violence, institutions – such as courts – have become sites for new enactments of citizenship.

The overall effect is highly ambiguous – in that the law and the leader speak mostly monologically, continuing to brook little dissent, even as the system allows new demands to pullulate. But as all of Myanmar becomes a site for roiling dissent, and when activists maintain focus on the aesthetic dimensions of rule – as shirt burnings, sobbing lovers and children, and riots within and outside of courts all call attention to the failure of the regime to produce thrall or at least quietude – the long-insulated system is drawn into the political realm, meaning that different normative conceptions clash against one another, producing a charged dissensus available for others to observe. This may not alter the approaches of state elites, such as Suu Kyi, or lead to reform of the law and those who carry it out, but it contests them on their terms, threatening to divest them of their potency.

Notes

1 Many critics have castigated Suu Kyi for "remaining silent" on the Rohingya issue. But this is a strange interpretation, given all that she has said in defense of the military and how little sympathy she has given the Rohingya. In the wake of the ethnic cleansing, Suu Kyi merely said there were "some things we could have done better." When asked later for specifics, she could not recall what those were: "I didn't at any time see that the situation . . . could have been handled better. And I don't quite understand the reference" (NHK, 2018). See Sardiña-Galache (2013) for a critique of the "remaining silent" trope made as early as 2013.

2 And it has proven to be more than idle threat. Cheesman has found that this "gift of conditional freedom" (ibid.) can be retracted: he relays how a police officer bringing a case against comedian Zaganar for actions in 2008 effected the reactivation of charges from 2007 pursuant to Zaganar's violation of his pledge (2015, p. 214).

3 The discussion in Steinberg (2001) is instructive: while he is perceptive to contest a literature that foregrounds the voting mechanism as the source of legitimacy in Burma, he still presumes that military elites desired to *legitimate* their rule by attenuating voting with "nationalism, Buddhism, socialism, [and] the military" (2001, p. 43).

4 This is perhaps not entirely fair to Weber, who had many varied thoughts on "legitimacy." We might say, instead, Weber*ian* – stressing the way that political thought has *interpreted* him. (I thank Charles Carstens for stressing this point – personal communication, 8 March 2018).

5 Weber writes, "What is important is the fact that in a given case the particular claim to legitimacy is to a significant degree and according to its type treated as 'valid'" (214). Critical here is the phrase "treated as valid," in which a field of assessment is referenced and ceded power to advance judgement.

6 "Alaung-hpaya and his sons respected the customs of captive Tavoyans, Europeans, Indians, Manipuris, Chins, Shans, Lus, etc. whom they required to appear in 'national' costume on ceremonial occasions. Indeed, Alaung-hpaya seems to have gloried in their diversity as a validation of his universal political pretensions" (Lieberman, 1978, p. 477).

7 Conversation 16 October 2018.

8 In the early 1990s, political prisoners were processed in military tribunals rather than courts. I thank Nick Cheesman for this clarification (personal communication, February 2019).

9 In addition to the four volumes discussed that I was able to find (listed in references), there are also "The Country Destroying Acts of BCP and KNU Sein Win" and "The Tangled Plan to Take Over the Country by the BCP UG, DAB, Some NLD Party Leaders"

10 Email correspondence with AAPPB, 17 October 2018.

11 Although opposition was voiced and even recorded in the pages of the court documents no less (Cheesman 2009/2010, p. 609), there was no audience, no public for those eruptions.

12 While this critique may appear to implicitly imagine a substantive rule of law that is lacking, see Prasse-Freeman (2016a) for a discussion of the underdetermined nature of "rule of law" as a sign in Burmese activist speech acts.

13 The following is a selection of what Thein Aung Myint said, recorded by another activist, which we together later transcribed and which I then translated.

14 "Because barbarity that is in opposition to all peoples and all countries cannot be accepted, culture, morals, discipline, and law are laid down and enacted and a society is made to have to follow them. Breaking the law, not following the rules, destroying the morals, if we are talking about those things, they are things we should not dare to think."
15 Cheesman reported that in 2010 a judge averred 'that whoever should have permission to enter or leave the courtroom is a matter of no relevance to the court,' holding instead that, "according to the judge, the guards, not he, held the keys of authority to the court gates." (2015, p. 118).
16 I thank Nick Cheesman for this clarification (personal communication, February 2019).

References

Agamben, G. (2004) *State of Exception*, trans. K. Attell. Chicago: Chicago University Press.

Althusser, L. (1971) "Ideology and Ideological State Apparatuses," in *Lenin and Philosophy and Other Essays*. New York: Monthly Review Press.

Amnesty International. (2018) "Myanmar: Aung San Suu Kyi in Shameful Defence of Reuters Journalists' conviction," 13 September. Available at: https://www.amnesty.org/en/latest/news/2018/09/myanmar-aung-san-suu-kyi-in-shameful-defence-of-reuters-journalists-conviction/

Aung-Thwin, M. (2013) "Those Men in Saffron Robes," *Journal of Burma Studies*, 17 (2), pp. 243–334.

Aye Thein. (2018) "Democratizing the Public Space in Myanmar," *Tea Circle Oxford*, 26 March.

Brac de la Perrière, B. (2017) "About Buddhist Burma: Thathana, or 'Religion' as Social Space," in Picard, M. (ed.) *The Appropriation of Religion in Southeast Asia and Beyond*. Cham: Palgrave Macmillan, pp. 39–66.

Butler, J. (2006) "Indefinite Detention," in *Precarious Life: The Powers of Mourning and Violence*. New York: Verso.

Campbell, S., and Soe Lin Aung. (2016) "The Lady and the Generals," *Jacobin*, 13 January.

Cheesman, N. (2010) "Thin Rule of Law or Un-Rule of Law in Myanmar?," *Pacific Affairs*, 82 (4), Winter 2009/2010.

Cheesman, N. (2015) *Opposing the Rule of Law*. Cambridge: Cambridge University Press.

Cheesman, N. (forthcoming) "Looking towards Burma through Memoirs of the Cocos Island Detention Camp," in Cribb, R., Twomey, C., and Wilson, T. (eds.) *Detention Camps in Asia*.

Cheesman, N., D'Costa, B., and Haberkorn, T. (2016) "Anticipating the Struggle against Everyday Impunity in Myanmar through Accounts from Bangladesh and Thailand," *Asia & the Pacific Policy Studies*, 3 (1), pp. 48–61.

Connelly, K. (2011) *The Lizard Cage*. New York: Spiegel & Grau.

Crouch, M. (2017) "The Everyday Emergency: Between the Constitution and the Code of Criminal Procedure in Myanmar," in Harding, A. (ed.) *Constitutionalism and Legal Change in Myanmar*. Oxford and Portland: Hart.

Dunant, B. (2018) "Outrage at Insein Court," *Frontier Myanmar*, 15 September.

Elgee, A. (2010) "Silencing the Sangha," *Irrawaddy*, 18 (11), November.

Foucault, M. (1995) *Discipline and Punish*, trans. A. Sheridan. New York: Vintage.

Geertz, C. (1980) *Negara: The Theatre State in Nineteenth-Century Bali*. Princeton, NJ: Princeton University Press.

Ginsburg, T., and Moustafa, T. (2008) "Introduction: The Functions of Courts in Authoritarian Politics," in *Rule by Law: The Politics of Courts in Authoritarian Regimes*. Cambridge: Cambridge University Press, pp. 1–22.

Guha, R. (1997) *Dominance without Hegemony*. Cambridge, MA: Harvard University Press.

Harding, A. (ed.). (2017) with the assistance of Khin Oo, *Constitutionalism and Legal Change in Myanmar*, Oxford and Portland: Hart.
Justice Base. (2017) "Behind Closed Doors: Obstacles and Opportunities for Public Access to Myanmar's Courts," Yangon, June, Available at: https://www.myjusticemyanmar.org/sites/default/files/Justice-Base-Behind-Closed-Doors.compressed-1.pdf
Leehey, J. (2010) *Open Secrets, Hidden Meanings: Censorship, Esoteric Power, and Contested Authority in Urban Burma in the 1990s*. Dissertation, Seattle: University of Washington.
Lieberman, V.B. (1978) "Ethnic Politics in Eighteenth-Century Burma," *Modern Asian Studies*, 12 (3), pp. 455–482.
Mann, M. (1984) "The Autonomous Power of the State: Its Origins, Mechanisms and Results," *The State: Critical Concepts*, 1.
Ma Thida. (1994) *Prisoner of Conscience: My Steps Through Insein*, Chiang Mai: Silkworm.
Moustafa, T. (2014) "Law and Courts in Authoritarian Regimes," *Annual Review of Law and Social Science*, 10, pp. 281–299.
NHK. (2018) "Exclusive Interview: Aung San Suu Kyi," 9 October. Available at: https://www3.nhk.or.jp/nhkworld/nhknewsline/backstories/aungsansuukyi/
Nyunt, K. (1989a) "Burma Communist Party's Conspiracy to Take Over State Power," Yangon: Government of Myanmar, 5 August.
Nyunt, K. (1989b) "The Grand Treachery of the Traitors From Inside Myanmar and the Axe Handles From Outside," Proceedings from press conference given by Khin Nyunt on 9 September, Yangon: Government of Myanmar, 9 October.
Nyunt, K. (1989c) "Scheming and Activities of The Burma Communist Party Politburo to Seize State Power," Yangon: Government of Myanmar, 16 November.
Nyunt, K. (1990) "The Protection Given by State Law and Order Restoration Council (Tatmadaw) for the People's Lives and Property and the Activities of Destructive Elements," Yangon: Government of Myanmar.
Osiel, M. (1995) "Ever again: Legal Remembrance of Administrative Massacre," *University of Pennsylvania Law Review*, 144 (2), pp. 463–704.
Pereira, A.W. (2008) "Of Judges and Generals: Security Courts under Authoritarian Regimes in Argentina, Brazil, and Chile," in Ginsburg, T. and Moustafa, T. (eds.) *Rule by Law: The Politics of Courts in Authoritarian Regimes*. Cambridge: Cambridge University Press, pp. 23–57.
Peterson, J. (2007) "Unpacking Show Trials: Situating the Trial of Saddam Hussein," *Harvard International Law Journal*, 48, pp. 257–292.
Prasse-Freeman, E. (2012) "Power, Civil Society, and an Inchoate Politics of the Daily in Burma/Myanmar," *Journal of Asian Studies*, 71 (2).
Prasse-Freeman, E. (2016a) "Grassroots Protest Movements and Mutating Conceptions of 'the Political' in an Evolving Burma," in Egreteau, R. and Robinne, F. (eds.) *Metamorphosis: Studies in Social and Political Change in Myanmar*. Singapore: NUS Press, pp. 69–100.
Prasse-Freeman, E. (2016b) "The New Burma Is Starting to Look Too Much Like the Old Burma," *Foreign Policy*, 28 July. Available at: https://foreignpolicy.com/2016/06/28/the-new-burma-is-starting-to-look-too-much-like-the-old-burma/
Prasse-Freeman, E., and Phyo Win Latt. (2018) "Class and Inequality in Contemporary Myanmar," in Holliday, I., Farrelly, N., and Simpson, A. (eds.) *The Routledge Handbook of Contemporary Myanmar*. Abingdon, UK: Routledge, pp. 404–418.
Reuters. (2018) "Suu Kyi Defense of Jailing of Reuters Journalists 'Unbelievable': Haley," *Reuters*, 12 September.
RFA. (2015) "Aung San Suu Kyi Urges Support For NLD Amid Myanmar Candidate Row," *Radio Free Asia*, 10 August. Available at: www.rfa.org/english/news/myanmar/support-08102015151253.html

RSF Myanmar. (2018) "RSF Calls for Release of Three Eleven Media Journalists," *Reporters without Borders*, 10 October.

Rudy, S. (2010) "Monistic Force at the End of the Line: Strategic De-Territorialization after Sovereign Capture," *theory@buffalo*, 14.

Rudy, S. (forthcoming) "'Human Rights' as Rule-of-Law as Violence," in Dogra, J. and Vashist, L. (eds.) *Violence and Law*. Oxford: Indian Law Institute [New Delhi], forthcoming.

Sardiña Galache, C. (2013) "The Lady Doth Protest Too Seldom," *Democratic Voice of Burma*, 10 November.

Schober, J. (2011) *Modern Buddhist Conjunctures in Myanmar: Cultural Narratives, Colonial Legacies, and Civil Society*. Honolulu: University of Hawaii Press.

Schober, J. (2017) "Belonging in a New Myanmar Identity, Law, and Gender in the Anthropology of Contemporary Buddhism," *Religion and Society: Advances in Research*, 8, pp. 158–172.

Shapiro, M. (1981) *Courts: A Comparative and Political Analysis*. Chicago: University of Chicago Press.

Steinberg, D. (2001) *Burma: The State of Myanmar*. Washington, DC: Georgetown University Press.

Weber, M. (1978) *Economy and Society: An Outline of Interpretive Sociology*. Vol. 1 and 2. Berkeley: University of California Press.

Win Tin. (2012) *What Is That? Man-Made Hell*. Yangon: Red Star Publishing.

Zarni Mann. (2015) "Activist Gets 6 Months for Protest against Journalist's Killing," *Irrawaddy*, 23 April.

Žižek, S. (2002) "Homo Sucker to Homo Sacer," in *Welcome to the Desert of the Real! Five Essays on September 11 and Related Dates*. New York: Verso.

Part III

Institutional practices

Chapter 8

The politics of judicial actors in the Philippines's "war on drugs"

Pablo Ciocchini

Introduction

In June 2016, Rodrigo Duterte became president based on a campaign promise of implementing, at the national level, the tough-on-crime policies he had applied as mayor of Davao. Upon being elected, he kept his promise and unleashed a massive and brutal "War on Drugs," which resulted in the deaths of 4,729 suspects in antidrug operations according to the Philippine National Police (PNP) with human rights organizations estimating the number at almost 20,000 (Gavilan, 2018). Although a majority of Filipino people disapprove of extrajudicial killings (EJK), Duterte continues to receive high approval ratings (Lamchek, 2017).

While EJKs have indubitably been the most striking feature of Duterte's "War on Drugs," it is not the only consequence. The "War on Drugs" has also been based on unprecedented arrests of a massive numbers of drug-related offenders, whether they were consumers or pushers. Thus, while the number of arrests for drug-related violations was relatively stable between 2005 and 2015, ranging from a low of 6,259 arrests in 2010, to a peak of 19,432 in 2015 (Philippine Statistics Authority, 2017); these figures grew exponentially to 28,056 individuals in 2016 and 75,008 in 2017 (Leonen, 2018). By May 2018, 102,692 individuals, or 70.88% of the total prison population, were serving sentences for drug-related offenses (Bureau of Jail Management and Penology (BJMP), 2018)

EJKs have only involved courts in a few cases in which the family members of the victims were brave enough to file a complaint. To date, no officer has yet been convicted (Patag, 2018a). However, courts have been actively involved in the "War on Drugs" on a daily basis through the handling of the massive number of arrests. Duterte's offensive has led to a serious backlog in a system already undergoing reforms aimed at improving efficiency. These reforms, initiated before Duterte's election, were regarded to be a much-needed measure to recover the people's confidence in the judiciary. However, the massive influx of drug-related cases threatened to bog down the system again, erasing gains in confidence made over the last few years. This problem was amplified by legislation explicitly banning plea bargaining for drug cases, forcing judicial actors to take those cases to trial. To understand the scale of the backlog according to the BJMP, only 648 of the 102,692 individuals in prison for drug-related offenses in May 2018 had been sentenced; the rest were awaiting their trial (BJMP, 2018). This serious congestion of courts and the prisons was not surprising since the prison system was overcrowded with defendants waiting for their trial even before the massive influx of detainees arrived as a result of the "War on Drugs" (Narag, 2018).

Several commentators have pointed out that the "War on Drugs" was less of a criminal policy than a political strategy (Iglesias, 2017; Quimpo, 2017; Johnson and Fernquest, 2018). According to them, the "War on Drugs" is a pretext to gain full control over the state's security apparatus and govern through crime. Although this analysis helps us to understand the rationality behind such a controversial policy, it focuses on EJK and the role of police without paying much attention to other key feature and actors involved in the "War on Drugs" – namely, the role of courts and criminal process. This chapter seeks to fill this gap. It is based on 50 interviews with judges, public prosecutors, and public attorneys conducted in Manila city between May and November of 2018. The chapter argues that judicial actors played a key role before and during the first stage of the "War on Drugs" by maintaining a certain level of legality by controlling indirectly police behavior through the dismissal of cases or acquittal of the defendants. However, facing the massive influx of cases and the political pressures exerted by the executive, they strategically sought to reduce their exposure, while maintaining their legalizing function – they did so by enabling plea bargaining for drug-related cases. This constituted a turning point for judicial actors, but also for the very "War on Drugs," although this was not apparent to the larger public.

The chapter is organized into three sections. The first section explores the precedents of Duterte's "War on Drugs." In this section, it is argued that the "War on Drugs" is the result of a continuum of state violence, the failure of elitist politics, and a political strategy based on fear. The second section reviews the explanations scholars have offered for Duterte's strategy. Scholars have focused their attention on EJKs. Although there are significant differences among them, they agree on two features of the strategy. First, the policy's primary aim is to galvanize support for the government through the construction of a threat for the Philippine society: drug personalities. Second, the widespread use of state violence, and particularly EJK, evidences the limited capacity of the state. This chapter argues that such an account fails to address the role that the courts and the law have played in this strategy. The third section analyzes the role judicial actors play in the "War on Drugs," based on interviews conducted in Manila in 2018. It describes the challenges these actors have faced and the strategies developed to cope with them. It is in this context that enabling of plea bargaining for drug-related cases can be fully understood. The interviews show that this has had two key consequences: on the one hand, weak cases end up in a conviction, but on the other, judicial actors are able to reinsert a rehabilitation focus in the antidrug campaign. The chapter concludes by reflecting on the significance that this strategy has had for the rule of law and state violence.

The precedents of Duterte's "war on drugs"

Duterte's "War on Drugs" is the result of a historical process. It is important to understand the politicization of the Philippines's approach to the drug problem, the suspicions among public officials it created, and the normalization of police violence as a key strategy to deal with it. Production, trafficking, and consumption of crystal methamphetamine, called "shabu" in the streets, has been a serious problem in Southeast Asia since the end of the 1990s (McKetin et al. 2008). The methamphetamine epidemic peaked in 2000 and 2001, and then declined and stabilized in the region (ibid.). However, in the Philippines, the production remained high, with police dismantling more than 25 clandestine laboratories between 2010 and 2015, and 10 laboratories in 2016 (UNODC, 2017, p. 38). The use of crystalline methamphetamine has also remained high in the Philippines in recent years (UNODC, 2017). In fact, the United Nations World Drug Report of 2008 stated that the Philippines had the highest percentage methamphetamine prevalence rate in the world (6%) (UNODC, 2008, p. 159), and, more recently, the latest drug use survey conducted by the Dangerous Drugs Board (DDB) of Philippines found that there were an estimated 1.8 million drug users in the country (UNODC, 2017, p. 37).

The "War on Drugs" strategy was not started by Duterte, but by former president Gloria Macapagal-Arroyo 15 years before in 2001. In the Letter of Instruction No. 1 (Republic of the Philippines, 2001) in which Macapagal-Arroyo established the government's strategy (the National Anti-Drug Program of Action) it is stated that drug syndicates were "engaging in narco-politics of bankrolling with drug money the candidacies of many politicians who shall protect them, once installed in government." Months later, her government publicly accused the former head of the police, and at that time senator and leader of the opposition, Panfilo Lacson, of being "involved in a plot by drug traffickers to take over the state" (The Economist, 2001). The "War on Drugs" in the Philippines, like in the United States, has legitimized the empowering of the police and has targeted the poorest sectors of the population. However, unlike the United States, it has, on the one hand, enabled the state's "illegal" violence (e.g., extrajudicial killings), and on the other hand, it has been politically used by the government to weaken the political opposition and to deflect any political responsibility by accusing collusion, corruption, and abuse of power to police officers, prison service officers, public prosecutors, judges, and mayors.

This 'institutionalized' distrust in the agencies of the criminal justice system was promoted by Macapagal-Arroyo's government and set the context for Congress to pass the Comprehensive Dangerous Drugs Act of 2002 (RA 9165). The two most notable features of the legislation were the extremely harsh penalties for offenses involving illegal drugs, which doubled prison sentences from the previous law (RA 6425 of 1972) and introduced life imprisonment and capital punishment for the possession of drugs based on quantity, and the banning of plea bargaining for drug-related cases to prevent prosecutors from receiving bribes to fix a case.

In addition to the organizational challenges of the enacted legislation, a key feature of the "War on Drugs" was that law enforcement agencies, and particularly the police, operated outside the law. The director general of the Philippine Drug Enforcement Agency (PDEA) for instance admitted that his agency was forced to "plant evidence" in "some special cases" (Garcia Desacada, 2008). Controversial figures were offered high positions. For example, Jovito Palparan, nicknamed "the Butcher," a retired general who had led in previous years a campaign against communist groups and who became infamous for the murder, disappearance, and torture of activists, was appointed to the DDB, the powerful agency that was in charge of defining and enforcing the government's antidrug campaign alongside the PDEA (Nery, 2009).

In 2010, the administration of Benigno Aquino III changed the government's focus from the "War on Drugs" to fighting corruption – particularly inside the police force. Aquino's emphasis on the rule of law was a direct attempt by the government to force police to operate under the law. However, such attempts were described in the media as superficial and fruitless (Koeppinger, 2013; Lopez, 2015). Under his administration, crime doubled and the smuggling of drugs and guns became a serious problem (Saludo, 2014). Furthermore, there was no real attempt to investigate and prosecute the EJK, tortures, and other abuses perpetrated by the military and security forces during Macapagal-Arroyo's presidency or his own. Thus, police continued to operate beyond the law (HRW, 2011, 2012) with death squads, killing hundreds of alleged drug dealers in Davao and Tagum under Mayors Duterte and Uy's respective support (HRW, 2014).

It was under these circumstances that Duterte started this presidential campaign in mid-2015 (Caduaya, 2015; Nawal, 2015). Duterte, originally a public prosecutor, made his name during his time as mayor of Davao City between 1988 to 1998 and 2001 to 2016. During his administration, he unleashed police violence against drug dealers and consumers, resulting in thousands of suspects being killed (HRW, 2015; Rauhala, 2016a; Iglesias, 2017). After winning the presidency in 2016, Duterte's "War on Drugs" built on the tactics he had previously implemented in Davao City (Rauhala, 2016b). His "War on Drugs" was called Project Double Barrel, consisting of a two-pronged approach: Project Tokhang and Project High Value Target (HVT) (Calisco et al., 2017). The project involves "the conduct of house to house visitations of alleged illegal drug users and pushers to convince them to voluntarily surrender and/or stop using illegal drugs." The program complemented this program seeking the voluntary surrender with the heavy deployment of the National Police to conduct a massive campaign of arrests of drug-related suspects. In the first year of the antidrug campaign, the police arrested around 86,933 drug dealers and users. Consequently, the prison population increased from 98,000 to 142,013 inmates a year later (Tupas, 2017).

Continuing the narrative of mistrust set by previous administrations, Duterte started his campaign accusing judges of corruption and collusion with drug dealers (Corrales, 2016). Chief Justice of the Philippine Supreme Court, Lourdes Sereno, responded with an open letter to the president in which she warned him that it was the function of the high court to penalize erring judges and asked him, in the sake of preserving public confidence in the judiciary, to avoid public allegations of that kind (Ramos, 2017). But Duterte did not tone down his discourse, and publicly threatened the Chief Justice. The confrontation between the two continued until Sereno was finally removed of her office in 2018, accused of tax evasion and unauthorized expenses.

Duterte's accusations against judges and his confrontation with the judiciary should be read together with Duterte's repeated public defense of police officers who kill suspects (Mendez, 2016). In this way, Duterte distanced himself from the discourse on the rule of law sustained by the Aquino administration, and he implicitly enabled police to operate beyond the law. As Curato argues,

> Duterte's predecessor, Benigno S. Aquino, prioritized programmes that fight crimes in a deliberate, programmatic and sustained manner to control crime . . . [while Duterte has promised] to overcome the corrupt bureaucracy in the justice system and deliver peace and order in a swift and decisive manner.
>
> (Curato, 2016, p. 96)

Thus, Duterte set the government's narrative on crime, presenting constitutional rights and courts as obstacles to punish criminals and provide safety. The evident consequence has been the unleashing of unfiltered state violence, which is even more problematic due to the alleged corruption pervading the police and other governmental agencies. Duterte's "War on Drugs," therefore, cannot be defined as something truly original, but it is rather an extreme intensification of previous policies. It is based in a profound mistrust in the capacity of the state to be effective in operating under its own legality. The next section reviews the analysis by critical scholars of the logic that drives Duterte's "War on Drugs." It then moves to analyze the conditions and factors that have shaped this policy and some of its most problematic consequences.

Explaining the "War on Drugs": from state vigilantism to business opportunities

Scholars analyzing the "War on Drugs" have focused on the extrajudicial killings. Kreuzer (2016) has argued that EJK are part of the political strategy of the elites to maintain their power based on the state's incapacity to legally prevent and punish crime. In a similar vein, Johnson and Fernquest argue that Duterte's is "governing through killing" (2018, pp. 17–18) and Quimpo (2017) that Duterte has securitized illegal drugs – i.e., convert them from a criminal to a security matter – to govern through bossism. These analyses assume, too, on the one hand, too much discretionary control from Duterte over police, and on the other, they understate the role prison plays in his strategy. Regarding the assumption of Duterte's complete control over police, we should be cautioned that the relationship between the government and the police is not one of complete submission, but rather of mutual benefits (Colonel, 2017), as evidenced by his withdrawal of the police force from his "War on Drugs" twice due to scandals and his recently public threat to kill corrupt police officers (Perper, 2018). According, to Colonel (2017), the "War on Drugs" has created (illegal) business opportunities for the police, such as bribing and kidnapping. Thus, while the government may be using the "War on Drugs" and the police to have tight control over the population, the police are using the "War on Drugs" to pursue their own interests. This highlights the relevance of the role that public prosecutors, and especially courts, should play indirectly in controlling the legality of police behavior. In relation to the assumption that prison is not as relevant as EJK in his strategy, it should be noticed, as mentioned earlier in this chapter, that according to the prison service authorities, in Duterte's first year, the prison population increased almost by 50% (Tupas, 2017).

Furthermore, these analyses are focused on the police, particularly their role in the EJK, without paying attention to the other agencies of the criminal justice system and the role of massive arrests. Whenever courts are brought into the analysis, it is merely to describe their inefficiency, without actually exploring what are the causes for such inefficiency and what is the role they are actually playing in the government strategy. This is problematic for several reasons. First, public prosecutors and courts can play an important role in controlling police behavior by dismissing cases or acquitting defendants. Thus, it is important to study them to understand how they have reacted to police illegal activities in the context of the "War on Drugs." Second, the relevance of the massive arrest campaign in the "War on Drugs" should be taken seriously. Dozens of thousands have been arrested under Duterte's administration. The vast majority of the prison population are detained for drug-related cases, and they are still awaiting their trials. Thus, courts play a significant role in the "War on Drugs." Lastly, public prosecutors' and courts' incapacity to handle the cases should be analyzed in-depth and not merely assumed. It is argued that an understanding of how judicial actors operate can help to develop a more sophisticated analysis of the "War on Drugs" in the Philippines.[1] The following section explores the challenges that courts handling criminal cases face and how the "War on Drugs" impacted them.

Maintaining the legality of the "War on Drugs"

As Kreuzer (2009, 2016, 2018) and Johnson and Fernquest (2018) have pointed out, Duterte's populism is a product of decades of elites ruling the Philippines with weak state's institutions. Thus, it is not surprising that the vast majority of the targets of the "War on Drugs" come from the poorest and most vulnerable sectors of the society (Aldama, 2018; Kreuzer, 2016). Furthermore, the state's incapacity is a result of decades of policies purposely neglecting or at least failing to address the institutional needs. Thus, Philippine courts have long been suffering from an endemic backlog, hampering their ability to offer timely solutions (Tadiar, 1980). Despite such serious problems, politicians designed campaigns, such as the original "War on Drugs" in 2001, without equipping the system to deal with the cases. For example, in 2005, three years after the enactment of the Comprehensive Dangerous Drugs Act of 2002 (RA 9165), the police commissioner at that time, Sanidad-Leones, stated,

> Problems relating to the government's campaign against illegal drugs include (. . .) the increasing number of drug and drug-related cases at the level of the prosecution and the courts and the resultant further clogging of dockets, the congested jails due to the growing intake or admission rate of drug offenders, and the growing pressure on the part of the rehabilitation centres to provide treatment and aftercare programmes and services.
>
> (Sanidad-Leones, 2006, p. 137)

The institutional limitations were openly recognized by previous administrations. Thus, in 2010, President Aquino admitted in an interview that there was a need to reform the judicial system because only 1% of the criminal cases involving drugs ended in conviction (CFR, 2010). However, five years later, at the end of his presidency, police reports indicated that while the number of reported crimes was rising year by year, the percentage of solved crimes out of reported crimes was dropping (Ranada, 2016). Meanwhile, the chief justice of the Supreme Court of the Philippines at that time, Justice Sereno, publicly admitted that courts were characterized by delay (Torres-Tupas, 2014), and the deputy director of the Asia Division at Human Rights Watch declared, "The judicial system, the court system, is broken in the Philippines" (Taub, 2016).

However, despite these apocalyptic statements, there is evidence that courts, with their severe deficiencies, were playing an important role in controlling police work. Thus, by 2014, 20% to 30% of the drug-related cases were dismissed by prosecutors or courts due to technical problems (De Jesus, 2014). This tells us much about police inefficiency but also about the role of judicial actors in controlling the legality of their behavior. In response, Aquino amended the law to allow police officers to do the physical inventory of the seized illegal drugs, which was a significant decision, considering the suspicions over police behavior. In fact, even with the empowerment of the law, police failure to observe the chain of custody continued to be pervasive. Thus, two years later, in 2016, a judge applying to be appointed to the Supreme Court, explained in public hearing that "she has acquitted 7 out of 10 in the drug cases in her court" and the reasons for those acquittals were that "the search warrant is not effectively implemented or the chain of custody is broken, or many doubts to entertain" (Francisco, 2016). In this context, Duterte's "War on Drugs" suddenly brought a combination of thousands of drug-related cases to the already clogged courts and the overcrowded jail system, and turned political pressures and media attention to the courts' decisions. This forced the judiciary to develop strategies to cope with the massive inflow of cases.

To better understand their situation, I conducted 50 interviews with public prosecutors (27), judges (9), clerks of courts (2), and public attorneys (12) working in regional trial courts in the City of Manila between May and November of 2018 (see Table 8.1). Half of the interviewees were female. Most of the interviews took place in the library of the building in which the courts are located, Manila City Hall, and the rest in the interviewee's office. The interviews were semistructured. They focused on the different judicial reforms recently implemented to reduce the courts' backlog (e.g., continuous trial, judicial affidavit, plea bargaining for drug-related cases), problems faced during the criminal procedure (e.g., nonappearance of witnesses, multiple hearings scheduled at the same time), and their working relationship with other agencies of the criminal justice system (e.g., police, prison service). The interviews were audio recorded and lasted between 15 minutes to 1 hour.

a) A massive influx of cases

In the district of the City of Manila, there are courts that specialize in drug-related cases. However, facing the massive influx of cases due to Duterte's "War on Drugs," these new drug-related cases were distributed among every court, regardless of their specialization. Public prosecutors and judges alike complained about this increment in their workload. According to a judge,

> The drug problem has increased so much, there are so many numbers of cases, and the special drugs courts cannot cope with the number (. . .) one court would have as many of more than 1,000 cases. So, we had to come up with a solution . . . but because of the number of cases being filed against drug traffickers, including users and possessors of drugs, there are more coming in than those that are being decided.
>
> (Interview #30)

These cases presented several challenges for the courts. First, because of the harsh penalties, the law establishes that these offenses are not bailable, so suspects must await their trial under detention. Second, in these cases, the claimant is the police force and the witnesses usually are police officers. This was problematic because police officers were very poor witnesses who tend to fail to appear in some cases because they were busy or have been relocated but in others suspiciously without any excuse. A prosecutor highlighted this issue:

> Policemen, they have many court appearances with cases to appear to testify on in other courts, not only one court a day [but] sometimes four courts they have to appear in drug cases.
>
> (Interview #5)

Given their heavy caseload, when they do take the stand, sometimes facts are forgotten or confused with other cases. According to one prosecutor,

> So many cases are dismissed because one, our police officers' witnesses are not smart enough in answering questions; they often say it is been a long time they forgot the details although as early as the first hearing if the police officers are around; we already tell them to go over the records of this case. (. . .) They say it is a long time when, in fact, it is just months since the arrest. But because of the numbers of accused arrested they are confused, they seem to mix up the facts from this case to this case; they are confused.
>
> (Interview #9)

At the same time, when police officers do take the stand, they do not always serve as good witnesses. Sometimes they lie or contradict evidence already established. According to the same prosecutor,

> Sometimes there are very disappointing police officers' witnesses, which compel us to report them to their authorities. (. . .) [There are] very abusive officers and those who are put on the witness stand and very clearly lie (. . .) despite their affidavits, despite the presence of the evidence. (. . .) [I]t is not uncommon that this police officer has traded their jobs into this (. . .). [W]e have big-time drug pushers who can even pay the police officers the price that they want.
>
> (Interview #9)

Judges themselves acknowledge the questionability of the officers who take the stand:

> Cases that came in starting 2016 up to today 2018, I would even say more than 90% of the cases involve what we call, in essence, and just general essence, planted evidence by the police. Although this doesn't necessarily mean that the accused were not selling that they were not drug addicts but as to whether they committed that offense the way the police said it that's a different matter.
>
> (Interview #31)

The last point by the judge highlights how bad witnesses and poor testimony can render many of these cases void. This is because to avoid planted evidence, the law is very strict with the maintenance of the chain of custody. Unfortunately, the police often neglect this requirement, and as a result, more than 90% of suspects had to be acquitted due to technicalities. According to a prosecutor,

> The rules are very strict, and the procedures are not being followed by the police officers, although we can say that it is not their fault because the rules are very strict, and if they follow the rule (. . .) it will be difficult for them to run after the illegal dealers as well as the users. (. . .) But we are trying to also educate the police officers that we must follow the law and the implementing rules to the letter because that is how we can convict.
>
> (Interview #26)

Judges acknowledge that when a case is tossed out, it is often because the police have mishandled evidence, either because they are new, inexperienced with the law, or just handing a large volume of cases. According to a judge,

> When the chain of custody is broken, there is already a doubt whether or not this illegal drug that they are presenting is the same drug that they recovered from the accused. (. . .) [T]he police sometimes forget or sometimes they intentionally forget, the circumstances of the arrest and the investigation.
>
> (Interview #32)

Besides, the problems with the quality of the police investigation, the massive influx of drug-related cases with the plea-bargaining ban presented judicial actors with an organizational problem. First, there were time requirements: the speedy trial act and the new reforms brought by continuous trials that required them to dispose of the cases in less than six months. Second, any delay, dismissal, or acquittal could potentially be read by the government or the media as collusion with the suspect.

> I think judges and prosecutors, especially in drug cases, are careful (not) to be branded that . . . They are afraid to be placed in the list of narco court prosecutors or narco judges.
>
> (Interview #19)

> If (public prosecutors) dismiss this case, we will be subjected to administrative cases (they will be questioned): "Why did you dismiss that? Do you know that the first goal of the government is to eradicate drug cases and drug-related crimes?" . . . And if you are very technical about it, and you dismiss it, then they will become suspicious and say, "Oh you might be in the pockets of the drug," (So), you don't know where to stand; you know

> it's like damned if you do, damned if you don't. So, what do we do? We just transfer the problem to the courts.
>
> (Interview #13)

Facing these problems, the different judicial actors involved in criminal justice, acted without official coordination, but with a clear common interest to find a solution to the organizational problem they were facing. This solution was going to be to appeal to the Supreme Court to enable plea bargaining. However, to understand the challenges the judicial actors faced, we have to understand the reasons behind the banning of plea bargaining.

b) *Enabling plea bargaining:* Salvador Estipona V. Lobrigo, *G.R. No. 226679 (15 August 2017)*

The integrity of the members of the police force, prosecutors, and judges is a long-standing question in the Philippines. Due to these suspicions of a corrupt judiciary and police force, legislators decided to ban plea bargaining in drug-related cases. This is a provision that sought to prevent prosecutors from negotiating with the drug pushers. Thus, it is not surprising that a central tenet of Duterte's campaign has been to identify and denounce corrupt officers, judges, or mayors who work in collusion with drug kingpins. These factors combine to create a serious problem. There has been a deluge of drug-related cases reported by police, which have flooded courts that were already strained with a significant backlog. Suspects in these cases were placed in already overcrowded jails. Furthermore, the backlog delays the disposal of the case, which means detainees accumulate in the jails. According to one public prosecutor,

> When the case was with the drugs court (. . .) before it becomes final or everything it will take around five, six, eight years . . . (. . .) in a drug case you have prior to the implementation of plea bargaining, you have already been detained in court for three or four years.
>
> (Interview #17)

This situation continued to deteriorate. In June 2016, only six months after Duterte's "War on Drugs" started, Salvador Estipona Jr., who was charged with possession of dangerous drugs (Section 11, Article II, R.A. No. 9165) and was represented by the Public Attorney's Office (PAO), filed a motion to enter into a plea-bargaining agreement. He offered the prosecutor a plea of guilty for a lesser offense – namely, the possession of paraphernalia for dangerous drugs (Section 12, Article II, R.A. No. 9165) – and requested a penalty of rehabilitation since he was a first-time offender and the quantity of drugs in his possession was minimal (Estipona, V. Judge Lobrigo, G.R. No. 226679). The prosecution opposed the motion and the judge denied it in July 2016. However, both the prosecution and the judge acknowledged there was merit in the request, especially considering that the intent of the law was to rehabilitate those accused of drug offenses. However, their decision was based on strict prohibitions prescribed by the law and the potential consequences of declaring its unconstitutionality. Facing such decision, Estipona submitted in September 2016 a petition for certiorari and prohibition challenging the constitutionality of Section 23 of R.A. No. 9165, which prohibits plea bargaining in drug cases before the Supreme Court of the Philippines. The petition argued that plea bargaining was a right of the defendant and that its denial was arbitrary and constituted an infringement of his right to equal protection of laws and to due process. It explained that by allowing plea bargaining, the claimant could benefit from a lighter sentence, even with probation, and avoid awaiting trial under detention.

At the end of the petition, it stated that under the "War on Drugs," the workload of the PAO has significantly increased, from handling 36,000 drug-related cases in 2011 to 82,000 in 2016. Thus, the petition argued that allowing plea bargaining will save financial resources to the state and benefit all stakeholders, including the courts, the jail system, and the accused, besides the PAO. This argument had nothing to do with the claimant's case, but it was rather an organizational claim inserted in the case discussion. Notably, the petition did not mention the benefit to the police or the prosecutors, despite the fact that plea bargaining essentially meant they will be getting sentences without having to prove their cases before a judge. This is particularly important since in the interviews, prosecutors, judges, and public attorneys stated that the vast majority of drug-related cases, some of them said more than 90%, ended with the acquittal of the defendant because of serious problems in the police investigation. According to a prosecutor,

> [Allowing plea bargaining for drug-related cases] is very good; it is a welcome move for us as prosecutors because it lessens the burden of prosecuting these cases. We don't have to present the police officers anymore; we don't have to present evidence anymore, and we are guaranteed with a conviction. It is a win for us.
>
> (Interview #16)

The Supreme Court of the Philippines ruled in favor of the petition on August 2017, and it declared unconstitutional the prohibition on plea bargaining (Section 23 of R.A. No. 9165). The Supreme Court enjoined judges to refrain from acting on motions and requests for plea bargaining in drug cases until the decision of the Court became final. The decision became final and executory on November 2017. The Philippine Judges Association presented to the Supreme Court a "Suggested Plea-Bargaining Framework in Drug Cases" that would prescribe in each sentence the acceptable plea bargain. This framework was discussed by the Court En Banc and adopted with some amendments in April 2018.

In *Estipona*, the Supreme Court drastically changed the conditions under which the "War on Drugs" has taken place. Interestingly, this decision was taken during a period in which the Supreme Court in particular, and the judiciary in general, was suffering from serious discursive attacks by Duterte himself. Nevertheless, while the government through the Office of the Solicitor General did argue against the unconstitutionality of the plea-bargaining ban for drug-related cases, the prosecutors and the police, principal claimants in drug-related cases, were generally favorable to plea bargaining as the interviews presented earlier have shown.

c) Managerial concerns and institutional limitations

The outcome in the *Estipona* case is clearly a significant change in the "War on Drugs." The decision of the SC allowing plea bargaining was a necessary adaptative strategy of the criminal justice system to deal with the organizational challenge that the "War on Drugs" represented. Managerial concerns internalized by judicial actors were prioritized in this strategy.

> We cannot avoid backlog because there are so many human factors. Number one is that there is an ongoing "War on Drugs," so many cases are piled in our courts. (. . .) But, fortunately, there is now a decision of certain (of the Supreme) Court (. . .) (about) plea bargaining (that) can be applicable (to drug cases), so I was able to dispose of all these drug cases of around 700 up. So, every day, I decided cases based on plea bargaining. The Supreme Court gives us that opportunity so that we can dispose of the case easily. (. . .) I had no backlog when there were no drug cases; I have a minimal number of cases.
>
> (Interview #34)

However, this strategy also significantly reduced the capacity of courts to control the police. In that sense, the adaptation showed the limits of the state capacity to deal with the drug problem under a criminal approach as Kreuzer (2009, 2016) and other scholars (Quimpo, 2017; Johnson and Fernquest, 2018) have argued before. However, it also shows the complexity of the state and the internal contradictions among the different agencies it is composed. In this sense, it rebuts the assumption that the government, under Duterte or other administrations, have complete control over the criminal justice system. Because this strategy is not merely "legalizing" state violence under the "War on Drugs" by helping police and prosecutors to increase their conviction rates, but it is also modifying the "War on Drugs" itself. This is because it has significantly reduced the de facto punishment drug users will face, bringing back "rehabilitation" policies. In that sense, many interviewees regarded plea bargaining in drug-related cases as a benefit for drug consumers that otherwise could face long sentences. According to a prosecutor,

> I have always agreed with plea bargaining; let's face it (. . .), some drugs cases are not ready. . . . In order to help the accused, I encourage them to enter into a plea bargain. They will admit the crime, but to a lesser offense; then they will reform. I always believe that a person should always be reformed, I do not believe (in the) capital punishment, the harsh punishment. As a prosecutor, as much as possible, I will give the person a chance to reform by entering into a plea bargaining (. . .) I am helping them in my own little way to change their ways.
>
> (Interview #6)

A judge agrees,

> We have applied (plea bargaining for drug-related cases because) it helps us on our drug docket (and) because that is favorable to the accused. Where the principle is favorable to the accused, you apply it, and that applies to the pending drugs cases.
>
> (Interview #33)

However, although enabling plea bargaining has indirectly enabled a rehabilitation policy, the facilities – i.e., rehabilitation centers – are not enough, so the problems with jails and courts remain. Prosecutors and judges highlighted this issue in their interviews.

> Some enter plea bargaining; they want to be rehabilitated (. . .) but, unfortunately, all the drug rehabilitation centers are already full. So that is now our dilemma. (. . .) The government should create more drug rehabilitation centers.
>
> (Interview #34)

And judicial actors are already using their power to "interpret" the law to readapt the strategy, so it can be fulfilled even without the improvement of the rehabilitation facilities.

> If the accused has already been in jail (and it should have) been sent to the rehabilitation center (for) six months, and then they were not sent because of the facilities in the drug center (then they time in), detention will be considered as they have been rehabilitated, considering that they were not exposed to drugs.
>
> (Interview #37)

By reducing the punishment drug users and small pushers face, without changing the law, the allowance of plea bargaining has permitted the government to formally maintain its "War on Drugs," while mitigating some of its problematic consequences, such as prison overpopulation or police abuse. Although there are no statics available at the time of writing this chapter (October 2018), since it has only been implemented months ago, a recently published report in a local newspaper claimed that 500 were released in the region of Tagaytay thanks to plea bargaining in July 2018, only months after it has been allowed for drug-related cases (Punay, 2018). This is consistent with the responses by the interviewees.

Conclusions: an emptied legality

This chapter has argued that the "War on Drugs" should not be analyzed only in terms of EJK. The massive arrests and the disposal of those cases are also integral to the strategy. It is important to recognize the strain this strategy has put on an already overwhelmed criminal justice system. An analysis of the challenges that the criminal justice system is facing and the strategies it has developed to cope with these challenges helps us understand the role it plays in the "War on Drugs." The expansion of plea bargaining is an example of these strategies.

The Estipona saga shows the importance that managerial concerns have for judicial actors, but also highlights a certain lack of commitment to ensure due process, and to cast oversights on police legality.

However, the expansion of plea bargaining to drug-related cases was also radical change led by judicial actors of the "War on Drugs." Although not publicly announced, it meant, in practice, a shift toward a rehabilitation strategy. A significant number of suspects were released on probation after a six-month treatment in a rehabilitation center; others were sent to prison but for short sentences. In this sense, this could be understood as an adjustment behind the doors of the judicial actors of the irrationality of the government's program.

Nevertheless, the Department of Justice and police acquiescence in the Estipona saga reveals the government may also be aware that the "War on Drugs" was not sustainable over time. The criticisms of judicial actors interviewed on the police behavior and the percentage of the cases that ended with acquittals demonstrate that the expansion of plea bargaining has lightened the consequences of the campaign on all the state's agencies.

In any case, the expansion of plea bargaining to drug-related cases underscores the importance of the legitimation of state violence that the criminal justice performs. As Kreuzer (2016) has argued in relation to how police vigilantism "legalized" EJK, plea bargaining legalizes police daily procedures, regardless of their illegalities and arbitrariness. But by doing so, judicial actors void the law of its content and pure force becomes legal.

While enabling plea bargaining was the only strategy judicial actors found to deal with the unrealistic demands of the "War on Drugs," the ultimate problem is it converts a problem of disproportionate, and in many cases illegal state violence, into a managerial problem (how to process the input).

Nevertheless, there are hopeful signs that the judiciary is assuming a more active role against police abuse. In October 2018, the Supreme Court set a mandatory policy on arrests and seizures related to illegal drugs. This is a significant development because the policy explicitly orders judges to refuse to issue warrants of arrest or even to dismiss cases if prosecutors have not properly controlled the legality of the police procedures (Patag, 2018b). Another hopeful sign was the conviction in November 2018 of three police officers for the murder of a Kian Loyd delos Santos, a 17-year-old boy. This was the first conviction of police officers for EJK in the "War on Drugs" (Lema and Perry, 2018). These events show that courts still have the power to mitigate, if not stop, state violence. It should be seen that this is the beginning of a fiercer defense of the rule of law by judicial actors.

Note

1 An additional criticism of their work can be found in their usage of the "weak state" and "strongman" framework, which others have found problematic. Although this chapter will not address the debate, it is worth noting. See Radics (2001).

References

Aldama, Z. (2018) "How Philippines War on Drugs Has become a War on the Poor," *South China Morning Post*, 20 January 2018. Available at: www.scmp.com/magazines/post-magazine/long-reads/article/2129538/how-philippines-war-drugs-has-become-war-poor (Accessed on: 19 October 2018).

BJMP (2018) "PDL with Drug Cases (As of May 2018)." Available at: www.bjmp.gov.ph/datstat.html (Accessed on: 9 October 2018).

Caduaya, E. (2015) "Duterte on SONA 2015: Aquino Should Stop Blaming Arroyo," *Rappler*, 27 July [Online]. Available at: www.rappler.com/nation/100687-duterte-aquino-stop-blame-arroyo-sona-2015 (Accessed on: 9 October 2018).

Calisco, R., Canare, T., and Garcia, E. (2017) *Shaping the Public Perception toward Local Authorities: The Role of Perceived Social, Economic, and Political Insecurities*. RSN-PCCWorking Paper, 17-004. Available at: https://ssrn.com/abstract=2941994 (Accessed on: 19 October 2018).

CFR (2010) "A Conversation with Benigno S. Aquino III," *Council of Foreign Relations*, 23 September [Online]. Available at: www.cfr.org/event/conversation-benigno-s-aquino-iii-0 (Accessed on: 19 October 2018).

Colonel, S. (2017) "Murder as Enterprise: Police Profiteering in Duterte's War on Drugs," in N. Curato (ed.) *A Duterte Reader: Critical Essays on Rodrigo Duterte's Early Presidency*, Manila: Ateneo de Manila University Press, pp. 167–198.

Corrales, N. (2016) "Duterte's New Drug List: 40 Judges, '1 Page' for Chinese Suspects," *Inquirer.net*, 21 September 2016. Available at: https://newsinfo.inquirer.net/817675/dutertes-new-drug-list-40-judges-1-page-for-chinese-suspects (Accessed on: 19 October 2018).

Curato, N. (2016) "Politics of Anxiety, Politics of Hope: Penal Populism and Duterte's Rise to Power," *Journal of Current Southeast Asian Affairs*, 35, pp. 91–109.

De Jesus, J. (2014) "High Conviction Rate of Drug Cases Seen with New Law," *Inquirer.net*, 4 August [Online]. Available at: https://newsinfo.inquirer.net/626229/high-conviction-rate-of-drugs-cases-seen-with-new-law (Accessed on: 19 October 2018).

The Economist (2001) "The Plots Thicken: Corruption in the Philippines," *The Economist*, 25 August 25, pp. 54–55.

Francisco, K. (2016) "Davao Judge Explains to JBC High Rate of Acquittal in Drug Cases," *Rappler*, 16 November [Online]. Available at: www.rappler.com/nation/152546-jbc-supreme-court-interview-adlawan-illegal-drugs (Accessed on: 19 October 2018).

Garcia Desacada, M. (2008) "PDEA: Some Agents Plant Evidence," *Philstar Global*. Available at: www.philstar.com/headlines/2008/05/30/64805/pdea-some-agents-plant-evidence (Accessed on: 19 October 2018).

Gavilan, J. (2018) "Justice Remains Elusive 2 Years into Duterte's Drug War," *Rappler*. Available at: www.rappler.com/newsbreak/in-depth/205921-justice-elusive-war-on-drugs-duterte-second-year (Accessed on: 19 October 2018).

HRW (2011) *"No Justice Just Adds to the Pain" Killings, Disappearances, and Impunity in the Philippines*, Human Rights Watch. Available at: www.hrw.org/report/2011/07/18/no-justice-just-adds-pain/killings-disappearances-and-impunity-philippines (Accessed on: 19 October 2018).

HRW (2012) *Philippines: Two Years Under Aquino, Abuses Go Unpunished*, Human Rights Watch, 27 June [Online]. Available at: www.hrw.org/news/2012/06/27/philippines-two-years-under-aquino-abuses-go-unpunished (Accessed on: 19 October 2018).

HRW (2014) *"One Shot to the Head" Death Squad Killings in Tagum City, Philippines*, Human Rights Watch, Available at: www.hrw.org/report/2014/05/20/one-shot-head/death-squad-killings-tagum-city-philippines (Accessed on: 19 October 2018).

HRW (2015) *Philippines: Probe Mayor's Alleged 'Death Squad' Links*, Human Rights Watch, 19 May. Available at: www.hrw.org/news/2015/05/19/philippines-probe-mayors-alleged-death-squad-links (Accessed on: 19 October 2018).

Iglesias, S. (2017) "The Duterte Playbook," *New Naratif*. Available at: https://newnaratif.com/research/the-duterte-playbook/ (Accessed on: 19 October 2018).

Johnson, D. and Fernquest, J. (2018) "Governing Through Killing: The War on Drugs in the Philippines," *Asian Journal of Law and Society*. https://doi.org/10.1017/als.2018.12

Koeppinger, P. (2013) "The Aquino Administration at Midterm," *Rappler*. Available at: www.rappler.com/nation/29822-the-aquino-administration-at-midterm (Accessed on: 19 October 2018).

Kreuzer, P. (2009) "Philippine Governance: Merging Politics and Crime," *PRIF Reports 93*, Frankfurt: Hessische Stiftung Friedens – und Konfliktforschung. Available at: http://nbn-resolving.de/urn:nbn:de:0168-ssoar-319699 (Accessed on: 19 October 2018).

Kreuzer, P. (2016) "If They Resist, Kill Them All: Police Vigilantism in the Philippines," *PRIF Reports 142*, Frankfurt: Hessische Stiftung Friedens- und Konfliktforschung. Available at: http://nbnresolving.de/urn:nbn:de:0168-ssoar-50187-0 (Accessed on: 19 October 2018).

Kreuzer, P. (2018) "Excessive Use of Deadly Force by Police in the Philippines before Duterte," *Journal of Contemporary Asia*, 48 (4), pp. 671–684.

Lamchek, J. (2017) "A Mandate for Mass Killings? Public Support for Duterte's War on Drugs," in N. Curato (ed.) *A Duterte Reader: Critical Essays on Rodrigo Duterte's Early Presidency*, Manila: Ateneo de Manila University Press, pp. 199–218.

Lema, K. and Perry, M. (2018) "Philippine Court Jails 3 Police Officers for Drugs War Murder," *Channel NewsAsia*, 29 November [Online]. Available at: www.channelnewsasia.com/news/world/philippine-court-jails-3-police-officers-for-drugs-war-murder-10979560 (Accessed on: 19 October 2018).

Leonen, J. (2018) "PDEA: 75,000 Drug Suspects Arrested in 2017," *Inquirer.net*. Available at: https://newsinfo.inquirer.net/960768/pdea-75000-drug-suspects-arrested-in-2017 (Accessed on: 19 October 2018).

Lopez, T. (2015) "BS Aquino's Two Biggest Failures," *Manilastandard.net*. Available at: http://manilastandard.net/opinion/columns/virtual-reality-by-tony-lopez/182783/bs-aquino-s-two-biggest-failures.html (Accessed on: 19 October 2018).

McKetin, R., Kozel, N., et al. (2008) "The Rise of Methamphetamine in Southeast and East Asia," *Drug and Alcohol Review*, 27 (3), pp. 220–228.

Mendez, C. (2016) "Duterte to PNP: Kill 1,000, I'll Protect You," *Philstar Global*, 2 July [Online]. Available at: www.philstar.com/headlines/2016/07/02/1598740/duterte-pnp-kill-1000-ill-protect-you (Accessed on: 19 October 2018).

Narag, R. (2018) "Understanding Factors Related to Prolonged Trial of Detained Defendants in the Philippines," *International Journal of Offender Therapy and Comparative Criminology*, 62 (8), pp. 2461–2487.

Nawal, A. (2015) "Duterte Vows to Fight Corruption, Criminality If Elected President," *Inquirer.net*. Available at: https://newsinfo.inquirer.net/743211/duterte-vows-to-fight-corruption-criminality-if-elected-president (Accessed on: 19 October 2018).

Nery, J. (2009) "Drugged (or, PDA for PDEA)," *Newsstand*, 27 January [Online]. Available at: https://johnnery.wordpress.com/2009/01/27/column-drugged-or-pda-for-pdea/ (Accessed on: 19 October 2018).

Patag, K.J. (2018a) "Parents of EJK Victim Feel Philippine Courts Are 'Paralyzed'," *Philstar*. Available at: www.philstar.com/headlines/2018/08/29/1846890/parents-ejk-victim-feel-philippine-courts-are-paralyzed (Accessed on: 19 October 2018).

Patag, K.J. (2018b) "SC Sets Rules on Drug-Related Seizures, Arrests," *Philstar*, 2 October [Online]. Available at: www.philstar.com/headlines/2018/10/02/1856660/sc-sets-rules-drug-related-seizures-arrests (Accessed on: 19 October 2018).

Perper, R. (2018) "Philippine President Duterte Lined Up 100 Cops Accused of Corruption in Front of the Media and Threatened to Kill Them," *Business Insider Singapore*, 8 August [Online]. Available at: www.businessinsider.sg/philippines-rodrigo-duterte-lines-up-threatens-allegedly-corrupt-cops-before-media-2018–8/?r=US&IR=T (Accessed on: 19 October 2018).

Philippine Statistics Authority (2017) *2017 Philippine Statistical Yearbook*, Quezon City: PSA.

Punay, E. (2018) "Plea Bargain Eases Drug Case Backlog," *Philstar Global*, 9 July [Online]. Available at: www.philstar.com/headlines/2018/07/09/1831871/plea-bargain-eases-drug-case-backlog (Accessed on: 19 October 2018).

Quimpo, N. (2017) "Duterte's 'War on Drugs': The Securitization of Illegal Drugs and the Return of National Boss Rule," in N. Curato (ed.) *A Duterte Reader: Critical Essays on Rodrigo Duterte's Early Presidency*, Manila: Ateneo de Manila University Press, pp. 145–166.

Radics, G. (2001) "Globalization, Corruption and the Structural Historical Perspective," *Philippine Sociological Review*, 49(1–2), pp. 39–58.

Ramos, M. (2017) "Days of Disquiet in Judiciary under Duterte," *Inquirer.net*, 24 July [Online]. Available at: http://newsinfo.inquirer.net/916532/days-of-disquiet-in-judiciary-under-duterte (Accessed on: 19 October 2018).

Ranada, P. (2016) "A Look at the State of Crime, Drugs in the Philippines," *Rappler*. Available at: www.rappler.com/nation/118004-crime-drugs-philippines (Accessed on: 19 October 2018).

Rauhala, E. (2016a) "A Manila Neighborhood Mourns Four Men Lost to Duterte's 'Drug War'," *The Washington Post*, 10 October [Online]. Available at: www.washingtonpost.com/news/worldviews/wp/2016/10/10/a-manila-neighborhood-mourns-four-men-lost-to-dutertes-drug-war/?utm_term=.13d1e8abd762 (Accessed on: 19 October 2018).

Rauhala, E. (2016b) "Before Duterte Was the Philippines' President, He Was 'the Death Squad Mayor'," *The Washington Post*, 28 September [Online]. Available at: www.washingtonpost.com/world/asia_pacific/before-duterte-was-the-philippines-president-he-wasthe-death-squad-mayor/2016/09/28/f1d1ccc4-800b-11e6-ad0e-ab0d12c779b1_story.html (Accessed on: 19 October 2018).

Republic of the Philippines (2001) *Letter of Instruction No. 1*, 4 July. Available at: www.officialgazette.gov.ph/2001/07/04/letter-of-instruction-no-1-s-2001/ (Accessed on: 19 October 2018).

Saludo, R. (2014) "Crime Has Double Under Aquino: Here's Why," *The Manila Times*, 8 September [Online]. Available at: www.manilatimes.net/crime-doubled-aquino-heres/125276/ (Accessed on: 19 October 2018).

Sanidad-Leones, C. (2006) The Current Situation of Crime Associated with Urbanization: Problems Experienced and Countermeasures Initiated in the Philippines," in *Resource Material Series 68*, Tokyo: UNAFEI, pp. 133–150.

Tadiar, A. (1980) "Some Role/Functions in the Administration of Criminal Justice," *Philippine Law Journal*, 55 (1), pp. 32–50.

Taub, A. (2016) "How Countries Like Philippines Fall into Vigilante Violence," *The New York Times*, 11 September [Online]. Available at: https://nyti.ms/2cF7kN6 (Accessed on: 19 October 2018).

Torres-Tupas, T. (2014) "Sereno Seeks for More Budget for Judiciary Reforms," *Inquirier.net*. Available at: http://newsinfo.inquirer.net/640461/sereno-seeks-more-budget-for-judiciary-reforms (Accessed on: 19 October 2018).

Tupas, E. (2017) "Jail Facilities Congested by 583 Percent," *Philstar Global*. Available at: www.philstar.com/headlines/2017/07/01/1715573/jail-facilities-congested-583-percent (Accessed on: 19 October 2018).

UNODC (2008) *World Drug Report*, Vienna: United Nations Office on Drugs and Crime. Available at: www.unodc.org/documents/wdr/WDR_2008/WDR_2008_eng_web.pdf (Accessed on: 19 October 2018).

UNODC (2017) *The Challenge of Synthetic Drugs in East and South-East Asia: Trends and Patterns of Amphetamine-Type Stimulants and New Psychoactive Substances: A Report from the Global SMART Programme*, Vienna: United Nations Office on Drugs and Crime. Available at: www.unodc.org/documents/scientific/Trends_and_Patterns_of_ATS_and_NPS_2017.pdf (Accessed on: 19 October 2018).

Annex

Table 8.1 Interviews

Interview #	*Role*	*Gender*	*Date*
1	Public Prosecutor	Female	21–05–18
2	Public Prosecutor	Female	21–05–18
3	Public Prosecutor	Male	21–05–18
4	Public Prosecutor	Male	21–05–18
5	Public Prosecutor	Female	21–05–18
6	Public Prosecutor	Female	21–05–18
7	Public Prosecutor	Male	21–05–18
8	Public Prosecutor	Male	21–05–18
9	Public Prosecutor	Female	22–05–18
10	Public Prosecutor	Male	22–05–18
11	Public Prosecutor	Male	22–05–18
12	Public Prosecutor	Female	22–05–18
13	Public Prosecutor	Female	22–05–18
14	Public Prosecutor	Female	22–05–18
15	Public Prosecutor	Female	22–05–18
16	Public Prosecutor	Female	22–05–18
17	Public Prosecutor	Male	22–05–18
18	Public Prosecutor	Male	23–05–18
19	Public Prosecutor	Female	23–05–18
20	Public Prosecutor	Female	23–05–18
21	Public Prosecutor	Female	23–05–18
22	Public Prosecutor	Male	23–05–18
23	Public Prosecutor	Male	23–05–18
24	Public Prosecutor	Female	23–05–18
25	Public Prosecutor	Male	23–05–18
26	Public Prosecutor	Female	23–05–18
27	Public Prosecutor	Female	23–05–18
28	Assistant Clerk of Court	Female	05–06–18
29	Branch Clerk of Court	Female	05–06–18
30	Judge	Male	05–06–18
31	Judge	Male	05–06–18
32	Judge	Female	05–06–18
33	Judge	Male	05–06–18
34	Judge	Male	06–06–18

Interview #	*Role*	*Gender*	*Date*
35	Judge	Female	06–06–18
36	Judge	Female	06–06–18
37	Judge	Female	06–06–18
38	Public Attorney	Male	06–06–18
39	Public Attorney	Male	06–06–18
40	Judge	Male	06–06–18
41	Public Attorney	Male	22–11–18
42	Public Attorney	Female	22–11–18
43	Public Attorney	Female	22–11–18
44	Public Attorney	Male	22–11–18
45	Public Attorney	Male	22–11–18
46	Public Attorney	Male	22–11–18
47	Public Attorney	Female	22–11–18
48	Public Attorney	Male	22–11–18
49	Public Attorney	Male	22–11–18
50	Public Attorney	Male	22–11–18

Chapter 9

Arresting a due process revolution

The reform of Indonesia's code of criminal procedure and the persistence of history

Jayson Lamchek

Introduction

The continued existence of Indonesia's Code of Criminal Procedure or *Kitab Undang-Undang Hukum Acara Pidana* (KUHAP) enacted in 1981 despite *reformasi* represents a puzzle in the recent history of Indonesian law. During the period of general political and legal reforms or *reformasi* following the fall of Suharto in 1998, both Indonesian and international actors targeted KUHAP for an overhaul, arguing that KUHAP was a relic from an authoritarian age unfit for a newly democratizing country. From an international perspective, the attempt to reform KUHAP in Indonesia was similar to reforms of criminal procedure in the Global South, particularly in Latin America, which undertook a "transition to democracy" in the 1990s and 2000s. During this period, 14 transitioning Latin American countries dramatically transformed their codes of criminal procedure, turning the inquisitorial system in these countries into something more adversarial (Langer, 2007; deLisle, 1999). Though led by expert reformers from those countries, Global Northern actors, primarily the United States, provided key support to their activities. This was also the case in Indonesia, where the United States and other Western countries lent technical assistance to the expert Indonesian team that drafted the revision of the code.

As Strang notes, many other factors made the reform of criminal procedure very likely to have been adopted in Indonesia at the time. First, Indonesia adopted the International Covenant for Civil and Political Rights (ICCPR) and the Convention against Torture (CAT), and hence was expected to implement their provisions through revision of its criminal procedure. Second, similar procedural legal changes, especially changes to the rules of evidence, have already been introduced into the country's legal system by special laws on terrorism, money laundering, corruption, human trafficking, and cyber-crime, as well as the Witness Protection Law. Third, important institutional reforms made the Indonesian judiciary, prosecutorial service, and police ripe for change to a more adversarial system (Strang, 2008). Yet despite these conditions, the KUHAP survived.

This chapter interrogates the significance of KUHAP's survival and seeks to contribute to the scant material on KUHAP reform. Robert Strang, a legal adviser to the United States Embassy in Jakarta who assisted the drafters of the proposed revised KUHAP, provides a valuable firsthand account of the process of drafting the proposed revision. However, his story ends on September 2008, when, he recounts, the Ministry of Law and Human Rights finally approved a draft revised KUHAP for presidential and parliamentary approval (Strang, 2008). Moreover, his account did not indicate any basis for pessimism about the prospect of the draft. Indeed, in his presentation, Indonesia was an example (from the largest civil law country no less) of the possibility of radical or fundamental changes to criminal procedure being effected through code-based, as opposed to judicial or judge-made, reform (Strang, 2008).[1] Ten years after, however, none of the dramatic changes that he anticipated for Indonesia have yet to come to fruition nor do they seem likely to take place in the near future. This chapter, therefore, offers a supplement and corrective to Strang's sanguine account by tracing the obstruction of the draft revised KUHAP after 2008 and exploring factors that allow KUHAP to survive the attempt to reform it.

Interviews with actors involved in the reform show that the main obstacle to the reform of KUHAP has been the police's unwillingness to give up its unfettered power under the status quo. To understand why the police have been so influential and such an important factor, in turn, it is necessary to have a fuller grasp of just how deeply entrenched police dominance and prosecutorial and judicial weakness were. For this, I turned to history. The failure of KUHAP reform, I argue, attests to the persistent influence of dispositions and outlooks on the criminal justice system that have been deeply ingrained as a result of colonialism and authoritarianism.

I develop this argument in the following manner. In the succeeding section, I explain the importance of KUHAP reform for the improvement of respect for human rights in the context of the country's criminal justice system. In the process, I introduce the substance of the main proposed reforms. In the third section, I review the events pertaining to the discussion of the draft revised KUHAP after 2008. This section is based in part on the recollection of events by a member of the drafting team and some of the civil society actors involved in lobbying for the enactment of the draft revised KUHAP by Parliament. I draw from interviews I conducted in September 2018 with Luhut Pangaribuan, a key member of the drafting team, representatives of five civil society organizations, and a prosecutor. In the remainder of the chapter, I engage in an exploration of some of the reasons that can account for KUHAP's survival. Thus, in the fourth section, I look at the historical roots of police dominance and prosecutorial and judicial weakness in the Indonesian criminal justice system. This section shows that police dominance and prosecutorial and judicial weakness are deeply entrenched features of Indonesia's criminal justice system brought about by historical circumstances of colonialism and authoritarianism. I round out this historical exploration with a survey of more contemporary realities showing a political trend encouraging a punitive attitude toward crimes in Indonesia.

The significance and substance of the proposed reforms of KUHAP

It was no secret that during the Suharto era, the criminal justice system was a major site of governmental abuse affecting ordinary citizens. Writing in 1999, Fitzpatrick noted repeated reports from several Indonesian and international human rights organizations in the 1990s regarding violations of criminal procedural rights recognized in KUHAP. Torture, mistreatment, and fabrication of evidence against the accused, among other abuses, were widespread in ordinary criminal cases (Fitzpatrick, 1999).[2] It was clear that authorities lacked respect for legal rights to begin with. But lawyers also argued that KUHAP itself may be part of the problem (Amnesty International, 2006; Anggara, 2014; Institute for Criminal Justice Reform, 2016). Although certain rights of the accused were recognized in KUHAP, these rights lack sufficient mechanisms for enforcement through, for example, the imposition of some legal penalty for their violation or were circumvented by permissive provisions that gave authorities too much leeway. In this way, KUHAP was seen as an internally defective national institution that easily lent itself to abuse by authorities.

To be sure, the defective design of KUHAP by itself does not sufficiently explain the occurrence of violations. Some authors, such as Fitzpatrick, prefer to locate an explanation for the violations in other factors, such as the ideology of the "integralist" state. But if the defective design of KUHAP was part of the problem, then plugging the loopholes of KUHAP – so that enforcement mechanisms are identified and permissive provisions are restricted – constituted part of a possible solution. In the process of fixing these loopholes (typically taken from features of the adversarial system of criminal justice), new procedural rights are introduced, and new standards are set that also function to articulate values or aspirations for the future. The approval of such provisions would constitute political acknowledgment, however superficial it may be, that previous practices should not take place anymore. Thus, although they may not suppress those practices, it would certainly delegitimize them and give victims some legal means to label those practices as violations and to attribute responsibility to offenders.[3]

Some illustrations will make this point clearer. The investigation stage led by the police has attracted a lot of concern since mistreatment and abuse, including torture, of the accused take place at this stage (Sheany, 2017; VOA News, 2011). KUHAP provides that arrests normally require a written warrant (delivered to the suspect's family), except in lesser crimes or offenses and when the offender is caught in the act. Moreover, the arrested person must be released after 24 hours if not subsequently ordered detained. Detention, when necessary, is allowed only for crimes punishable with greater than five years' imprisonment or crimes "with great impact on public order and general safety" (art 21(4)), with the written order provided to the defendant and his family. Legal experts attribute the main defect of KUHAP with regard to detention to the fact that it allows such long periods of detention that are not in accord with international standards. Police, prosecutors, and judges may order detention or extend one already granted up to 60 days (without judicial involvement) or 90 days (with judicial involvement) (Fitzpatrick, 1999, p. 345). In 1999, legal experts opined that KUHAP's allowance of lengthy detention that exceeded "a few days," as provided in the United Nations Human Rights Committee General Comment 8, art 9 (1982), did not comply with art 9(3) of the ICCPR.[4] Lengthy detentions and the fact that detention can be ordered by police were conducive to mistreatment and abuse of the accused. The power of the police to order detention allowed suspects to be pressured by police to make admissions under threats that they will be detained if they don't admit the crime (Fitzpatrick, 1999, p. 345). Notwithstanding the establishment of the pretrial mechanism, KUHAP did not provide for a right of the accused to be brought promptly before a court (Fitzpatrick, 1999, p. 345). The Ministry's draft revised KUHAP responded to these expert criticisms. It brought down the period of police detention without judicial intervention to 5 days, although the judge could still extend the detention to 15 days to allow police to further investigate (Strang, 2008, p. 213). This then is an example of a permissive provision in KUHAP that reformers tried to restrict.

Access to a lawyer (recognized as a right in arts. 55, 56, 69, 70, 115(1), KUHAP), another measure that could guard against abuse during the investigation phase, is often disregarded. This is largely because there is simply a dearth of lawyers, especially in rural areas. Aided by a government regulation that restricts access to lawyers to within regular office hours, the police are also known to actively deny access to lawyers by conducting investigations at night and in the absence of lawyers (Amnesty International, 2006, pp. 347–348). However, access was also denied even when lawyers were available because free legal aid wasn't mandated in all cases.[5] Moreover, KUHAP doesn't oblige the police to inform the accused of this right. Here, the strengthening of the right to access a lawyer by mandating it in all cases and by requiring the police to inform the accused of this right is seen as helpful. This is then an example of a right being strengthened through some kind of enforcement mechanism.

The reform of KUHAP offers some further solutions so as to guard against abusive practices of unlawful warrantless arrests, forced confessions and torture, and denial of access to a lawyer. First, it is proposed that the right of the accused to be brought promptly before a court be recognized. Second, a rule excluding illegally obtained evidence is proposed (Fitzpatrick, 1999, p. 345). Third, the draft also provided that the newly created office of the commissioner judge had the power to suppress illegally obtained evidence (Strang, 2008, p. 217).

More drastic were the changes proposed in the draft regarding the rights to remain silent and against self-incrimination. The right to remain silent was at best implied in art. 66 of KUHAP (suspect shall not be burdened with providing evidence). But there was no penalty for violation of this right. Furthermore, art. 175, which provides that "[i]f the accused declines to answer or refuses to answer a question addressed to him, the head judge at trial shall suggest that he answer and thereafter the examination shall be continued" undermines the right during trial. Also, lack of obligation to prosecute multiple offenders in the same trial (art. 141, 142) allows for the practice of "splitting" trials, which can be used to circumvent the right against self-incrimination (Fitzpatrick, 1999, p. 349). In the draft revision, the right against self-incrimination was made explicit. Miranda-like warnings were required to be provided by the investigator informing the person of his right to remain silent, and it was provided that no adverse inference could be drawn against a suspect exercising the right to remain silent (Strang, 2008, p. 212).

The pretrial under KUHAP (arts 77–83), which was meant as a mechanism available to the accused to protect themselves against illegal arrest and detention, also couldn't function as envisioned. Experts observe that the main problem was related to the lack of lawyers especially in rural areas who could make use of the pretrial mechanism. Also, pretrial was easily circumvented by nonappearance of authorities at pretrial, as there was no penalty for ignoring the same (Fitzpatrick, 2009, p. 346; Anggara, 2014, pp. 5–6). Thus, in practice, pretrial is greatly underutilized by defendants, and defendants who do make use of them often fail.[6] The Ministry's draft revised KUHAP tried to solve the problem by strengthening the pretrial provisions primarily through the grant of more enforcement power to a commissioner judge in charge of pretrial (Strang, 2008, p. 217).

The draft's proposals regarding the prosecution and trial stages were also clearly premised on moving the criminal process away from the rigidity of the inquisitorial system. Joinder of multiple defendants in a single indictment was allowed, and the prosecutor is given discretion over whom to charge in which indictment. Strang asserts that this potentially changes the role of the prosecutor, who under the inquisitorial system was almost reduced to a functionary who passed on dossiers from the police to the court (Strang, 2008, p. 218). The draft also explicitly provided that in the trial, like in an adversarial system, the examination of witnesses initially rests with the prosecutor and the defense counsel, not the judge, although the judge can still ask clarificatory questions (Strang, 2008, p. 219).

While being only the first steps to changing a culture of disregard for procedural rights of the accused, the envisioned changes in the draft revised KUHAP were, nevertheless, so comprehensive and in spirit so courageous. Strang remarked that the proposal potentially institutes "fundamental" changes that responded to the demand of "many Indonesians" for "comprehensive legal reform" of the criminal justice system (Strang, 2008, pp. 192, 202). It is not an exaggeration to say that to this package of reforms is attached the aspirations of human rights advocates for Indonesia to move closer to international human rights standards. They also articulate the efforts of reformers within government to change the system toward a more rational system of cooperation among the police, prosecutors, and judges.

Obstructing reform: discussions of the draft revised KUHAP after 2008

Although the work of the drafting team formed in 1999 has been extensive and a complete draft was finished by 2008, the draft revised KUHAP did not reach Parliament until 2013. Then President Susilo Bambang Yudhoyono submitted a draft revised KUHAP to the House of Representatives in March 2013 together with a draft revised Penal Code (Kitab Undang-undang Hukum Pidana, KUHP) in order to have simultaneous discussions on both substantive and procedural criminal law. Discussions were held before the Third Committee of the House of Representatives until March 2014.[7] During this brief period, the Corruption Eradication Commission (Komisi Pembarantasan Korupsi, KPK) expressed strong opposition to the joint bill (Halim & Saragih, 2014). Following the election of the new president Joko Widodo in the July 2014 elections, the contentiousness of the draft revised KUHAP led the government to decide to prioritize the enactment of changes to the substantive criminal law – i.e., KUHP, before discussing proposed changes to the criminal procedural law. This decision then doomed the prospect of the draft revised KUHAP being considered by Parliament in the foreseeable future. The draft has since been returned to the executive department and shelved.

On one level, the long wait for the changes to KUHAP to be adopted is simply a function of the slow grind of the legislative mill in Indonesia. On another level, it is determined by the strength of the interests behind the preservation of the status quo. As leaders of civil society organizations saw it, the most significant obstacle to the adoption of the draft revised KUHAP was simply the dissatisfaction of the police with the loss of power that it had to endure with a revamped KUHAP.

According to Arsil,[8] an activist with LEIP (*Lembaga Kaijan dan Advokasi untuk Independensi Peradilan*), one of the nongovernmental organizations (NGOs) that formed the coalition that monitored and supported KUHAP reform since 2007, action by high-ranking officials of the National Police caused the delay in the transmission of the draft to Parliament. A member of the drafting team Dr. Luhut Pangaribuan confirmed that when the draft revised KUHAP reached the Office of the Secretary of the Cabinet, high-ranking officials of the National Police tried to block further movement of the draft revised KUHAP by raising objections with the Ministry of Law and Human Rights. He said that the police objected to the provisions of the draft pertaining to the judge commissioner (*hakim komisaris*) who was empowered to oversee the arrest and detention of the accused during the investigation stage. This caused the Ministry to require the drafting team to rediscuss the concept of the judge commissioner with representatives and academic advisers of the National Police. Eventually, Luhut Pangaribuan said, the drafting team rewrote those provisions of the draft to the satisfaction of the police.[9] As a result, the 2012 version of the draft no longer mentioned the judge commissioner (*hakim komisaris*), and instead the term preliminary examining judge (*hakim pemeriksa pendahuluan*) was adopted. The authority of the preliminary examining judge was more limited than the judge commissioner.

Contention, however, did not end with the 2012 draft. It is true that in 2013, when the draft revised KUHAP was discussed in the House of Representatives, the police were not heard in public arguing against it. Instead, it was the KPK that took the cudgels for opponents of the bill. The KPK argued that the draft revised KUHAP was intended to weaken the institution and the fight against corruption by diminishing its powers of investigation. It took particular issue with the removal of the investigator's power to conduct preliminary investigation and the need for investigators to obtain judicial warrant to conduct wiretapping (Amelia & Sihaloho, 2013).

The KPK's objections really related to the fear that corruption was no longer being considered an extraordinary crime that would require extraordinary procedural measures. Then KPK chairman Abraham Samad explained that the draft revised Penal Code included corruption offenses in the general criminal offenses, eliminating its nature as an extraordinary crime (Atmaja, 2013). The KPK's objection then seemed external to the draft revised KUHAP itself and could be assuaged, among other possibilities, by ensuring that KPK's own statute and special rules of procedure continued to be good law. In this way, whatever changes that would result from the revised KUHAP would be *lex generalis* subject to the KPK's own procedural rules which would then be the *lex specialis* (Harkrisnowo, 2014, p. 53).

The KPK's rejection of the draft revised KUHAP on the supposition that it weakened anticorruption efforts was an overly dramatic and oppositional position to take toward a reform that was not specifically about corruption cases. As Erasmus Napitupulu, a program coordinator at the Institute for Criminal Justice Reform (ICJR), emphasized that KPK's argument was really irrelevant to the letter of the draft revised KUHAP. Yet it cast KUHAP reform in such a bad light. The popularity of the KPK as a government agency that ran after the corrupt helped further the misimpression that the draft revised KUHAP was alien to the needs of the public. Significantly, some NGOs like the Indonesia Corruption Watch supported the KPK on the issue. Despite the irrelevance of the KPK's arguments, Erasmus and Arsil recalled pleading with representatives of the KPK not to reject the bill altogether but to try and find a compromise. Arsil also emphasized the point that KPK's objections were really an echo of the police's misgivings about the diminished power of investigators over the accused. Thus, the larger significance of the KPK's objections to the draft revised KUHAP was its articulation of the point of view of the criminal justice system, shared with the police, which favored keeping the status quo.

We next turn to the historical roots of this status quo in order to get a sense of its strength and deep entrenchment in official culture.

The historical roots of police dominance and prosecutorial and judicial weakness

One might think that the criminal procedure law in Indonesia during the Dutch colonial period was patterned after the law that applied in the Netherlands at the time. This is, however, only partly true. During the Dutch colonial period until 1949, as far as criminal procedure was concerned, a kind of apartheid system existed in Indonesia in the sense that there were two sets of laws that applied, one for Europeans and another for the natives. The *Reglement op de Strafvordering* (RS) which applied to Europeans indeed reflected Dutch law. But the law applicable to the natives called the *Indlansch Reglement*, later called *Herziene Indonesisch Reglement* (HIR), was in comparison, far simpler and recognized less rights and opportunities for the accused to defend themselves than the RS or Dutch law. This dual system moreover meant the natives were allowed in the first instance to dispose of their criminal cases through indigenous courts staffed by local officials rather than trained colonial judges. This made economic sense to the colonial state administration that rid itself of the financial burden of administering criminal justice upon natives. Moreover, while the Dutch allowed independent courts for Europeans, they did not countenance independent courts for the natives, preferring to control their affairs through strong government (Pompe, 2005, pp. 28–31).

In 1949, the Japanese colonial government unified the criminal procedure law by choosing to make the HIR, rather than the RS, applicable universally throughout the country. When Indonesia became an independent state in 1951, the HIR was thus carried into the postcolonial legal system. According to Pompe, the advent of Guided Democracy under Sukarno confirmed the HIR as the applicable code of criminal procedure. The Sukarno government chose the HIR over the RS because it feared that the lack of skilled personnel and lack of familiarity might make the application of RS to Indonesians unworkable (Pompe, 2005, p. 47). The perpetuation of a colonial legal system is not at all unique to Indonesia but is in fact a common feature in many countries in the Global South. A clear parallel is with Latin America in the 1810s to 1830s when Latin American countries were newly independent. Langer observes that most of these countries chose to retain the less liberal – i.e., classic inquisitorial – system that was applied to them under colonial Spanish law, rather than adopt reforms, featuring a mix of inquisitorial and adversarial features that were sweeping many civil law countries in Europe at that time (Langer, 2007, pp. 627–628).

Moreover, Sukarno instituted Guided Democracy in 1959 until his fall in 1965, a period of authoritarian experimentation with nationalist and integralist ideology (Butt & Lindsey, 2012).[10] Among its legacies is the imbalance of powers between police, prosecutors, and judges that marked the country's criminal justice system ever since. During the parliamentary period from 1950–1959, Sukarno had already tried to subdue judges' aspirations as an independent branch of government by making the status and salary of prosecutors equal to judges (Pompe, 2005, pp. 43–50). Under the succeeding period of Guided Democracy, the independence of judges and the principle of separation of powers among executive, legislative, and judicial branches were formally declared no longer applicable to Indonesia. This was symbolized by the appointment of the chairman of the Supreme Court to Sukarno's Cabinet, a move that subordinated the highest magistrate to the president and conveyed the appearance that the court has joined Sukarno's authoritarian project (Pompe, 2005, pp. 52–62). Sukarno also created the Office of the Attorney General, with the attorney general occupying a cabinet-level post. He also placed the National Police directly under his authority. These actuations made the judiciary, prosecutorial service, and police equal organizationally. In reality, this meant a diminished status for judges and an elevated sense of importance for the police, which now thought of itself as no longer a mere helper or subordinate to prosecutors in the investigation of crimes.

Narendra Jatna, a prosecutor and lecturer in criminal procedure at the University of Indonesia, posits that Guided Democracy also gave birth to the idea that the criminal justice system can be compartmentalized into three distinct and successive stages of investigation, prosecution and adjudication.[11] Each stage was controlled, respectively, by the police, prosecutor and judge, which therefore again confirmed their functional equality. These three groups were also seen as criminal law enforcers, each contributing to the singular goal of suppression of crimes. Narendra Jatna added that the chief of the National Police under Suharto, Awaluddin Jamin, was later to articulate this into a theory of the criminal justice system as a kind industrial production line. In practice, the supremacy of the police in the investigation stage meant that the supervision from prosecutors and judges over interrogation and detention of individuals by police was rendered unnecessary. Moreover, prosecutors and judges were almost reduced to relaying and accepting evidence assembled by the police in the investigation stage (see also Supreme Court of Indonesia and Faculty of Law, University of Indonesia, 2005, p. 88ff).

The ideas that permeated Indonesia's criminal procedure until then reflected quite closely the logic and values of the so-called crime control model of criminal justice. Herbert Packer, writing about the American criminal justice system in the 1960s, posited a set of intuitions about criminal justice that he called "crime control model," which he contrasted with the so-called due process model. The crime control model valued the efficient suppression of criminal conduct. It imagined the police as chiefly responsible for identifying and weeding out criminals from society. The faster the police are able to carry out this task, the sooner criminals are locked up, the better for society. Thus, the image of the ideal criminal justice system as an assembly line. This meant that rights for the accused were seen as potential obstacles that slowed down the work of police; lengthy and expensive trials are, therefore, frowned upon. The assumption is that the police can be trusted to differentiate between the factually guilty and the factually innocent. In contrast to the crime control model, the due process model was concerned with ensuring the quality of criminal convictions and not simply the quantity of crimes suppressed. The due process model gave importance to the supervision of police by legal experts and emphasized the need to abide by the standard of legal guilt. It valued the rights of the accused and a scrupulously fair trial as protections against wrongful conduct by law enforcers. Because of the emphasis on considered deliberation and rigorous processes, in contrast to the haste of the assembly line, Packer identified this model with the image of an obstacle course (Packer, 1964; Stribopoulos, 2010, pp. 197–199).

When KUHAP was enacted in 1981 under the succeeding Suharto administration, the dominant institutional arrangements and ideas about criminal justice already favored a system in which the police were given almost unchecked powers over ordinary citizens while prosecutors and judges were almost reduced to mere functionaries supporting the police. These undoubtedly shaped the contents of KUHAP and the way it was enforced.

Indeed, Suharto's was only too willing to perpetuate the disempowerment of the court during his own authoritarian rule and showed no interest in changing the imbalance of power among the police, prosecutors, and judges. As Pompe notes, the administration of the judiciary, as in Guided Democracy, continued to be done through the Department of Justice which in time completely ignored the suggestions of the Supreme Court. This undermined merit-based assessments and personnel management system in the court and instead fostered personal connections between judges and the executive (Pompe, 2005, p. 119ff). Especially when politicians or their relatives were involved, judges became accustomed to taking dictations from the Justice Department or from senior judges close to the government about how they should decide criminal cases (Pompe, 2005, pp. 126–128). Executive interference became so prevalent that their official instructions to judges on how to decide cases were given openly and in writing. Judges even noted such instructions in their written decisions, sometimes as a form of protest to expose to the public that they had no free hand on the matter (Pompe, 2005, pp. 140–141).

KUHAP, even today, is often celebrated in nationalist discourse as a "masterpiece" of Indonesian legal thought because it significantly improved on the colonial era HIR, making it more humane while being reflective of Indonesian values.[12] However, this is a highly misleading proposition. The HIR imposes such a low standard in terms of rights protection that it was so easily surpassed anyway at least in letter. More significantly, the enactment of KUHAP did not really intend to introduce a new vision of the criminal justice system that would be significantly more oriented to a "due process model." Rather, it codified the dominant practices and ideas of the time which hewed closely to a "crime control model." Ironically, and the nationalist rhetoric notwithstanding, the adoption of KUHAP reenacted the disdain for or lack of confidence in Indonesians' capacity to administer a more complicated rights-respectful criminal justice system that Suharto exhibited when he sustained the Japanese colonial government's decision to continue imposing the Dutch colonial era HIR on Indonesians.

An increasingly punitive attitude toward crime in the Global South

In many countries around the world, an increasingly punitive attitude toward crimes is pushing back gains in the improvement of respect for human rights and due process. While this is also true for the Global North, the expression of this tendency in the Global South takes more extreme forms because of a number of factors, including the need to reform criminal procedure codes, address rising judicial backlogs, or the purported rise of social pandemics (i.e., drug use or terrorism). Furthermore, rising crime rates do not always translate to, and are sometimes unrelated to, the institution of more punitive measures; rather, political actors play a crucial role in fomenting fear of crime and manipulating such fear in order to govern (Simon, 2007). Scholars in the Global North who work on "penal populism" suggest that politicians respond to public anxieties about crime by encouraging punitive laws and sentences in order to increase their electoral chances or popularity (Pratt & Clark, 2005). "Penal populism" also exists in the Global South, but it is further complicated by the fact that the state typically wields much more lethal power toward civil society in the South than in the North. This final section will explore these issues in the context of Latin America and Southeast Asia and ascertain their impact on the prospect for increasing due process protection in Indonesia.

In his account of the reform of Argentinian criminal procedure, said to be typical of the "due process revolution" that swept Latin America beginning in the 1980s, Ciocchini emphasized the interrelation between punitive public attitude to crimes on the one hand and the managerialist logic of reforms supported by the West on the other hand (Ciocchini, 2017; see also, on managerialism in the Global North, Resnik, 1982; Feeley & Simon, 1992; Kohler-Hausmann, 2014). In Argentina, the shift to the adversarial system was originally intended to increase due process not only for the protection of the accused but to ensure "accountability" and "efficiency," but the actual reforms that were introduced instead emphasized punitive methods of crime control that only minimally involved adjudication (Ciocchini, 2017). Indeed, "efficiency" and "accountability" are highly mutable ideas that can mask the tension between competing conceptions of crime control and due process (Packer, 1964). The emphasis on "efficiency" can jive with the values of the due process model as much as the crime control model, which, as we have mentioned, interprets efficiency as the ability to process the maximum number of factually guilty persons in the least amount of time. It is such efficiency that demands broad and unfettered instead of restricted discretion on the part of police to "separate the innocent from the guilty as early in the process as possible" and values resolution through guilty pleas in order to avoid "wasteful and needlessly time-consuming trials" (Stribopoulos, 2010, pp. 197–198). As the Argentinian example also suggests, the demand for the criminal justice system to be tougher on street-level crimes brought on by pressures from politicians and the media is an important factor that eventually oriented reforms toward the values of a crime control model.

In the Philippines, the politicization of crime can and has been taken to such an extreme that what is demanded by politicians is no longer just more punitive laws and court sentences as has been observed in the Global North, but the outright extrajudicial killings of street-level criminals. In the past few years, the president of the Philippines has openly encouraged extrajudicial killings of small-time drug peddlers and users, a move that buoys up his popularity among frustrated and anxious publics. In this connection, Johnson and Fernquest make the interesting observation correlating recent human rights advances abolishing the death penalty with the rise of extrajudicial killings sanctioned by the state. "[S]tate killing often survives and sometimes thrives after capital punishment is abolished (see Mexico, Brazil, Nepal, and Cambodia)" (Johnson & Fernquest, 2018, p. 3). They also observe that extrajudicial execution rates rise when judicial executions in countries that still adopt them in their statutes rarely carry them out in practice, citing Bangladesh, India, and Indonesia as examples. Thus, they argue for a greater attention to the sort of state-led vigilantism observed in the Philippines, expecting the same pattern especially in countries with "weak law, strong executives, and fearful and frustrated citizens" (Johnson & Fernquest, 2018).

The foregoing considerations allow for reflection on some contemporary political trends that encourage an increasingly punitive attitude toward crimes and that therefore keep the prospect of an Indonesian "due process" revolution through KUHAP reform bleak. Compared to Argentina, Indonesia is a simpler, more straightforward case of frustration of reform. In Argentina, the intended goals of reform were perverted as a result of the existing conditions; in Indonesia, the proposed reforms were not perverted but were simply not carried out. In the Indonesian case, NGOs also often do point out that the prisons were already operating beyond capacity. They argue that less punitive and more creative new ideas for dealing with the accused and convicts other than imprisonment would serve the efficient administration of justice better.[13] However, unlike in Argentina, these arguments were not appropriated but were simply ignored by the government.

Furthermore, much like in the Philippines, Indonesian political leaders are aware that appearing to get tough on at least certain crimes, even at the expense of individual rights of the accused or indeed when it is precisely in contravention of such rights, can elicit political capital among certain audiences. The

KPK Chairman's actuation toward KUHAP reform exhibits this; he has framed his objection to KUHAP reform as "protection of the rights of perpetrators" of corruption at the expense of weakening the anticorruption effort (Atmaja, 2013). The rhetoric is premised on the awareness that getting tough on crime sells; conversely, protecting human rights is a hard sell, especially if they pertain to the perpetrators of corruption. This is also true in the case of terrorism (Butt, 2009) and drug crimes (Pisani, 2015; Hunt, 2016). In all three cases, as in the Global North, Indonesia's laws have been or are being adjusted so that authorities are further empowered to deal with suspects more aggressively through such means as longer periods of arrest and detention than are allowed under KUHAP and wiretapping (Butt, 2009; Anti-Narcotics Law, art. 76).

But even more concerning are the extrajudicial killings that have recently been witnessed against terrorism and drug crimes suspects in Indonesia. In the case of terrorism, often the suspects' connection to terrorist networks or activities have been invoked by police as if that was enough to justify extrajudicial killings (KomnasHAM, 2011; Lamchek, 2019, pp. 266–268). In the case of drug crimes, President Widodo has not only routinely refused to stop judicial executions of drug convicts to project an image of toughness on the drug problem. He has also ratcheted up the punitive rhetoric of his "War on Drugs" by encouraging police not to hesitate to shoot to kill drug offenders, especially foreigners (Reuters, 2017). The result: 60 fatal shootings by police against drug suspects as of August 2017 (Hamid, 2017). Thus, while an increasingly punitive attitude and penal populism may be seen throughout the world, its manifestation in the South is profound and distinct. In this regard, Indonesia serves as an excellent case study highlighting many of the issues seen in Southeast Asia and Latin America.

Conclusion

This chapter has provided a picture of a due process revolution that has been arrested. KUHAP's proposed overhaul would have affected significant improvements toward the protection of the rights of accused while empowering prosecutors and judges vis-à-vis the police. I have argued that the resistance of the police to the diminishment of its dominance had been crucial in obstructing discussions about reform and, hence, the reform itself and in keeping the status quo. The chapter turned to history to account for the strength of this conservative disposition. Briefly surveying current trends showing an increasingly punitive attitude toward crime, I show further troubles for the prospect for reviving KUHAP reform today.

Twenty years into *reformasi*, the Indonesian criminal justice system continues to dwell under the long shadow of colonialism and authoritarianism, a fact that is masked by nationalist rhetoric. What I have ultimately shown is that the reform of KUHAP is a matter of decolonization and the uprooting of antidemocratic forces. In Indonesia, like many countries of the Global

South, colonialism continues to exert its influence on laws that subsequent authoritarian governments have perpetuated. We have also seen that an increasingly punitive attitude toward crimes in Indonesia is expressed in more extreme terms, including extrajudicial killings, than scholars in Global Northern countries are familiar with.

Given the deeply ingrained nature of the forces opposed to criminal justice reform, the chapter also indicates the limits to expert-led efforts that may have worked to an extent in the Latin American context but was easily frustrated in Indonesia. Perhaps if a due process revolution were ever to occur in the archipelago, it will have to be ignited by more broad-based social mobilization that also confront the rising punitive attitude toward crimes. The challenges of KUHAP reform are then similar to what peoples all around the Global South and beyond are experiencing with rising right-wing nationalism and populism.

Notes

1 "The civil law tradition . . . has been seen as more rigid than the common law system because it deprives judges of the capacity to shape procedures in response to new facts and developments. This perception is wrong. The very code-based systems that are less flexible in the short term have proven to be more capable than common law systems of adopting broad new legal paradigms over time" (Strang, 2008, p. 188).

2 These practices were also rampant in cases involving political or regional unrest; the Anti-Subversion Law operated to suspend many provisions of KUHAP with respect to these cases. Law No. 11/PNPS/1963; Law No. 5 of 1969.

3 I thank Pablo Ciocchini for the formulation in the last two sentences.

4 Report of the Working Group on Arbitrary Detention on its visit to Indonesia (31 January–12 February 1999), UN Doc. E/CN.4/2000/4/Add.2, para. 99. In 2008, the UN Human Rights Commission reiterated the recommendation to Indonesia of a maximum 48-hour period of detention without judicial intervention. UN Doc. A/HRC/7/3/Add.7 (Mar. 10, 2008) 20.

5 Right to counsel is provided only for crimes the penalty for which exceeds five years. Art. 56 KUHAP.

6 In the study of 80 pretrial decisions made by ICJR, the success rate was only 3% (Anggara, 2014, 53).

7 A summary of the proceedings in Parliament is provided in Komite untuk Pembaharuan Hukum Acara Pidana (KuHAP), *Mengawal RUU KUHAP* (Komite untuk Pembaharuan Hukum Acara Pidana (KuHAP) 2014) 5–13.

8 Interview with the author, 19 September 2018.

9 According to Luhut Pangaribuan, the discussions were often heated, as the representatives or advisers of the police would express views indicating that there was no need for any change to the existing KUHAP. In at least one occasion, out of frustration, the chairman of the drafting team, Andi Hamzah, threw fruit at an interlocutor.

10 Sukarno dissolved the Constituent Assembly that was drafting a constitution for Indonesia and instead reverted to the bare-bones revolutionary era 1945 Constitution. Originally intended as a temporary measure, the 1945 Constitution did not provide for a bill of rights and contained very little protection for individual rights. Absent constitutional protection of rights for the accused, the court then had no capacity to shape criminal procedure so as to enforce those rights.

11 Interview with the author, 22 September 2018.
12 The further misleading claims are made that KUHAP "utilized the accusatorial system where[as] the HIR applied the inquisitorial system" and that KUHAP abolished the use of torture in the investigation of crimes (Supreme Court of Indonesia and Faculty of Law, University of Indonesia, 2005, 87).
13 Some data on Indonesia's crime rate and incarceration rate up to 2016 can be found in United Nation Surveys (UNS) on Crime Trends and the Operations of Criminal Justice Systems, www.unodc.org/unodc/en/data-and-analysis/United-Nations-Surveys-on-Crime-Trends-and-the-Operations-of-Criminal-Justice-Systems.html.

References

Amelia, R. & Sihaloho, J. (2013). KPK Demands Govt to Revoke the Revised Criminal Code Procedures Draft. *Jakarta Globe*, 22 March [Online]. Available at: http://jakartaglobe.id/news/kpk-demands-govt-to-revoke-the-revised-criminal-code-procedures-draft (Accessed: 26 September 2018).

Amnesty International (2006). Indonesia: Comments on the Draft Criminal Procedure Code. ASA 21/005/2006. Available at: https://www.amnesty.org/download/Documents/72000/asa210052006en.pdf

Anggara, S. (ed.) (2014). *Pretrial Hearing in Indonesia: Theory, History, and Practice in Indonesia*, Jakarta: Institute for Criminal Justice Reform. Available at: http://icjr.or.id/data/wp-content/uploads/2014/02/Pretrial-Hearing-in-Indonesia.pdf

Atmaja, Y.C.D. (2013). KPK: RUU KUHP-KUHAP Lemahkan Pemberantasan Korupsi. *Satu Harapan*, 18 December [Online]. Available at: www.satuharapan.com/read-detail/read/kpk-ruu-kuhp-kuhap-lemahkan-pemberantasan-korupsi (Accessed: 16 October 2018).

Butt, S. (2009). *Indonesian Terrorism Law and Criminal Process*. University of Melbourne Centre for Islamic Law and Society. Islam, Syari'ah and Governance Background Paper (ARC Federation Fellowship). Available at: http://papers.ssrn.com/abstract=1400506 (Accessed: 29 October 2013).

Butt, S. & Lindsey, T. (2012). *The Constitution of Indonesia: A Contextual Analysis*, Oxford: Hart Publishing.

Ciocchini, P. (2017). The Relevance of Criminal Courts in the Global South. *Laws*, 6 (4), p. 29.

deLisle, J. (1999). Lex Americana: United States Legal Assistance, American Legal Models, and Legal Change in the Post-Communist World and Beyond. *University of Pennsylvania Journal of International Economic Law*, 20, p. 179.

Feeley, M. & Simon, J. (1992). The New Penology: Notes on the Emerging Strategy of Corrections and Its Implications. *Criminology*, 30 (4), pp. 449–474.

Fitzpatrick, D. (2009). Culture, Ideology and Human Rights: The Case of Indonesia's Code of Criminal Procedure. In Lindsey, T. (ed.), *Indonesia: Law and Society* (2nd ed.), Sydney: The Federation Press, p. 344.

Halim, H. & Saragih, B.B.T. (2014). KPK Delivers Strong Words for SBY on KUHAP. *The Jakarta Post*, 24 February. Available at: www.thejakartapost.com/news/2014/02/24/kpk-delivers-strong-words-sby-kuhap.html (Accessed: 26 September 2018).

Hamid, U. (2017). Indonesia: At Least 60 Killed as Police Shootings of Drug Suspects Skyrocket. *Amnesty International*, 16 August [Online]. Available at: www.amnesty.org/en/latest/news/2017/08/indonesia-at-least-60-killed-as-police-shootings-of-drug-suspects-skyrocket/ (Accessed: 11 August 2018).

Harkrisnowo, H. (2014). KPK Tidak Usah Galau. In *RKUHP: Kodifikasi atau Kompilasi?*, Jakarta: Bidang Studi Hukum Pidana FHUI, p. 53.

Hunt, L. (2016). Executions Cast a Pall over Indonesia and Its 'War on Drugs'. *The Diplomat*, 4 August [Online]. Available at: https://thediplomat.com/2016/08/executions-cast-a-pall-over-indonesia-and-its-war-on-drugs/ (Accessed: 16 October 2018).

Institute for Criminal Justice Reform (2016). Torture Remains a Part of Criminal Law Enforcement in Indonesia, 30 June [Online]. Available at: http://icjr.or.id/torture-remains-a-part-of-criminal-law-enforcement-in-indonesia/

Johnson, D. & Fernquest, J. (2018). Governing through Killing: The War on Drugs in the Philippines. *Asian Journal of Law and Society*, pp. 1–32.

Kohler-Hausmann, I. (2014). Managerial Justice and Mass Misdemeanors. *Stanford Law Review*, 66, p. 611.

Komisi Nasional Hak Asasi Manusia (2011). *Laporan Pemantauhan Dan Penyelidikan Penanganan Tindak Terorisme*, Jakarta: Komisi Nasional Hak Asasi Manusia.

Lamchek, J. (2019). *Human Rights-Compliant Counterterrorism: Myth-Making and Reality in the Philippines and Indonesia*, Cambridge: Cambridge University Press.

Langer, M. (2007). Revolution in Latin American Criminal Procedure: Diffusion of Legal Ideas from the Periphery. *The American Journal of Comparative Law*, 55 (4), pp. 617–676.

Packer, H.L. (1964). Two Models of the Criminal Process. *University of Pennsylvania Law Review*, 113, p. 1.

Pisani, E. (2015). Widodo's Desperate Executions. *The New Yorker*, 1 May [Online]. Available at: www.newyorker.com/news/news-desk/widodos-desperate-executions (Accessed: 16 October 2018).

Pompe, S. (2005). *The Indonesian Supreme Court: A Study of Institutional Collapse*, Southeast Asia Program, New York: Cornell University.

Pratt, J. & Clark, M. (2005). Penal Populism in New Zealand. *Punishment & Society*, 7 (3), pp. 303–322.

Report of the Working Group on Arbitrary Detention on its visit to Indonesia (31 January–12 February 1999). UN Doc. E/CN.4/2000/4/Add.2, para. 99.

Resnik, J. (1982). Managerial Judges. *Harvard Law Review*, 96, p. 374.

Reuters (2017). Indonesian President Orders Officers to Shoot Drug Traffickers. *Reuters*, 22 July [Online]. Available at: www.reuters.com/article/us-indonesia-drugs/indonesian-president-orders-officers-to-shoot-drug-traffickers-idUSKBN1A708P

Sheany (2017). Torture Remains a Serious Problem in Indonesia: AHRC. *Jakarta Globe*, 30 June.

Simon, J. (2007). *Governing through Crime: How the War on Crime Transformed American Democracy and Created a Culture of Fear*, Oxford: Oxford University Press.

Strang, R.R. (2008). More Adversarial, But Not Completely Adversarial: Reformasi of the Indonesian Criminal Procedure Code. *Fordham International Law Journal*, 32, pp. 188, 203–209.

Stribopoulos, J. (2010). Packer's Blind Spot: Low Visibility Encounters and the Limits of Due Process versus Crime Control. In Tanguay-Renaud, F. and Stribopoulos, J. (eds.), *Rethinking Criminal Law Theory: New Canadian Perspectives in the Philosophy of Domestic, Transnational and International Criminal Law*, Oxford: Hart.

United Nation Surveys (UNS) on Crime Trends and the Operations of Criminal Justice Systems. *United Nations Office on Drugs and Crime*. Available at: www.unodc.org/unodc/en/data-and-analysis/United-Nations-Surveys-on-Crime-Trends-and-the-Operations-of-Criminal-Justice-Systems.html

VOA News (2011). Indonesian Police Accused of Systematic Torture of Prisoners. *VOA Voice of America*, 2 January [Online]. Available at: www.voanews.com/a/legal-aid-group-accuses-indonesian-police-of-systematic-torture-of-prisoners-112796219/133029.html

Chapter 10

Sacrificing justice for efficiency?

Examining premature dismissal rates in Peruvian corruption cases

Wilson Hernández

Introduction

In Peru, corruption is not new and is based on historical legacy (Quiroz, 2013). Therefore, it is unsurprising that one out of four Peruvians admits to having bribed a public servant (Proética, 2017). Since 2000, four democratically elected presidents are now in prison or under investigation for corruption. Moreover, half of the population would still vote for a local government candidate who might steal from the national budget so long as he or she invests in infrastructure (*que robe, pero que haga obra*) (Datum, 2014). In attempting to address this major problem of corruption since the 1990s, the criminal justice system throughout Latin America has been identified as the cause of widespread corruption, as well as an object of reform (Langer, 2007). It was argued that the existing inquisitorial model was too bureaucratic, lacked transparency, and created incentives for corruption (De la Jara, Del Mastro, Mujica, & Ramírez, 2008). Following this trend, in 2007, Peru introduced a new Criminal Procedure Code, promising greater justice and efficiency. This chapter argues, however, that justice itself may have been sacrificed in the search for, and the implementation of, increased efficiency measures in the new Criminal Procedure Code.

In this chapter, a critical examination on how the Criminal Procedure Code encourages the premature dismissal of corruption cases will be presented. The main hypothesis is that premature dismissals are the result of deficiencies in the public prosecutors' work, as pressures for increased efficiency were heightened under the new Criminal Procedure Code. In order to test this hypothesis, a total of 315 complaints related to embezzlement and collusion – two of the most commonly reported cases of corruption in Peru – were analyzed to ascertain the probability of erroneously dismissed cases. The results of this analysis demonstrate two important issues. First, one out of every three complaints should not have been dismissed in the name of efficiency. The numbers are alarming when considering that these cases deal with allegations of corruption among public officials. Second, premature dismissals are principally linked to the quality of the public prosecutors' work. Even though case complexity and the disconnect between the alleged acts and the type of crime specified in the formal charges also increase the possibility of a premature dismissal, the factors that most affect the likelihood of a premature dismissal are deficiencies in the public prosecutors' work.

This chapter will be organized in five parts. It will first discuss the new rules of the criminal procedure game, discussing criminal justice reform in Peru and how it led to heightened dismissals. Next, it will explore where the mistakes of public prosecutors occur by first discussing the characteristics of their work and institutional incentives to promote "efficiency." The third section will discuss the methodology used to make sense of the 315 cases reviewed, and the fourth section will discuss results. The final section will provide a few concluding remarks on the situation in Peru and how it relates to other nations in Latin America.

The new rules of the criminal procedure game

The fight against corruption in the Peruvian criminal justice system has had two major milestones in the 21st century. First was the creation of the anticorruption legal subsystem in 2000. The subsystem consisted of a new prosecutorial team and designated a specialized chamber to hear the most complex corruption cases. The formation of the anticorruption legal subsystem was politically motivated. It was created in response to the noticeable presence of corruption, particularly during the Fujimori[1] regime. The subsystem allowed for the provision of more resources and training for judges and criminal public prosecutors, who previously investigated cases from their nonspecialized criminal jurisdictional bodies. The subsystem gained notoriety with some emblematic cases, but at the same time, it suffered from the same problems as the judiciary. The large procedural burden quickly became a problem, along with the lack of personal and logistical support, and – paradoxically – insufficient training despite its formation as a specialized jurisdiction. These problems continue to this day.

The second milestone was the adoption of new procedural rules in the new Criminal Code of 2007. This reform was applied to the anticorruption legal subsystem. This new code replaced the old written and inquisitorial system with an oral and less bureaucratic one based on adversarial models. This reform was part of the most recent wave of criminal procedure reform in Latin America. Unlike procedural reforms from prior decades in which respect for the rights of the involved parties was prioritized, this latest wave focused on providing efficient justice (Langer, 2007). In Peru, the basis of the justification for criminal justice reform mirrored reasons given over decades in other countries in the region: higher standards of due process, increased transparency and less corruption, protection of human rights, and efficiency (Bergman & Langer, 2015; Ciocchini, 2017). However, Peru prioritized the latter factor above all in its reform process.

Under the previous system, almost all reported crimes had to go through each phase of criminal procedure – including resolution by a judge. The fact that this system was based on written documents generated incentives for delaying the case with unnecessary bureaucratic procedures, which, in turn, promoted illegal payments to avoid delays and to "speed up" the decision. With the new Criminal Procedure Code, the system changed in an important way. Orality was introduced, and with it, a series of changes occurred that reduced the quantity of audiences, eliminated unnecessary steps in the processes, thus reducing opportunities for bribery. At the same time that the functions of investigating and judging were separated, plea bargains were created, and the public prosecutor – not the police – was given a central role in overseeing the investigation of the crime. These changes, in addition to early dismissal of cases by the public prosecution, took place in the latest wave of reforms.

Under the objective of efficiency, it was thought that when fewer cases reach the judge, the system would work better. Therefore, a series of filters were created so that certain complaints would not reach the judge. This creates a funnel effect that incentivizes the presentation of solid cases that can progress through the criminal justice system and is thought to reduce the amount of work performed by judges, allowing them to dedicate more time to each case. Therefore, the idea behind the use of the early dismissal is to filter out those cases that have a low probability of garnering a conviction. In turn, this mechanism contributes to one of the three objective probabilities in reducing crime: that of increasing the likelihood of punishment (though it does not alter the probability of being detained and processed) (Robinson & Darley, 2004). However, as I will argue next, this funnel effect ultimately creates poor incentives and will lead to the premature dismissal of cases.

The new dismissal mechanism

Not all filters have the same weight (i.e., the risk of dismissal is not linear). The most relevant filter is the first one. The new Criminal Procedure Code gave public prosecutors the ability to dismiss cases early (during preliminary investigation) after a minor investigation has been carried out and without a judge needing to intervene in (and therefore be aware of) the case. This procedure is what I refer to as an early dismissal. Early dismissals were common in other criminal procedure reforms in Latin America and were developed in response to the notion that the justice system has limited resources, and only those legally relevant cases should advance through the system. In this regard, the reform and its funnel effect have been successful. The early dismissal became the most common form of closing cases in Peru and in other countries in the region. Official data demonstrate that 50% of complaints (for embezzlement and collusion) were dismissed by public prosecutors (Defensoría del Pueblo, 2014). This is higher than the 30% originally projected (Ministerio Público, 2005). The amount of dismissals has been taken as a positive sign in a new procedural system focused on judges and efficiency; however, a question remains as to of the cases that are in fact *premature* dismissals, were the facts of the cases examined critically? In a similar case, when 77% of cases were dismissed in El Salvador, the dismissal rate was met with concern (Riego, 2003). In Chile, the amount of dismissals reached 54% (Ministerio de Justicia, 2011, p. 99), which also provoked concern and calls for quality control measures for dismissals (Castillo, Tapia, & Urzúa, 2011).

Given the context of these reforms, it is important to examine if those cases dismissed without further investigation were due to the desired result of efficiency (i.e., the dismissal of cases with little legal relevance). These dismissals could be a result of mistakes in the system caused by poor work on the part of the public prosecutor or due to exacerbating institutional incentives and could in fact be premature. These incentives may have used efficiency as an end goal without regard for quality control over the decisions leading to the dismissal of cases.

Speedy dismissal and more prosecutorial discretion lead to mistakes

Under the recent changes in the Criminal Procedure Code, public prosecutors are granted a wide range of power and discretion (Luna, 2014). Ever since the reforms took place, public prosecutors decide what to investigate, under which procedures, and which evidence is used and discarded. Their expanded authority is particularly evident in the first stage of criminal justice procedure, which is the focus of this chapter. At this stage, the public prosecutor has broad powers and discretion in deciding whether cases proceed via further investigation or are dismissed. This first stage is especially important due to the lack of transparency and a little regulation in Peru (Defensoría del Pueblo, 2014), but also in Argentina (Duce, 2018), Colombia, and El Salvador (Langer, 2007). In the United States, the power and discretion of the public prosecutors is intensified by scenarios of little transparency and accountability (Sklansky, 2018), and inadequate sanctions of wrongful actions (Sullivan & Possley, 2016).

The lack of control over this power and discretion increases the probability of erroneous decisions, or, in the case examined in this chapter, prematurely dismissed cases. In this sense, power and discretion allow for the possibility of errors in the processing of complaints. This issue is not only relevant in terms of achieving fair decisions in individual cases but also on the influence those decisions may have on the politics and strategies of the whole criminal justice system (Sklansky, 2018). Incorrect decisions leading to the premature dismissal of cases may stem from the characteristics of the public prosecutors' work or from the institutional incentives that designated early dismissals (marginalizing their quality) as a sign of efficiency. Both characteristics are discussed in the following sections in more detail.

Public prosecutors and their multiple responsibilities

A premature dismissal may come from different sources, one of them being the prosecutors' use, or misuse, of expert testimony. As evidentiary material is central to an investigation, certain documents produced during this phase are of great importance. This is the case with expert reports. These technical documents lose reliability when they are based on subjective criteria or junk science, when they generate conclusions without an empirical basis, or when they are overvalued by judges (Duce, 2018). However, in the Chilean experience, these weaknesses are rarely mentioned in cases that involve more objective expert reports, such as those pertaining to financial crimes which are usually used in corruption cases (Duce, 2018). Another weakness relates to the quality of experts and fulfillment of their duties. A study of the dismissal of corruption cases by the public prosecution in Peru (Defensoría del Pueblo, 2014) demonstrated that specialization, availability, delays in delivering reports, and the use of technical language that is not adapted to judicial language and thinking are problems with expert testimony in Peru.

Beyond reliance on expert testimony, the prosecutor's investigation itself may lead to premature dismissals. Errors in the investigation process can be considered involuntary so long as they are not related to the desire to dismiss a case. Rather, they are indicative of a lack of competence in investigating and/or extracting sufficient information from the evidence to demonstrate that a crime has occurred. Apart from their origin, this lack of capacity makes it difficult for prosecutors to identify evidence in and of itself that would allow an investigation to proceed. The policies of the specialized bodies that train judges and public prosecutors are also part of the measures used in the legal systems in Latin America (Pásara, 2004). The training of public prosecutors was a central factor in the implementation of criminal justice reform in the region. However, there is little evidence regarding how effective these trainings were. Many studies suggest they were insufficient when faced with the general needs for training and the abilities of public prosecutors to work within the new model. A study by the Office of the Ombudsman (2014) revealed that the initial investigations of cases that were later dismissed were superficial and left certain evidence uninvestigated. They also found that public prosecutors had difficulties in establishing the functional relationship correctly (association between the accused, their role as a public official, and their responsibility in the crime).

Lastly, errors coming from the public prosecutors' work may not always be explicitly manifested. Implicit bias may also play a role in erroneously dismissed cases. This type of bias subconsciously attributes stereotypes to certain groups. In the United States, many studies demonstrate that African Americans, when compared to Caucasian Americans, are charged more often, offered less favorable plea bargains, and are characterized negatively in prosecutors' reports (Tucker, 2018). An experimental study in the United States also found that judges are more prejudiced against Asians and Jews than against Caucasians, given that the latter typically receive lighter sentences (Levinson, Bennett, & Hioki, 2017). The literature on implicit bias in the public prosecution's work is limited and has only focused on race. There are no studies that examine implicit bias in areas related to corruption. However, one could argue that corruption can trigger bias in public prosecutors when complaints are lodged by ordinary citizens or by the media. Nonexperts may see signs of corruption or irregularity where none exists, leading public prosecutors to implicitly undervalue and dismiss these complaints. On the other hand, public prosecutors may be less likely to dismiss cases brought by the media given the possibility of a publicity scandal.

Institutional incentives

Criminal convictions are not only the result of individual action but also a social product (Martin, 2004). This construction is conditioned by institutional and cultural pressures that mold individual conduct (Findley & Scott, 2006). Therefore, there is no reason why a premature dismissal could not also be conditioned by institutional pressures to pursue speedier justice, at the expense of its quality. In many judicial systems, the use of financial incentives is nothing new. During the judicial reform period of the 1990s in Peru, judges who sentenced more were given financial incentives, allowing for an increase in productivity by 252% (Hammergren, 2004). However, we do not know if this increased efficiency sacrificed the quality of judicial decisions. The emphasis on efficiency that was brought about via the new Criminal Procedure Codes created the expectation of quicker processes, and along with them unforeseen incentives regarding the idea of dismissing a case. This type of context was exacerbated due to the installation of quantitative management goals (Castillo, Tapia, & Urzúa, 2011), which in Peru measured and rewarded prosecutors without distinguishing between dismissals (easy to produce) or a more difficult case which could reach an oral hearing (Defensoría del Pueblo, 2014).

Institutional pressures, however, may also come from different origins, while it enhances individual work rather than coordinated work. The system and its incentives act not only through presence but also through omission. The lack of effective controls over actors' interventions (decisions and sentences) represents a large incentive for corrupt practices, but also for other incentives that reduce the quality of the public prosecutions' work. Public prosecutors not only follow general rules that do not create the need to coordinate their criteria but also work in a hierarchical work culture that weakens general coordination (Hernández, 2017). It is no surprise that there are no regulations, guides, or quality controls for the use of early dismissals, which in Chile have been associated with wrongful convictions (Duce, 2018). All the responsibility for correcting any errors on behalf of the public prosecution was left in the hands of the litigating parties. Even worse, this possibility is diminished, as according to criminal code, once a case is dismissed, it can only be reopened if new evidence is presented.

Ultimately, cases may be dismissed for reasons unrelated to institutional incentives, prosecutorial deficiencies, or desires for efficiency. A complaint regarding an actual crime may be dismissed when certain problems with the complaint (clarity, identifiable acts, identification of the crime, and with evidence) or with the case in itself (complex or voluminous) are present. However, none of these characteristics should determine a premature dismissal if the public prosecutor dedicates enough time to finding a relationship between the alleged acts and the commission of a crime. In other words, premature dismissals can be avoided with quality investigative action on the part of the prosecutor, despite the characteristics of the case or complaint itself. Thus, this chapter aims to examine if and how often cases are prematurely dismissed. The next section will discuss the methodology used to explore this important question.

Methodology

Peru is divided into 25 governmental regions and 30 judicial jurisdictions. The cases in this study come from four judicial districts (Lima, Ayacucho, Junín, and Ancash). In order to disentangle the causes of these prematurely dismissed cases, a database of 315 premature dismissals from 2012 and 2013 was constructed. This database consists of complaints and the respective prosecutors' investigations in the anticorruption legal subsystem of the Peruvian criminal justice system. Random and representative samples for each judicial district and each crime in this study were used. Fieldwork took place between January and March of 2013. The cases were selected randomly from the central archives of the Public Prosecutor's Office. Cases of embezzlement and/or collusion were selected, as they were the most common in the anticorruption subsystem.[2]

Variables

The evaluation of the public prosecutor's work – as a way to identify the factors that were associated with the premature dismissal of a case – should not focus entirely on the work of the public prosecutors. As previously mentioned, certain characteristics of the case or the crime report may impact whether the case was properly dismissed. Therefore, an adequate evaluation of these cases consists of considering both the characteristics of the case and the work of the public prosecution.

Incorrect dismissals (dependent variable)

Our principal variable of interest is the description of each decision to dismiss as correct or incorrect (the variable takes a value of 0 in the former and 1 in the latter). This decision was made after having scored each of the independent variables. Three criteria were used in labeling a dismissal as incorrect: 1) clear and directly established evidence in the complaint or report, 2) mistakes in the construction of the prosecution's argument (regarding alleged acts and the type of charges), and 3) legal relevance of the complaint.

Characteristics of the public prosecutor's decision to dismiss the case (independent variables)

Four variables were created for this purpose:

1 Order, clarity, and completeness in the narration of the alleged crimes
2 Completion of the evidence list – both evidence that is present and absent
3 Coherence in the information extracted from evidence
4 Clarity in the determination of the causes of the dismissal

While the first aspect relates to the way in which the public prosecutor understands the reported crimes, the three following aspects evaluate the quality of the investigation. Each of the criteria was scored ranging from 1 to 5. A coding guide was developed in order to have homogenous criteria while analyzing each case. Examples of this scale are "the dismissal decision mentions all the documents received by the parties and presents conclusions for each of them separately" (score 3 on coherence in the information extracted from evidence scale); "the dismissal decision clearly indicates the reasons for dismissing the case but does not explain them properly or the explanation is unclear" (score 2 on clarity in the determination of the causes of the dismissal scale). Lower scores correspond to lower quality in the prosecution's work. Factor analysis was implemented to assess the reliability of the used measures. Cronbach's Alpha was satisfactory (0.85) and loadings were higher than 0.69 (being 0.30 the minimum acceptable standard), suggesting an important correlation toward measuring a unique latent construct related to the decision guiding an erroneously dismissed case. In other words, our items of erroneous dismissals measure well what it was meant to as they are internally consistent.

Characteristics of the crime report (complaint)

A very similar list of four variables was used to evaluate these characteristics:

1 Lack of order and clarity in the narration of the alleged acts
2 Few details of the alleged acts
3 Disconnect between the alleged acts and the charge
4 Little evidence of the alleged crime

They were rated with a coding guide and scores ranging from 1 to 5. Cronbach's Alpha was also important (0.81). Loadings on each factor were high (>0.62), which suggests that measures tap aspects of the same latent construct.

Characteristics of the case (independent variables)

Four aspects case were examined. A dichotomous variable was used to identify the cases that were described as complex (1 for complex cases and 0 for the remainder). The complexity of a case is a designation that the public prosecutor makes based on criteria that are subjective more than anything, but also related to the quantity of attributed crimes and number of people investigated. The denoting of case complexity allows for the prosecutor to take more time to investigate the complaint. Additionally, another dichotomous variable was used to indicate whether (1) or not (0) the complaint had expert reports. These reports are carried out by qualified experts in the subject area. Normally, they are reports that are a result of previous administrative requests or investigations. In theory, a case with an expert report has a greater ability to identify evidence of a crime, and therefore, a lower probability of being prematurely dismissed. The number of pages of the entire file was also included (including the complaint and its appendices, prosecution reports, and general writings). A thicker file could coincide with a diminished ability to find adequate proof, delay the work of the public prosecution, and, in general, make good prosecution work more difficult. Finally, a variable to identify the judicial district of each file was included.

Procedure

Each case was coded by a group of five lawyers. The group was trained to score each case based on the guides described in the earlier section. A pilot study was carried out in which the first version of the datasheet was tested. Each member of the research team participated. Several team meetings were held to improve the quality of the datasheet used to catalogue the data and refine the criteria set to identify erroneously dismissed cases. The fieldwork lasted approximately ten weeks. Each case was assigned and reviewed by one lawyer.

No matter how much effort was put into identifying an erroneous case, certainty about this decision can be controversial. Quality control checks were, therefore, necessary. These quality control checks were implemented when it was not clear whether the case was (or not) a correct decision taken by the prosecutor. First, the case was discussed between the research leader and the lawyer who reviewed the case. Second, more complex cases were discussed with the whole fieldwork group, the research leader, and, on occasion, experienced criminal justice lawyers. The difficult cases whose examination created useful guidelines for those remaining were shared in the group examining the sample. Sometimes these new guidelines forced us to re-examine cases that had already been evaluated. Third, when there was no agreement on whether a case was correctly or incorrectly dismissed, the case was discarded. Only 10% of the cases were not included in the final sample. Though this loss might be a more delicate matter for studies with a smaller N, fortunately, this was not the case for our sample. Furthermore, forcing these cases to remain in the analysis would have introduced unwanted bias and affected the consistency of our estimators. If quality control checks were to be successful, correct and erroneous dismissals would be (statistically) different from doubtful dismissals (those removed from our sample) on the four characteristics of prosecutors' work. This was achieved in the comparison between correct and doubtful dismissals (1% confidence level) and in the comparison between erroneous and doubtful dismissals (in which only one difference was significant at 13% confidence level).

Analytic strategy

Due to the dichotomous nature of our variable of interest, linear regression models are inappropriate. In their place, logistic regression was employed. This model allows for the identification of the probability that a case was prematurely dismissed in function of the variation of each of the variables included in the model. To identify the goodness of fit of the model, Bayesian and Akaike Information Criterion were used. There was no presence of collinearity between variables, nor the need to use robust standard errors due to correlation in observations between judicial districts.

Results

Results are presented in Table 10.1 Each column represents an independent estimate of the subsamples of embezzlement, collusion, and cases in which both crimes allegedly occurred. The predictors of a premature dismissal are grouped as a function of their source of origin (public prosecutor, complaint, case).

In general, the results support our hypotheses: incorrectly dismissed cases are due to individual or systemic incentives fostered by the efficiency impetus which could be mitigated given regulatory and additional training measures for public prosecutors. The factors that increase the probability that a case is prematurely dismissed are strongly linked to the characteristics of the resolution that determined the dismissal (and the previous work), and only partially associated with deficiencies in the complaints or the characteristics of the case. The goodness of fit statistics present additional useful information as a relevant amount of variance is explained in every model (McFadden's $R2 > 0.38$).

Among the factors of the public prosecutors' work that lead to a premature dismissal, the most frequent across all three models was the lack of clarity in the arguments used to dismiss the case. Given our results, they allow us to connect the prematurely dismissed cases with problems in the formation and investigation by the public prosecution at the moment of investigating and ruling on each individual case.

Also, the results demonstrate that the (statistically significant) factors leading to an incorrectly dismissed case are similar across the crimes examined in this study. This suggests that the error in dismissing a case shares some cross-cutting characteristics that are not related to the type of crime investigated, but rather to the public prosecutor (and likely their investigative capacity) and not whether the crime reported is embezzlement, collusion, or a combination of the two. For example, complaints related to embezzlement and collusion share two

Table 10.1 Probability that a case is prematurely dismissed (odds ratios)

	Embezzlement	*Collusion*	*Embezzlement and Collusion*
Characteristics of the ruling (decision to dismiss):			
Lack of order and clarity in the narration of the alleged acts	0.337**	0.826	0.394
Not all evidence is mentioned or related to the type of charge	2.905***	4.327	13.94**
Lack of coherence in the information taken from evidence	2.238**	17.14***	1.614
Unclear argumentation in favor of dismissal	3.487***	6.261**	13.70**
Characteristics of the crime report (complaint):			
Lack of order and clarity in the narration of the alleged acts	1.180	0.236	1.384
Few details of the alleged acts	0.946	0.411	1.819
Disconnect between the alleged acts and the charge	0.566	11.32***	0.253
Little evidence of the alleged crime	0.860	0.620	0.685
Case characteristics:			
Expert reports	1.009	0.551	0.0111**
Case was deemed to be complex	0.972	5.703**	0.268
# of pages in the case	0.999	1.001*	1.001
Judicial district	1.271	0.709	0.699
Number of observations	156	80	79
AIC	138.3	75.04	59.78
BIC	177.9	106.0	90.58
McFadden's R2	0.389	0.489	0.667

*p < 0.1
**p < 0.05
***p < 0.01

deficiencies in the work of the public prosecution as factors that significantly affected the probability of being dismissed: incoherence in the information extracted from the evidence and lack of clarity in the argumentation supporting the dismissal. At the same time, prematurely dismissed cases of collusion and embezzlement and collusion combined share the latter factor, as well as that of not mentioning all the evidence or their relation to the type of charge.

Given the ease in interpreting similarities in the factors that contribute to a premature dismissal by type of crime, the differences in these factors also allow for direct interpretation. For example, allegations of embezzlement are much more likely to be dismissed prematurely. All factors relating to the public prosecution's work have a significant impact on the decision to dismiss. On the other hand, the dismissal of cases of collusion are only influenced by two factors. These differences suggest that premature dismissals are partially related to the characteristics and implications of the type of crime investigated. Collusion is a crime that is, by nature, difficult to detect. Therefore, it is no surprise that a failure to mention evidence or the relation of said evidence to the type of charge are not significant. In these cases, prematurely dismissing the case is more critically related to the existence of incoherence in the information taken from evidence. In other words, the public prosecutor did not know how to find enough information in the evidence for the investigation to continue, rather than be dismissed.

Existing literature attributes a certain responsibility in the mistakes of the public prosecution to experts and their expert report. When strictly examining cases of corruption, these results refute this hypothesis. The uniqueness of the results lies in the fact that the expert reports for this type of crime are based on documentary evidence, and are, for the most part, more objective. The existence of an expert report reduces the probability of dismissal in a significant manner only in cases involving both embezzlement and collusion.

This study also finds that it is difficult for some characteristics separate from the work of the prosecution to influence a premature dismissal. The thickness of the case file (number of pages) could be associated with a more difficult case to investigate. However, this variable was only significant, and with a much smaller effect size, for allegations of collusion. On the other hand, the complexity of the case did have a significant effect, but only for premature dismissals of collusion. This finding suggests that the prosecution could "lose control" over some cases due to the multiplicity of pieces that the allegation entails, the diversity of documents and evidence presented, and the difficulty of proving an agreement to collude (which generally does not leave a document trail). The best explanation of these results may be via the lens of implicit biases. Some public prosecutors may dismiss complicated cases of collusion that they suspect that, despite the evidence, may be very difficult to win, or would take too much time given the pressures of efficiency under which they work.

Finally, in the models that examine embezzlement and cases that involve allegations of both embezzlement and collusion, none of the characteristics of the complaint influenced premature dismissals. In the model regarding collusion, only the disconnect between the alleged crime and the charges were significant. This is likely because these cases require more work from the prosecutor in the examination of the alleged acts and need further investigation. In any case, these results demonstrate that the incorrect dismissal of cases should be of institutional concern, particularly in order to improve the ability of public prosecutors to do their jobs, as well as identifying the institutional incentives that may diminish the quality of their work.

Conclusion: implications for Peru and Beyond

This study examined the factors that heighten the risk of premature dismissals of cases regarding criminal allegations of corruption. Three types of allegations were investigated (embezzlement, collusion, and the presence of both crimes) using a representative sample of cases in Peru, a country with high and historical levels of corruption, and which underwent the latest wave of criminal justice reform in the region. This reform prioritized efficiency over other factors in the ensuring of high-quality work among judges and public prosecutors. The results demonstrate that the majority of factors that increase the risk of a premature dismissal are direct results of the public prosecutors' work. The main reason for dismissals across the three types of crimes was the lack of clarity in the arguments used to dismiss the case. This demonstrates critical failures in the prosecutor's reasoning behind their decisions. Other characteristics, such as those relating to the complaint or the case itself, had little explanatory power. The results of this study provide support for this chapter's central working hypothesis: incorrectly dismissed cases are due to individual or systemic incentives fostered by the efficiency impetus which could be mitigated given regulatory and training measures for public prosecutors.

While the case of Peru indicates that adopting efficiency measures in criminal justice reforms can actually erode justice itself, this situation is not in isolation and can be seen throughout much of Latin America. For instance, early dismissals are acts that created similar incentives such as those related to plea bargaining in Argentina. There, actors were not trained to deal with this stage of the criminal justice process, nor did they anticipate how pleas were to be negotiated, opening the door to inappropriate use of sentencing negotiation (Ciocchini, 2017). Future reform processes or measures that aim to create filters that determine which cases advance through the criminal justice system should also focus on the quality control measures surrounding these decisions. More transparency is needed, but transparency alone may not be enough. In many Latin American legal systems, public prosecution dismissals are provisional, as they can be reopened. However, given that the conditions for reopening a case are very restrictive (the presentation of new evidence), the cost of doing so is very high. This is particularly damaging with respect to the reporting crimes of corruption among public officials, which very rarely leave documentary evidence.

Furthermore, results demonstrate that public prosecutors do make mistakes and that the pressures that encourage these mistakes should be monitored in order to prevent them from undermining the quality of prosecutorial work and promote impunity – particularly in the very important case of corruption. Dismissals should promote preventive and proactive actions for the mitigation of the underlying causes of the dismissed cases (Blanco, 2010). In Chile, the problem was initially addressed with normative regulations regarding when cases were to be dismissed, but these were only later complemented with instructions on how to arrange for a dismissal (Castillo, Tapia, & Urzúa, 2011). The objective of these regulations included an early warning for certain cases that would not be able to be investigated, and the dismissal of the case was communicated not in writing but by telephone to the person who reported the crime.

According Castillo, Tapia, and Urzúa (2011) this brought about higher rates of satisfaction among those who reported crimes.

Ultimately, there is no clear answer regarding what the correct percentage of dismissals should be. At least in Chile, where concern for the high level of prosecutorial dismissals went hand in hand with limitations placed on their use, dismissals have persisted at high rates (Duce, 2018). On the one hand, this supports the notion of prosecutorial dismissal as an adequate filter (assuming that the number of premature dismissals has been controlled for) and suggests that the majority of crimes reported should not be investigated due to the difficulty in finding supportive evidence (Blanco, 2010). On the other hand, this also suggests that many crimes could, by nature, leave little trace and documentary evidence, such as the crime of collusion.

Our results are important for criminal justice reforms in Latin America as well as for similar process in other regions that look forward to implementing measures that would change the structure of prosecutors' or even judges' discretional powers. As erroneous dismissals are inevitable, three policy implications must be considered. First, the introduction or redistribution of discretional powers directly creates new incentives that can erode the initial goals of these changes. Human behavior is difficult to anticipate, but at the same time, it offers a narrow range of possible outcomes (in our case erroneous dismissals). Second, efforts to increase efficiency and quality can create an opposite outcome. This highlights the importance of measuring reforms not only by indicators that take into account the length of proceedings but also the need of measuring the quality of the said outcomes (e.g., prosecutors' as well as judges' decisions). Finally, both implications make sense only if they are constantly monitored through time as decision makers need evidence as feedback to improve ongoing public policies. These policy implications suggest that rule of law must be sustained not only on macro-level orientations but also on how criminal justice actors (prosecutors, judges, etc.) implement it or change it in day-to-day justice.

Lastly, it is important to note that this study is not without its limitations. In evaluating the decisions of the public prosecutors, this study did not attempt to reconstruct their work, but rather evaluate it under certain conditions and with a particular objective in mind. Though several rules were created in this study in order to properly identify erroneously dismissed cases, the results could contain at least two types of bias. First, I assume that public prosecutors dedicated more time per dismissed case than our team. This could have increased our odds of finding false positives (identifying cases that were dismissed correctly as erroneously dismissals) and may affect the reliability of the results. Second, corruption cases could have been dismissed not due to an erroneously traceable decision but by external variables (defendants' lawyer prestige, corruption, etc.). While this also could affect the reliability of our results, these cases may involve a minor proportion of those analyzed. Additionally, the set of items used to evaluate the complaints and the decisions to dismiss them are not comprehensive. More items could have been introduced, though I suspect that their capacity of explaining additional variance would be very limited. Finally, the predictors of erroneously dismissed cases could be criticized because of the subjectivity they imply. Fortunately, support for our selection of measures exists as consistency (Cronbach's Alpha) was shown to be satisfactory. Notwithstanding these limitations, the data and scope of this research is novel and important, especially in a region struggling to reform its criminal procedures to promote efficiency, all the while battling the negative consequences of corruption. As this chapter has demonstrated, the effects of emphasizing efficiency in Criminal Procedure Codes has important ramifications in Peru and the rest of Latin America.

Notes

1 Alberto Fujimori was president of Peru from 1990 to 2000. He escaped to Japan and was in self-exile to avoid prosecution for charges involving corruption and human rights violations. Fujimori was extradited to Peru in 2007 to face criminal charges.

2 The Peruvian Legal Code defines these crimes as follows:

> Embezzlement (Article 387) "The official or public servant who appropriates or uses, in any way, for themselves or for a third party, any public goods or funds with which they are entrusted in matters of payment, handling, or safekeeping, shall be incarcerated for a period of no less than two nor more than eight years."
>
> Collusion (Article 384): "The official or public servant who, intervening directly or indirectly, given their position, in any stage of the acquisition or hiring of public goods, works, or services, concessions or any operation on behalf of the State conspires with an interested party to defraud the State or any State entity or organism, according to the law, shall be incarcerated for no less than three, nor more than six years."

References

Bergman, M., & Langer, M. (2015). *El proyecto de Código Procesal Penal Nacional Acusatorio: aportes empíricos para la discusión en base a la experiencia en Provincia de Buenos Aires* (Documento de Trabajo CELIV-UNTREF). Buenos Aires: UNTREF.

Blanco, J. (2010). "Aportes desde la sociedad civil al proceso de cambio en el sistema de enjuiciamiento criminal chileno". In Ministerio de Justicia (Ed.), *A 10 años de la reforma procesal penal: Los desafíos del nuevo sistema*. Santiago de Chile: Ministerio de Justicia, pp. 161–189.

Castillo, I., Tapia, M., & Urzúa, M. (2011). *Estudio sobre la aplicación de los archivos provisionales. Informe final*. Santiago de Chile: Universidad Andrés Bello.

Ciocchini, P. (2017). Reformers' Unfulfilled Promises: Accountability Deficits in Argentinean Criminal Courts. *International Journal of Law in Context*, 14 (1), pp. 22–42. https://doi.org/10.1017/S1744552317000593

Datum. (2014). *Encuesta de opinión pública en Lima Metropolitana*. Lima: Datum, August.

Defensoría del Pueblo. (2014). *El archivo fiscal de denuncias por Peculado y Colusión. Estudio realizado en distritos fi scales de Lima, Áncash, Ayacucho y Junín*. Lima: Defensoría del Pueblo.

De la Jara, E., Del Mastro, F., Mujica, V., & Ramírez, G. (2008). *La aplicación del Nuevo Código Procesal Penal en Huaura. Una experiencia positiva*. Lima: Instituto de Defensa Legal.

Duce, M. (2018). Una aproximación empírica al uso y prácticas de la prueba pericial en el proceso penal Chileno a la luz de su impacto en los errores del sistema. *Política Criminal*, 13 (25), pp. 42–103.

Findley, K. A., & Scott, M. S. (2006). The Multiple Dimensions of Tunnel Visions in Criminal Cases. *Legal Studies Research Paper Series*, 24 (1023).

Hammergren, L. (2004). "La experiencia peruana en reforma judicial: tres décadas de grandes cambios con pocas mejoras." In L. Pásara (Ed.), *En busca de una justicia distinta. Experiencias de reforma en américa latina*. Lima: Justivia Viva, pp. 289–333.

Hernández, W. (2017). Gerencialismo en un ambiente de regulaciones débiles y cultura fuerte: El caso de las Fiscalías Corporativas en Perú. *Derecho y Ciencias Sociales*, 17, pp. 145–163.

Langer, M. (2007) Revolution in Latin American Criminal Procedure: Diffusion of Legal Ideas from the Periphery. *American Journal of Comparative Law*, 55, pp. 617–676.

Levinson, J. D., Bennett, M., & Hioki, K. (2017). Judging Implicit Bias: A National Empirical Study of Judicial Stereotypes. *Florida Law Review*, 69 (1), pp. 63–52.

Luna, E. (2014). Prosecutor King. *Stanford Journal of Criminal Law and Policy*, 1 (48), pp. 48–103.

Martin, D. (2004). Lessons about Justice from the "Laboratory" of Wrongful Convictions: Tunnel Vision, the Construction of Guilt and Informer Evidence. *The Canadian Review of Policing Research*, 1, pp. 847–864. https://doi.org/10.3868/s050-004-015-0003-8

Ministerio de Justicia. (2011). *Informe Estadístico Nacional 2006–2010. Reforma Procesal Penal. Hacia una Justicia Rápida y Transparente*. Lima: Ministerio de Justicia.

Ministerio Público. (2005). *Propuesta del Ministerio Público para la Implementación del Nuevo Código Procesal Penal*. Lima: Ministerio Público.

Office of the Ombudsman (2014) El archivo fiscal de denuncias por Peculado y Colusión. Estudio realizado en distritos fiscales de Lima, Áncash, Ayacucho y Junín. Lima.

Pásara, L. (2004). *Reformas del sistema de justicia en América Latina: cuenta y balance*. México DF. Retrieved from: http://www2.congreso.gob.pe/sicr/cendocbib/con3_uibd.nsf/8A4D533AA4DB5A48052578C7005BBF07/$FILE/U9Pásaracuentabalance.pdf

Proética. (2017). *Encuesta Nacional sobre Percepciones de la Corrupción en el Perú*. Lima: Proética, 2016.

Quiroz, A. (2013). *Historia de la corrupción en el Perú*. Lima: Instituto de Estudios Peruanos.

Riego, C. (2003). Seguimiento de los procesos de reforma judicial en América Latina. *Sistemas Judiciales*, pp. 34–76.

Robinson, P., & Darley, J. (2004). Does Criminal Law Deter: A Behavioural Science Investigation. *Oxford Journal of Legal Studies*, 24 (2), pp. 173–205.

Sklansky, D. A. (2018). The Problems with Prosecutors. *Annual Review of Criminology*, (1), pp. 451–469.

Sullivan, T., & Possley, M. (2016). The Chronic Failure to Discipline Prosecutors for Misconduct: Proposals for Reform. *The Journal of Criminal Law & Criminology*, 105, pp. 881–946.

Tucker, D. (2018). Modern Hegemony: Implicit Bias, Media, and the Criminal Justice System. *Tennessee Journal of Race, Gender, & Social Justice*, 7 (1), pp. 125–160.

Chapter 11

Sexual crimes and transitional justice before courts in Brazil

Accountability for crimes against humanity

Emilio Peluso Neder Meyer and Claudia Paiva Carvalho

Introduction

This chapter aims to analyze the long delay of transitional justice in Brazil in responding to sexual crimes committed during the dictatorship of 1964–1985 and the lack of criminal liability. The research is focused on a criminal case study related to the political opponent, Inês Etienne Romeu. The research is based on a document analysis methodology that examines the main legal arguments of the case, particularly the criminal complaint and the federal court decision. The analysis takes into account the category of crimes against humanity and its nonrecognition by the Brazilian judiciary as well as the debate on sexual crimes and the incorporation of a gender perspective to transitional justice, aiming at showing the difficulties of this debate in Brazil. The text seeks to answer two main questions: why it took so long for state authorities to account for sexual crimes committed during the dictatorship and what the barriers to prosecution and punishment are.

In December 2016, the Federal Public Prosecutor's Office filed a criminal complaint against the individual accused of torturing and raping Inês Etienne Romeu while she was being held in a detention and disappearance center known as "House of Death" ("Casa da Morte"). It was the first attempt in addressing criminal accountability for sexual crimes committed during the dictatorship. The Brazilian judiciary rejected the complaint, and the decision was appealed by the Federal Public Prosecutor's Office.

The analysis of the Inês Etienne Romeu case illuminates relevant aspects of transitional justice in Brazil, particularly concerning criminal accountability. Brazilian judges and courts have refused to adequately address and to allow for prosecution of the dictatorship's crimes as crimes against humanity. This refusal reflects a precarious application of concepts and categories of international law, but also a political and ideological position. Our hypothesis is that the difficulties are even greater when it comes to sexual crimes, which must also be prosecuted as crimes against humanity.

In Brazil, until 2009, the Criminal Code of 1940 considered sexual crimes as "crimes against the customs," which revealed a protection of the society's morality and not the victims' integrity. Through the Criminal Code, law played the role of reinforcing the gender inequalities when authorities dealt with sexual crimes. These were most of the time considered crimes that belonged to the private sphere, offending patriarchal honor instead of women's dignity. When those crimes were committed under authoritarian rule, this situation was aggravated even further.

Brazil faced a civilian-military dictatorship from 1964 to 1985 – the most enduring authoritarian regime in the region in the second half of the 20th century. As we shall see, this dictatorship relied upon an authoritarian legality conception that tried to legitimize the government through an appearance of institutional normality. The relationship between the dictatorship and the justice system was a mixture of repression and cooptation. The regime dismissed judges, suspended judicial guarantees, changed jurisdiction rules, and used court-packing techniques. But the justice system also collaborated with the goals of political repression, as the courts tried political opponents and covered up violations committed by the state. Although the Brazilian Constitution of 1988 gave prominence to judicial activity, it only did so insofar as individual prerogatives were expanded without any purge or broader institutional reforms. No accountability device was brought into existence and only in 2004 did the creation of the National Council of Justice allow for slight internal control.

The chapter intends to a) discuss the process of incorporating sexual and gender-based violence into the transitional justice agenda and how it had the effect of reshaping the field –it implies not only a change of theoretical stance but also a reform of law and institutions, especially the judicial system; b) consider the position of the Brazilian judiciary during the dictatorship and after the political transition, particularly regarding the human rights violations committed under the authoritarian rule, and confront the national jurisprudence vis-à-vis the obligations set by international law, especially in convictions suffered by Brazil; c) examine the Inês Etienne Romeu case, considering its circumstances, the delay in filing the complaint, and the strategies and legal arguments of the Federal Public Prosecutors' Office; and d) critically analyze the federal judge's decision that rejected the complaint in the Inês Etienne Romeu case and demonstrate the conservative positions and gender biases behind the legal barriers.

Sexual crimes and transitional justice: reshaping a field

Critical approaches to transitional justice have demonstrated how the field was originally tied to a liberal conception of democracy. During the transitions, the main goal was to reestablish the political normality and the rule of law. The efforts to address human rights violations committed during the dictatorships and armed conflicts were focused on criminal proceedings and truth commissions. In general, those accountability mechanisms offered individual responses to individual violations. Structural aspects and consequences of the violations were not considered (Nagy 2008, p. 276). And the violations were narrowed to a small group, with emphasis on executions and enforced disappearances. This prevailing view neglects the specificities of gender violence, as Nagy argues,

> Until very recently women and gender have been glaringly absent from transitional justice programmes. Masculinist determinations of the transitional problem have centered on political violence with (. . .) an emphasis on 'extraordinary' violations of civil and political rights. This construction disregards and treats as 'ordinary' the private or intimate violence that women experience in a militarised, unequal society.
>
> (Nagy 2008, pp. 285–286)

The idea that victims as a whole – that is, regardless of any specificity – would have suffered *generic* and *homogeneous* violations reflects power relations and gender hierarchies. As a consequence, the differences and specificities of the violence practiced against bodies sexed as masculine or feminine were not considered. Sexual violence was not treated as a violation as serious as torture or as the assassination of political opponents. The gender deficit in transitional policies has failed to consider gender as "one of the most significant determining factors in one's experience of conflict" (O'Rourke 2012, p. 44). Forms of violence against women specifically involve state agents as perpetrators and the contexts of deprivation of liberty[1] and of armed conflict are factors that increase the victims' vulnerability.[2]

Until recently, in many countries, rape was classified as a crime against the (male) honor and as a private violation (Balardini et al. 2011, pp. 181–182) so it could not constitute a political crime. It did not belong to the public sphere and to the public confrontation. This understanding reinforced the shame and embarrassment of the victims in reporting what they have endured.

This scenario began to change in the 1990s with the advancement of gender studies in Brazil and of international law rulings on sexual violence. On the one hand, gender studies have offered a powerful tool to interrogate the dominant paradigm of transitional justice. It has shown that when the experience of women is taken into account, it is frequently narrowed to some kinds of sexual violence, and it is still seen through an individual lens. On the other hand, the International Criminal Tribunal for Rwanda (ICTR) and International Criminal Tribunal for the former Yugoslavia (ICTY) have played an important role in recognizing sexual violence and rape as crimes against humanity. In the context of the armed conflicts in those countries, rape was used as a war weapon and constituted a form of torture and an instrument of genocide. The ICTR and the ICTY were important in changing the previous landscape of impunity and in advancing the debate in a transitional justice context.[3] The ICTR and ICTY case law also influenced the development of international criminal law. The 1998 Rome Statute, which created the International Criminal Court (ICC), adopted a broad concept of sexual violence that may amount to war crimes, genocide, and crimes against humanity. Another significant change was the inclusion of gender-based persecution as a crime against humanity.

In the mid-1990s, the topic of sexual violence also gained prominence in the Inter-American Human Rights System. Especially after the adoption of the Convention of Belém do Pará in 1994, the Inter-American Commission on Human Rights (IACHR), and the Inter-American Court of Human Rights (IACtHR) were called upon to decide cases of sexual offenses. Important decisions have incorporated a gender perspective that examines sexual violence within the contexts of structural discrimination against women. Another aspect strongly developed in the decisions refers to the obligation of the state to act with due diligence in investigating cases and guaranteeing access to justice for victims.

Sexual crimes, whether committed in times of repression or not, have a number of specificities. One is that the only available evidence, as a rule, is the victim's testimony, since the crimes are committed clandestinely and are not witnessed by others. When it comes to crimes committed decades ago, it is also not possible to perform physical examinations to prove sexual assault. The context of the crimes during periods of dictatorship makes it even harder to obtain evidence, as described by Balardini and others (2011, pp. 203–204). Another peculiarity of the cases of sexual violence is the difficulty that the victims face in reporting the violations. Fear, shame, and embarrassment are common feelings among victims of sexual crimes. The obstacles are aggravated by the victims' distrust of the justice system and the fear of new violence when they give their testimony. As a result, in addition to the material and practical difficulties in proving the violations, discriminatory factors also influence the appreciation of evidence of sexual crimes. Along with the lack of preparation to assist and hear the victims of sexual violence, the personnel often cast doubt on the reports and try to blame victims for the harm they have suffered. Keeping silent is, overall, a matter of safety and a measure to prevent further violence. The delay in reporting the violations indicates the failures of the justice system, not any loss of the testimony's credibility.

In response to this scenario, specific rules of procedure and evidence in cases of sexual crimes were developed. ICTY and ICTR set important standards to increase sensitivity in the handling of evidence and testimony of sexual offenses. These standards have been reinforced by the Rome Statute and by the jurisprudence and reports of the Inter-American Human Rights System. Such rules of international law establish that the sexual history of the victim cannot be taken into account; absence of consent may be presumed or inferred from the coercive context in which sexual violence had taken place; any inaccuracies or gaps in the reports do not undermine the credibility of the testimony but represent effects of the psychological trauma itself caused by the violation. In the Inter-American Human Rights System, a fundamental concern has been to guarantee access to justice for victims of sexual crimes, which is considered the first line of defense for the human rights of women victims of sexual violence (IACHR 2007, 2011).[4] A victim's testimony is especially valuable for the regional court based on a simple assumption: sexual violence is usually committed in a circumstance that only involves the perpetrator and the victim.

These changes had an impact on domestic law and legal practice. Countries in the southern cone of Latin America that for decades had kept silent about the sexual violence committed during the dictatorships between the 1960s and 1980s began to address the issue. Truth commissions and criminal cases have come to investigate and punish sexual violence as a serious violation of human rights. In Brazil, the first transitional mechanism to name sexual and gender-based violence was the National Truth Commission (NTC). The NTC created a working group that was dedicated to address such violations and to disclose its findings on a specific chapter of the final report, released in December 2014. The final report concluded that the rapes were committed systematically, involving a widespread practice of sexual violence. As a rule, female prisoners were stripped naked, devices were inserted into their anuses or vaginas, genitals were clipped, and even nuns were raped. In all torture centers, sexual violence was reported.[5]

Brazilian judiciary and dictatorship's crimes: then and now

The dictatorship in Brazil maintained a strong appeal to legality. Typical institutions of the rule of law continued to function, such as the parliament and the judiciary, albeit under threat and coercion. Some repressive instruments, such as censorship and espionage, had a large bureaucratic and legalized structure. Alongside this "legal face," the state also operated illegally and clandestinely, notably against political militants who engaged in armed resistance. Centers for torture and disappearance of opponents were controlled by the intelligence services of the armed forces and became the scene of massive and systematic violations.

Unlike the strategies of other authoritarian regimes, in Brazil, the judiciary was integrated into the repressive apparatus. The regime opted for a broad submission of political repression to that branch. For Anthony Pereira (2010), the regime's option to bring its political opponents to justice was justified by its interest in demobilizing, intimidating, and criminalizing the opposition on the one hand and legitimizing and stabilizing repression on the other. In addition to trying political opponents, the judiciary also had a role in shielding allegations of human rights violations. The report of the NTC discloses cases in which the justice system was complicit in repressive practices and rights violations (Comissão Nacional da Verdade 2014, 2.257). Pereira understands that the participation of the judiciary was made possible because of the high levels of integration between military and judicial elites. Such integration would have made it difficult to hold perpetrators criminally responsible after the political transition.

Brazilian judges have been reluctant to accept the very idea that the crimes perpetrated by state agents during the military dictatorship of 1964–1985 were tantamount to crimes against humanity. Against their neighbors in Argentina and Chile (with all the contextual differences that one must bear in mind), federal judges and regional and "superior" courts magistrates do not accept the idea that agents used the state apparatus against its civil population in a widespread and systematic way. Even worse, judges with limited training in international human rights law (IHRL) ignore the normative demands postulated by this field and treat those cases as regular criminal deeds.

In April 2010, the Brazilian Supreme Court was asked to decide if the Amnesty Law of 1979 (Statute Law nº 6.683 of 1979) was in accordance with the Brazilian Constitution of 1988. The court ruled that there was a supposed political agreement in 1979 that could not be violated, legitimizing the blanket or auto-amnesty enshrined in the controversial expression "connected crimes" present in statute law.[6] This kind of narrative reinforces the dictatorship's aim of creating an idealized transition wherein continuity prevailed against rupture and a forced conciliation took place. One cannot avoid connecting it with the authoritarian role played by Brazilian judiciary during and after the dictatorial rule.

Against this background, the IACtHR ruling in *Gomes Lund* (IACtHR 2010a) recognized the dictatorship crimes as gross violations of human rights that require investigation and prosecution. The Brazilian national courts are obliged to follow the decision of the IACtHR. One must bear in mind that the Brazilian Constitution of 1988 establishes in the article 7 of its complementary part that Brazil must pursue the formation of an international tribunal of human rights. Also, the domestic enactment . . . submitted Brazilian courts and judges to IACtHR jurisdiction via the domestic enactment of the Declaration of Recognition of the Obligatory Competence of the Inter-American Court of Human Rights (Decree 4.463 of 2002).

In accordance to the IACtHR decision, Brazilian federal prosecutors created a working group on transitional justice and started filing criminal lawsuits. This was done under the pressure of civil society groups in Brazil and abroad, revealing that there is a field where judiciary and prosecutors dispute the correct understanding of criminal liability in Brazil's transitional justice process. From 2011 on, when the federal prosecutors' efforts started, few lawsuits came to limited success.[7] Most of the time, Brazilian courts are sympathetic to defendant's arguments to recognize the extinction of criminal liability on grounds like statute of limitations, nonretroactivity of the idea of crimes against humanity, and, in a great part of the decisions, the amnesty supposedly granted by the Amnesty Law of 1979.

Of the 37 criminal complaints that were filed until February 2019, only 7 of them had a first positive ruling from federal judges, recognizing that at least the procedure should go on and that there were basic elements to support it. Of the seven partially successful criminal complaints, five were ruled by first-degree federal judges and two by appeals courts. At least 17 rulings rejecting or suspending the criminal complaints were held by first-degree federal judges (Ministério Público Federal 2017, p. 28). Most of the rejection rulings relied on the Brazilian Supreme Court's decision that validated the Amnesty Law in 2010. Few rulings that accepted the cases mentioned IHRL as obiter dicta. A clear pattern in rejecting the complaints may be observed, with an average of 81%. However, several Brazilian institutions, like the NTC, the Amnesty Commission of the Ministry of Justice,[8] and the Federal Attorney Office (*Procuradoria-Geral da República* or the head of the federal prosecutors) refused the interpretation that an auto-amnesty could include crimes against humanity.

There is a recent additional fact to be faced by Brazilian judiciary branch. As seen in the *Gomes Lund* case, the IACtHR was able to again rule against the interpretation that avoided accountability for dictatorship's crimes against humanity in the *Herzog* case (IACtHR 2018). The court ruled that UN Convention on the Non-applicability of Statutory Limitations to War Crimes and Crimes Against Humanity of 1968 only codified previous customary law and *jus cogens* norms, something that would make unnecessary the signature by the Brazilian State. Referring to different precedents from its own repertoire and from other regional and supranational courts, as well as the work of the 69th session of the International Law Commission of the United Nations,[9] the IACtHR concluded that the *jus cogens* (peremptory) prohibition on crimes against humanity proscribe states from invoking statutes of limitation, *ne bis in idem* norms (double jeopardy), amnesty, or any other clause that could avoid criminal liability.

Concerning specifically the Brazilian dictatorship, the IACtHR recollected federal prosecutors' arguments to demonstrate the systematic and general characters of political repression. For the purposes of this chapter, sexual abuse and sexual violations were recognized as part of the physical and psychological methods of torture (IACtHR 2018, p. 60). The ruling goes clearly against what was decided in Inês Etienne Romeu case by the Brazilian federal judge, as we will demonstrate, since all statute of limitations clauses were rejected, reinforcing the obligation to investigate, prosecute, and sanction crimes against humanity. The IACtHR ruling in the *Herzog* case does not mean that the Brazilian judiciary will automatically accept the interpretation that the crimes of the dictatorship are crimes against humanity. However, it depicts the situation of a huge Latin American country not concerned with international human rights norms, recommendations, and rulings.

Inês Etienne Romeu case

The *Inês Etienne Romeu* case is representative of Brazilian transitional justice policies, specifically toward gender violations, in many aspects. Being the first and only complaint of sexual crime against female imprisoners during the military dictatorship, and filed as late as December 2016, the case demonstrates the delay and the difficulties of incorporating a gender perspective to transitional justice in Brazil. Although the public prosecutors have engaged efforts to press charges against state agents that committed crimes during the dictatorship, until December of 2016, there was no criminal case related to sexual crimes. The judiciary's reluctance to adjudicate cases considered more complex seems to be one of the reasons why public prosecutors had not tried, until recently, to put on trial suspects of having committed sexual offenses (Carvalho 2016). The Federal Public Prosecutors' Office followed a strategy of initially attempting to bring to courts cases of enforced disappearances, executions, and torture. The victims themselves and their families shared the view that priority should be given to the cases considered most urgent, especially involving missing persons.

The first prosecution of sexual crimes concerns the violations suffered by Inês Etienne Romeu, the only survivor of the "House of Death" (*Casa da Morte*). The "House of Death" was a clandestine detention center situated in the city of Petrópolis, in the state of Rio de Janeiro, and held by the Brazilian Army intelligence service from 1971 to 1974. It was the place where at least 22 political opponents disappeared. The Federal Public Prosecutors' Office indicted the ex-sergeant Antonio Waneir Pinheiro Lima (nickname "Camarão") for having kidnaped and raped Inês Etienne Romeu while she was held captive (Otavio 2016).

Inês Etienne Romeu was born in the city of Pouso Alegre, state of Minas Gerais, Brazil, in 1942. She worked in a bank, was a student union leader, and the coordinator of the organization of resistance against the dictatorship called *VPR* (*Vanguarda Popular Revolucionária* or Revolutionary Popular Vanguard). She was arrested in São Paulo on 5 May 1971, without previous judicial warrant. After being tortured, she revealed where she used to live, and when the agents tried to take her to that place, she tried to commit suicide by throwing herself under a bus. She was hospitalized in a military hospital to recover from severe injuries. Even in the hospital, military agents tried to interrogate her (Comissão Nacional da Verdade 2014, p. 790).

She was then taken to the "House of Death" on 8 May 1971, again tortured, and was isolated and prevented from speaking to anyone else for more than three months. That same day, she was raped for the first time. Only on 7 November 1971 was the prison officially recognized. After that, Inês was only released because public officials thought she would become an undercover agent. That is how she managed to become the sole survivor from the "House of Death." On the 5 September 1979, Inês delivered a report to the Brazilian Bar Association. After the end of the dictatorship, Inês Etienne Romeu confirmed her statements several times in different criminal investigative procedures and before different truth commissions.[10] In 2002, she filed a civil lawsuit, which resulted in the Union being held liable for the injuries she suffered.

In the criminal sphere, the Federal Public Prosecutors' Office began to carry out investigations that resulted in the filing of the complaint on December 2016. The complaint accused Antonio Waneir Pinheiro Lima for two rapes against Inês. The prosecutors classified rape as a crime against humanity based on international law and emphasized that rape represents "*one of the most serious violence a woman can suffer*, directly offending her dignity, her freedom, her honor and her physical and moral integrity" (Ministério Público Federal 2016, p. 11). The complaint also recognized rape as a form of gender discrimination: "The act was committed for discriminatory reasons, because of the political ideology opposed to the dictatorial regime, adopted by the victim, *and also because she was a woman*" (Ministério Público Federal 2016, p. 12).

The complaint followed the tendency, already identified by previous studies, "to focus exclusively on sexual violence, and within that frame, on a narrow range of penetrative sexual acts" (Aoláin and Turner 2007, p. 260). This approach examines harms against women from an individual perspective and may marginalize other experiences of violence, which cannot be narrowed to sexual offenses. Despite those limitations, the complaint is significant in the context of transitional justice in Brazil. In a country that still lives with the absolute impunity of torturers, the struggle for accountability for sexual violence is not only necessary but also important to challenge the still common view in society that the dictatorship was soft and the military incorruptible and guardians of morality.

The prosecutors carried out the meticulous work of cross-examining and obtaining data from one of the few sources of information about the "House of Death," Colonel Paulo Malhães, a former member of torture detention center and maybe one of the singular cases of military who recognized the heinous methods used at that time (Comissão Nacional da Verdade 2014, p. 750). Inês Etienne Romeu was also able to name some of the perpetrators and to identify "Camarão" before the prosecutors through a photograph. The criminal complaint accused "Camarão" of committing the crimes of kidnapping and two counts of rape. Therefore, the prosecution was able to determine the direct perpetrator on the basis of solid evidence. One of the greatest procedural difficulties in cases of sexual violence, which is the identification of authorship, was overcome.

Additionally, the federal prosecutors (Ministério Público Federal, 2016, pp. 28–49) affirmed that no amnesty, prescription, or other statutes of limitations could avoid the criminal liability of the accused. The conduct was perpetrated in the context of a generalized and systematic attack against the civilian population, being a crime against humanity already at the time when it was committed. The prosecutors also reminded that the NTC had already considered sexual violence as a crime against humanity when committed during the Brazilian dictatorship. Once the characteristics of a systematic or widespread attack against civil population were present, the prosecutors argued that sexual violence was already a crime against humanity by *jus cogens* at the time they were committed.

According to the prosecutors, Inês was subjected to psychological and physical torture. During her arrest at the "House of Death," her relatives had no idea of her whereabouts. She suffered the most common methods of torture during that time[11] but also confronted unique situations, like being obliged to lay naked on a cement floor in temperatures lower than 10° C (Ministério Público Federal, 2016, p. 6), having to clean the kitchen of the "House of Death" while naked and subjected to profanities, and being raped by "Camarão" on two occasions.

Finally, the federal prosecutors argued that there is no conflict between what the Brazilian Supreme Court ruled in the Arguição de Descumprimento de Preceito Fundamental (ADPF) 153 and what the IACtHR decided in *Gomes Lund*.[12] For the prosecutors, the Brazilian Supreme Court ruled in the field of constitutional review, whereas the IACtHR decided in the field of conventional review. In other words, the blanket amnesty aimed by the Amnesty Law of 1979 directly violated the American Convention of Human Rights.

The judicial ruling on the *Inês Etienne Romeu* case: legal conservatism and gender-biased views

Brazilian criminal procedure depends on a first judicial decision to start. Judges and courts can avoid the burden of a criminal accusation by refuting that there are minimal conditions for the identification of the authorship of the crime and what is called "materiality," in other words, basic proofs that confirm that a crime was committed. In the *Inês Etienne Romeu* case, this type of ruling was the duty of Federal Judge Alcir Luiz Lopes Coelho. On 8 March 2017, the federal judge rendered the decision rejecting the complaint on the grounds that the crimes would not be punishable due to the application of the Amnesty Law and the statute of limitations. At this point, the decision follows the lack of preparation of the judiciary and the disregard of international obligations concerning the investigation of crimes against humanity. It also reflects the general understanding of Brazilian judges on amnesty as a pact that characterized a conciliatory, peaceful, and nondisruptive political transition.

But the federal judge also shared authoritarian and conservative political views that aimed to discredit the evidence submitted by the prosecutors, particularly Inês Etienne Romeu's testimony, to disqualify the prosecutors' investigations and to reverse the human rights discourse in favor of the defendant. The judge thus expressed a revisionist position in relation to the Brazilian dictatorship and displayed gender-biased views that are prejudicial to the effective and sensitive handling of the case.

Federal Judge Coelho disqualified the evidence submitted by the prosecutors: except for two documents of the military tribunals, none of the evidence (interviews, newspaper articles, rulings from foreign courts, etc.) was accepted as valid. The judge specifically disqualified the testimony Inês Etienne Romeu gave to the Brazilian Bar Association in 1979 and considered it useless as evidence. He expressly pointed out that the victim's statements were provided "EIGHT YEARS after the time of the crime, according to the complaint" (1st Federal Court of Petrópolis 2017, 1.589). What he suggested is that the testimony lost credibility because of the delay, contrary to the sound position of international law. Not only did the judge disregard the difficulties, both subjective and institutional, to report sexual offenses in general, but he also ignored the particularity of the repressive context in which the crimes occurred.

If one takes into account that gender defines more than the context where sexual violence is reproduced (a worst context if it is a dictatorship), then it is not possible to set aside the institutional dynamics that are also permeated by gender domination. Barriers to reporting, investigating, and trying gender crimes turn sexual violence into invisible acts and reinforce the process of victim's stigmatization (Carvalho 2016, pp. 18–19). The decision of the judge contributes not only to the impunity of sexual crimes but also to the silencing of victims who fear suffering the violence of being doubted or blamed.

In addition, the judge's position relativizes the authoritarian nature of the dictatorship in Brazil insofar as it recognizes as valid the convictions handed down by the military courts against Inês Etienne Romeu in that period. The decision mentioned that Inês was sentenced for crimes against the national security by the Brazilian Superior Military Court and by other military courts during the dictatorship. It is clear that such convictions cannot be understood as legitimate expressions of the judiciary, but rather as acts of political persecution based on authoritative national security laws and on the expanded jurisdiction of military justice to try civilians.

Conversely, the federal judge accused the prosecutors of engaging in the creation of an ad hoc tribunal through a group especially dedicated to implementing transitional justice measures. The judge reversed the positions of the defense and prosecution and thereby falsified the historical facts. The military justice ruling that, back in the 1970s, convicted Inês Etienne Romeu was considered by him a legitimate decision, while the transitional justice unit of the Federal Public Prosecutor's Office was seen as an exceptional body.

More broadly, the judge reversed and distorted the discourse of human rights to use it against the very goals it aims to defend. Human rights were not accepted in defense of the victim, but of the aggressor. In other words, the perpetrator was treated as a victim. According to the judge, the defendant accused of raping Inês Etienne Romeu suffered three human rights violations. The first was to be investigated by an ad hoc body set up by the prosecution service. The second violation was directed against the accused's right to benefit from the 1979 amnesty. The third violation would be the disrespect to a statute of limitations and the retroactivity of the criminal law in defiance of the accused.

The decision's final quote is telling. The judge cited a controversial Brazilian conservative journalist stating that no one would be against human rights as long they are "true" human rights "and not mere pretexts to give advantages to selected minorities that attend to global interests" (1st Federal Court of

Petrópolis 2017, 1.590). That was the comprehension of Olavo de Carvalho, an obscure figure who describes himself as philosopher, although he does not bear any degree in the field. More recently, he has acted as an informal councilor to the elected President Bolsonaro, being responsible for indicating the new minister of foreign affairs.[13] Olavo de Carvalho is representative of a conservative thinking based on polemizing statements with little or no substratum of validity. His thoughts resonate in society because they present an easy and superficial discourse that reflect negative images about what human rights are. Facts, data, and history themselves become a matter of opinion. What is stunning is that a judicial decision uses this reference as its basis.

It may be observed that the federal judge accepted the arguments traditionally invoked by the judiciary to reject the criminal complaints against the dictatorship agents for crimes against humanity. The federal judge accepted the validity of the Amnesty Law in its supposed auto-amnesty effect and the applicability of the statute of limitations, ignoring the international norms. This comprehension, based on the Brazilian Supreme Court jurisprudence, reveals the complete failure in applying the IHRL and the authoritarian remnants that are present in the Judiciary education and legal practice. However, his position brings stronger legal and ideological consequences, both in the sense of relativizing the Brazilian dictatorship and of defaming the work of the prosecutors responsible for the case and the victim, with clear gender preconceptions involved.

The judge's arguments demonstrate the risks of politicizing the judiciary, which, being a power that is not elected by popular vote, is not subordinated to the mechanisms of control and accountability typical of powers with representative functions. The subordination of the judge to the law and to the legal principles is the basis of legitimacy. From the moment the judge is allowed to base his decisions on political preferences and on personal opinion without legal consistency, an important check on judicial arbitrariness becomes lost.

Conclusion

The outcome of the first complaint filed for a sexual crime committed during the dictatorship, the outcome in this case is emblematic. The victim – Inês Etienne Romeu – was a political opponent who was the only survivor of a torture and disappearance center known as the Death House. Based on extensive investigative work, the Federal Public Prosecutors' Office sought to convict the man who was the direct perpetrator of rapes against the victim. Although the complaint did not reach the broader and more structural dimension of gender violence, we can understand that focusing on sexual crimes and, within them, on rape was a strategy to introduce this debate into the judiciary. In addition, the complaint included important advances in considering rape as violence against the integrity, freedom, and dignity of women, and particularly as a form of discrimination against women. Therefore, the *Inês Etienne Romeu* case reflects the changes that have reshaped the field of transitional justice in order to incorporate a gender perspective and to offer appropriate responses to sexual violence practiced during dictatorships and armed conflicts.

On the other hand, the delay in filing the complaint and the refusal of the judiciary to receive it demonstrate the obstacles and deficiencies of the justice system in Brazil. To date, no crime committed under the dictatorship has been tried by the Brazilian judiciary. The reluctant application of the 1979 amnesty and of other statutes of limitation serves as a barrier to the very filling of complaints of sexual offenses, often considered harder cases. Despite the development of international norms and institutions, and the international condemnations of Brazil, the judiciary has been hostile to the application of the category of crimes against humanity and to the integration, therefore, of international law into domestic law.

The *Inês Etienne Romeu* case reveals more serious consequences. The denial of the complaint by the judiciary was not limited to the typical grounds for rejection – application of the statute of limitations and amnesty for dictatorship crimes. The federal judge disregarded international law not only by ignoring the category of crimes against humanity but also by disrespecting the specific rules of evidence and procedure in cases of sexual violence. He not only cast doubt on the credibility of the victim's testimony and disqualified the accusation of rape but also treated Inês Etienne Romeu as a condemned terrorist. The mere fact that a court decision contains such discourse demonstrates the limits of institutional reforms that should follow the process of political transition. The democratization of the judiciary has not succeeded in guaranteeing a commitment to human rights, let alone a gender expertise.

In a broader sense, one can conclude that Brazilian judges are not prepared to deal with the gross violations of human rights committed during the dictatorship – especially those related to sexual crimes. If any transitional justice education is lacking, one that could consider gender rights (Nagy 2008; Carvalho 2016) in the transitional justice field would be something very ambitious to demand on Brazilian judges, considering this simple picture. Specialized training in human rights and, more than that, perspectives that are sensitive to the different elements that take part in defining sexual violence, appears clearly, for instance, in the composition of the ICC. Not only plural gender composition matters in the way article 36 of the Rome Statute determines but also that judges must be experts in themes such as violence against women (Carvalho, 2016, p. 47).

In the Brazilian courts' composition, none of these demands appear. Beyond that, in the course of a federal judge career, few are the opportunities for continuing education that embraces those demands from IHRL. The National Council of Justice (Conselho Nacional de Justiça, CNJ), the constitutional organ responsible for functional and administrative matters relating to judges in Brazil, established few norms demanding concrete judicial politics related to human rights. Most of them institute "awards' for judicial rulings that promote human rights. Only one is concerned with the implementation of the Statute Law No. 11.340 of 2006, which defines policies and criminalize conducts related to domestic violence.

However, the matter is more complex than it appears at first sight. An immediate answer to this problem could be that institutional reforms in a broader sense than those required by transitional justice practitioners would be helpful. Indeed, they cannot be disregarded if we take into account that none of them happened in Brazil (Pereira 2010), meaning that many judges who held their positions during the dictatorship would remain there after the 1988 democratic Constitution.

Notes

1 Discussing the consequences of a rape committed by public agents against someone who is detained, the IACtHR affirmed that this is an act especially gross and reprehensible, as long as the victim is in a position of vulnerability and abuse of power by the authority (Carvalho 2016, p. 57).
2 See § 38 of the Vienna Declaration and Programme of Action (1993) and Article 2°, 'c' of the Convention of Belém do Pará (1994). For a different analysis on the *Inês Etienne Romeu* case, focusing on the antifeminist biases of the judicial ruling, see Possolo and Holl (2018).
3 One must be aware of the feminist criticism of IHRL and international criminal law treatment on sexual crimes inaugurated with ICTY and ICTR holdings (O'Rourke, 2013, pp. 11–41).
4 See *Espinoza Gonzáles vs. Perú* (IACtHR 2014), *Case of J. v. Peru* (IACtHR 2013), and *Fernández Ortega y Otros v. México* (IACtHR 2010b). This jurisprudence, as Carvalho (2016, p. 59) shows, indicates that the IACtHR has been adopting gender criteria to define accountability for sexual crimes. Such criteria take into account cultural and social patterns of discrimination against women that leads to specific violations.
5 Although undoubtedly a significant event of the country's transitional justice, the work of the NTC has been criticized, particularly in the treatment of sexual and gender-based violence (Duque 2018; Carvalho 2016). Lack of transparency, inadequate methods for hearing women's testimonies, and the inability to include marginalized groups of women are some of the critiques that can be made. But perhaps the NTC's biggest mistake has been the missed opportunity to foster social mobilization around human rights violations, especially sexual and gender-based violations.
6 For more information on this subject, see Meyer (2017, 2012).
7 For the criminal complaints filed by the Brazilian federal prosecutors, see https://cjt.ufmg.br/index.php/ditadura-e-responsabilizacao/acoes-criminais/, access on 6 February 2016, and Meyer (2017).
8 According to Statutory Law n° 10.559/2002, the Amnesty Commission of the Ministry of Justice has the duty to evaluate applications for a federal reparations program to all of those who were affected by exceptional acts of the military dictatorship of 1964–1985, following what states the Article 8° of the Provisory Constitutional Provisions Act of the Brazilian Constitution of 1988. From 2007 to 2016, the Amnesty Commission was a strong policy maker on transitional justice matters, being severely damaged by the Temer administration and facing worst obstacles after Bolsonaro took office.
9 See United Nationons (2018).
10 Following the work of the NTC, Brazil had several other state and private truth commissions. For the work of the NTC, see http://cnv.memoriasreveladas.gov.br, access on 5 July 2018.

11 Electrical shocks, *pau de arara* (the imprisoned was hanged naked by hands and feet in a post horizontally sustained by a wooden structure) and *cadeira do dragão* (or dragon's chair, a metal chair where the victims received electrical shocks). For diverse methods systematically used by the dictatorship to torture political opponents, see IACtHR (2018, pp. 57–59).

12 The "Arguição de Descumprimento de Preceito Fundamental" (ADPF), or Petition for Non-Compliance with a Fundamental Precept, is a kind of concentrated constitutional review procedure that must be filed in the Brazilian Supreme Court, basically following the kelsenian or concentrated method of control. Brazil adopts a mixed model of constitutional review, influenced by both American and Austrian proposes and allowing for a diffuse and a concentrated way of arguing the unconstitutionality of statute laws.

13 A glimpse of Olavo de Carvalho's view can be seen in a recent interview he gave to *Folha de S. Paulo* newspaper:

> "*What do you think about sex education in schools?*
>
> The more sex education, the more naughtiness in schools. In the end, the school is teaching children how to take it in the butt, how to suck cock, they end up touching each other's breasts in public. They think that sex education is a good thing, but it's only doing harm. The state has no business giving sex education to anyone" (ZAREMBA 2018, p. 1).

References

1st Federal Court of Petrópolis. Criminal Complaint n° 2016.51.06.170716–2. Judgment of 6th March 2017.

Aoláin, F.N. & Turner, C. (2007) "Gender, Truth and Transition." *UCLA Women's Law Journal* 16, pp. 229–279.

Balardini, L., Orbelin, A., & Sobredo, L. (2011) "Violencia de género y abusos sexuales en los centros clandestinos de detención: Un aporte a la comprensión de la experiencia argentina." In: Centro de Estudios Legales y Sociales (CELS), *Hacer justicia: nuevos debates sobre el juzgamiento de crímenes de lesa humanidad en la Argentina*. 1a ed. Buenos Aires: Siglo Veintiuno Editores, pp. 167–226.

Carvalho, C.P. (2016) *Crimes sexuais e justiça de transição na América Latina: judicialização e arquivos*. Florianópolis: Tribo da Ilha and Secretaria Executiva da Rede Latino-Americana de Justiça de Transição.

Comissão Nacional da Verdade. (2014) *Relatório final*. V. 1. Comissão Nacional da Verdade. Brasília: CNV.

Duque, A.P.D.V. (2018) *Gênero e justiça de transição no Brasil: a construção da figura da "vítima" no relatório final da Comissão Nacional da Verdade*. 136 f., il. Dissertação (Mestrado em Direito) – Universidade de Brasília, Brasília.

IACHR (2007) "Access to Justice for Women Victims of Violence in the Americas." OEA/Ser.L/V/II. Doc. 68, 20 January. Available at: http://www.cidh.org/women/Access07/tocaccess.htm

IACHR (2011) "Access to Justice for Women Victims of Sexual Violence in Mesoamérica." OEA/Ser.L/V/II., Doc. 63, 9 December. Available at: http://www.oas.org/en/iachr/women/docs/pdf/WOMEN%20MESOAMERICA%20ENG.pdf

IACtHR. Inter-American Court of Human Rights. (2010a) *Case of Gomes Lund et. al. ("Guerrilha do Araguaia") v. Brazil*. Judgment of November 24. Available at: www.corteidh.or.cr/docs/casos/articulos/seriec_219_ing.pdf.

IACtHR. Inter-American Court of Human Rights. (2010b) *Fernández Ortega et al. v. Mexico*. Judgment of August 30. Available at: www.corteidh.or.cr/docs/casos/articulos/seriec_215_ing.pdf.

IACtHR. Inter-American Court of Human Rights. (2013) *Case of J. v. Peru*. Judgment of November 27. Available at: www.corteidh.or.cr/docs/casos/articulos/seriec_275_ing.pdf.

IACtHR. Inter-American Court of Human Rights. (2014) *Caso Espinoza Gonzáles vs. Perú*. Sentencia de 20 de noviembre. Available at: www.corteidh.or.cr/docs/casos/articulos/seriec_289_esp.pdf.

IACtHR. Inter-American Court of Human Rights. (2018) *Caso Herzog e Outros v. Brasil*. Sentença de 15 de março. Available at: www.corteidh.or.cr/docs/casos/articulos/seriec_353_por.pdf.

Meyer, E.P.N. (2012) *Ditadura e Responsabilização: Elementos para uma Justiça de Transição no Brasil*. Belo Horizonte: Arraes Editores.

Meyer, E.P.N. (2017) "Criminal Responsibility in Brazilian Transitional Justice." *Indonesian Journal of International and Comparative Law* 4, pp. 39–69.

Ministério Público Federal. (2016) Criminal Complaint n° 2016.51.06.170716-2. Preliminary Statements. 1st Federal Court of Petrópolis.

Ministério Público Federal. (2017) "2nd Chamber of Coordination and Revision." In *Crimes da Ditadura Militar*. Brasília: MPF.

Nagy, R. (2008) "Transitional Justice as Global Project: Critical Reflections." *Third World Quarterly* 2, pp. 275–289.

O'Rourke, C. (2012) "Dealing with the Past in a Post-Conflict Society: Does the Participation of Women Matter? Insights from Northern Ireland." *William and Mary Journal of Women and the Law* 19(1), pp. 35–68.

O'Rourke, C. (2013) "International Law and Domestic Gender Justice, or Why Case Studies Matter." In M. Fineman and E. Zinsstag (eds.), *Feminist Perspectives on Transitional Justice: From International and Criminal to Alternative Forms of Justice*. Cambridge: Intersentia Publishing, pp. 11–41.

Otavio, C. (2016) "Carcereiro da Casa da Morte é denunciado pelo MP." *O Globo*. Available at: https://oglobo.globo.com/brasil/carcereiro-da-casa-da-morte-denunciado-pelo-mp-20585511#ixzz4S1HfqOe2, (Accessed on: 10 October 2018).

Pereira, A.W. (2010) *Ditadura e Repressão: o autoritarismo e o estado de direito no Brasil, no Chile e na Argentina*. São Paulo: Paz e Terra.

Possolo, R.C.G. & Holl, J. (2018) Por que uma crítica feminista ao Direito? Reflexões a partir do caso Inês Etienne. Manuscript with the authors. Belo Horizonte: UFMG.

United Nations (2018) "Sixty-ninth Session of the International Law Commission," *United Nations*. Available at: http://legal.un.org/ilc/sessions/69/

Zaremba, J. (2018) "Bolsonaro's Guru Says That Are No Left-Wing Intellectuals at His Level." *Folha de S. Paulo*. Available at: https://www1.folha.uol.com.br/internacional/en/brazil/2018/11/bolsonaros-guru-says-that-are-no-left-wing-intellectuals-at-his-level.shtml (Accessed on: 5 December 2018).

Conclusion

Seeking commonalities from across the South

George Radics

In *Law and Disorder in the Post-Colony* (2006: vii), Jean and John Comaroff ask, "Are the postcolonies in Africa, Asia, Europe, and Latin America haunted by more unregulated violence, un/civil, and random terror than other twenty-first-century states?" They answer this question, along with a string of other similar ones, with the statement, "The reflex answer to this brace of questions – is yes" (ibid.). Although they follow-up to say that there is something deeper happening, brilliantly explore the paradox of the postcolonial fetish with the rule of law, and how neoliberalism has bred lawlessness, their ultimate argument that the South creates a "simulacra of social order" or that "criminality with violence has become endemic to the postcolonial condition" (Comaroff and Comaroff, 2006: 7) is *not* what this edited volume has explored. The preceding chapters did not start with the assumption that "lawlessness" or the "simulacra of order" is the condition to be studied, but rather how criminal laws and institutions are in themselves historical constructs that attempt to define, control, and regulate behaviors in Southern societies that are constantly shifting and that many times have origins and cultural understandings different from the laws and institutions themselves. This edited volume, therefore, should instead be seen as exploring laws in the "frontier" (de Sousa Santos, 1995: 574). As opposed to studying the periphery to foreshadow the unfortunate future of the center, this volume explored laws in the South to expose

> very selective and instrumental use of the traditions brought to the frontier by pioneers and emigrants; invention of new forms of sociability; weak hierarchies; plurality of powers and juridical orders; fluidity of social relations; promiscuity of strangers and intimates; mixes of heritage and inventions.
>
> (ibid.)

By providing a wide range of perspectives, instead of focusing on violence and disorder, this edited volume serves as a spectacle of sorts, rejoicing in the vast array of difference and questioning established canons and the "fetish of the rule of law" by turning formal law on its head, suspending formal hierarchy, deconsecrating inequality, and allowing for a frank and free communication between all (Bakhtin, 1934 [1984]).

Yet to ignore the geopolitics of power and the totalizing effect of the state onto all aspects of one's life would be naïve. From "predatory extractivism" (Hollender, 2015: 75) to *naked laborers*, "stripped of all juridico-political rights or status in natural or divine law" (Whyte, 2009: 58), it is undeniable that economic and political changes suffered in the Global South "have had unintended, highly destabilizing effects on the fragile political and economic arrangements . . . that developed in many nation-states across the global south" (Comaroff and Comaroff, 2006: 4). Moreover, the increasing power of the state as manifested through officers of the law has become "permanent, exhaustive, omnipresent surveillance, capable of making all visible while it remains invisible" (Foucault, 1977: 214). In the South, far from serving as a liberating and empowering institution, many times, the state itself reproduces the same systems of oppression thrusted upon it as a colony, even after independence, abandoning citizens in the margins or overpolicing them (Auyero and Sobering, 2017; O'Donnell, 1993). Beyond these international and national political dimensions lies the even more enigmatic dilemma of the power of the law to entrench such structures and generate cultural confrontations that are rarely smooth or uncomplicated. In this regard, Said's (1978: 20) important concept of discourse reminds us that power as manifested through the state is "by no means in direct, corresponding relationship with political power in the raw, but rather is produced and exists in an uneven exchange with various kinds of power." Therefore, power – colonial or post-independent – must confront head on the power of the people, their history, culture, and traditions.

From a criminological perspective, the situation becomes even more complex. Large sections of Southern populations are economically and politically marginalized, while mass consumption and individualism exacerbate such marginalization due to an exponential increase of crime (Wacquant, 2009; Patalinghug, 2011; Müller, 2012). In response, much of the South is experiencing a "punitive turn" – with mass incarceration, racialized policing, and the decline of the emphasis on rehabilitation – similar to the phenomenon found in the Global North (Carrington et al., 2016). How the South attempts to define the boundaries of crime, manage its rise, and conceptualize what type of rights should be afforded its citizens prompts the question of whether a Southern criminology could investigate these issues more carefully (ibid.). Yet in the past few decades, not all regions of the South have moved in the same direction when it comes to the rights of criminal defendants or updating their criminal laws and judicial systems. While many countries in Africa, Asia, and the Middle East have increasingly rejected "Western" notions of judicial due process and human rights either due to cultural or religious differences (Radics and Ciocchini, 2018; Lorway, 2014; Aydin, 2007), those in Latin America experienced a revolution in criminal justice procedures, a rise in constitutionalism, and the emergence of an entire network of "transitional justice" scholars and activists (Langer, 2007; Huneeus, 2010; Skaar, 2016). Furthermore, there is vast diversity within these regions and within nations themselves. On vexing criminal issues that entail gender, sexuality, immigration, race, or issues that are deemed of national importance, such as drugs, corruption, or gambling, as can be seen in this edited volume, we return to the vast and bewildering diversity of the frontier as we seek commonalities from the Global South.

It is in this context that we have ventured to explore criminal legalities in the Global South. In compiling the preceding chapters, we intentionally sought to present topics on "criminal" issues in peripheral and semi-peripheral societies, specifically those that are understudied or found in underrepresented jurisdictions – and we believe such a project was enormously rewarding. The chapters in this volume cover a wide range topics from a diverse set Southern societies, from smaller nations like Peru or Bangladesh that exist in the shadow of larger nations, to large nations like Brazil or Indonesia that should be more powerful and influential yet still exist in the geopolitical margins. And the topics covered were equally diverse – from personal vices to state violence. Despite dramatically different histories and societies, this volume demonstrated a consistent emergence of themes between the Global South nations explored. These themes include colonial legacy, modernity vs. tradition, role of courts, relationship with the state, conceptualization and enforcement of rights, and economic and political inequality. Each chapter approached its topic differently, from the personal and creative angle of Danish Sheikh in "Privacy in Public Spaces" to the structural and international dimensions of immigration in Carolina Yoko Furusho's "(Cr)immigration in the Dominican Republic?" Finally, each chapter brought its own unique spin to understanding criminal law in the Global South, while enhancing our overarching understanding of the Global South's complexity through different perspectives, from economics to anthropology, and sociology to the law. This conclusion will thus develop these topics, beginning with the common history, then moving on to thematic similarities, and then ending with an overview of some of the theoretical contributions that emerge from the preceding chapters.

History from below: common experiences across the South

The "history from below" approach, otherwise known as "social history," can be traced to E. P. Thompson's seminal 1963 work *The Making of the English Working Class* in which he sought to rewrite history not from the perspective of those in power but those marginalized by it (Thompson, 1963 [1980]). According to historian Bryan D. Palmer, this sensitivity to class difference and the demand to write history with attention to sexuality, gender oppression, and rural labor ultimately charted Thompson's foray into the historiography of crime (Palmer, 1994; see Thompson, 2001). But Thompson was certainly not the only scholar who endeavored to study history from the perspective of the oppressed. Scholars such as Ranajit Guha (1983), Partha Chatterjee (1993), and Sumit Sarkar (1997) were all part of the Subaltern Studies Group which attempted to also build histories from below by uncovering the stories, sentiments and activities of those who resisted the colonial and nationalist project in India. Most, if not all, of these studies, however, have focused on the national or perhaps regional histories – which should be expected since a deep and methodical reconstruction of events has always been tied to national borders in traditional historical studies.

It was not until the 1980s that world history and global history emerged to challenge this predominantly national focus. According to historian Jerry Bentley in the inaugural issue of the *Journal of World History*,

> The predominantly national focus of historical scholarship has served the discipline well . . . It has required that historians master the languages and investigate the cultures of the various national traditions . . . [and] enabled scholars to place social, economic, and cultural developments in a meaningful political context.
>
> (Bentley, 1990: iii)

He adds, however, "Many powerful historical forces simply do not respect national or even cultural boundary lines, but work their effects instead on a regional, continental, or global scale" (iv). In 2006, the *Journal of Global History* emerged to address the growing emphasis on globalization by studying history in a matter that does not pursue "spurious claims [of] scientific objectivity and personal impartiality, but [instead] to moral purposes, connecting to the needs of a globalizing world" (O'Brien, 2006: 38). At the same time, it was acknowledged that "global history has to start with the acceptance of the 'spatial turn,' the refusal of Eurocentrism, and the realization that knowledge of the non-Western regions of the world is fundamental" (Middell and Naumann, 2010).

How a "global social history" looks, or how it works, has yet to be established. However, two trends have emerged in global history, the first of which entails the exploration of transnational confrontations and connections through events such as trade, war, or migration (O'Brien, 2006: 4). The other trend entails comparative histories on topics that might be the subject of a study across parish, regional, and national boundaries, as well as continents, oceans and separable cultures (O'Brien, 2006: 5). While this conclusion does not offer any pretense that the preceding chapters consistently produced a "history from below," it is undeniable that many of the chapters explored histories of continuities and ruptures between the North and the South, or colonial and postcolonial societies. It can further be argued that experiences across the South also share a similar global history, from disproportionately receiving the cultures, languages, and laws of the North, to the complex process of untangling itself from these foreign impositions. With regards to the preceding chapters, despite vast geographical distances, significant commonalities in histories and experiences can be found.

One commonality was the process of decolonization – though it should be acknowledged that many nations in the South decolonized in different ways, points of time, and in response to various triggers. As a result of the enlightenment and its concepts of rights and of the citizen, many Latin American nations witnessing such advancements in Europe demanded similar autonomy and achieved independence by the mid-19th century (Mignolo, 2005: 55). In other parts of the world, the New Imperialism period of the late 19th and early 20th centuries led to the scramble for Africa and the Opium Wars (Hobson, 1988). For nations captured in the New Imperial web, many remained colonies up to World War II when the cost of rebuilding, in addition to the rise of multilateralism, led to their eventual decolonization. Yet regardless of when decolonization took place, the process created an instability of borders, the rise of competing nationalisms, and ethnic strife. Moreover, by the 1970s, neoliberal economic policies aimed at spurring growth exacerbated inequality (see Connell & Dados, 2014; Bello, 1990). To maintain power during the growing disorder, a number of nations in the Global South endured military regimes – many times ironically supported by the "liberalizing" West – that initially were aimed at forcefully controlling the chaos that followed the economic and social instability (LaFeber, 2002). Thus, while in the 1960s and 1970s, the West was opening up and exporting their expanding conceptions of civil and human rights to the rest of the world,[1] nations of the Global South were still reeling from centuries of exploitation and political repression, or dealing with harsh military regimes left in the wake of independence. Although not all nations in the Global South experienced these conditions in the same way, such conditions created similar trends throughout the South when it came to rights and civil liberties.

Colonization profoundly affected the moral fabric of the Global South and in most cases created a deep-seated tension between the values of the colonizer and the colonized (Nandy, 1988). What was considered "modern," "developed," or "civilized" became associated with the colonial metropole, with nations of the Global South being seen as at best capable of becoming civilized, or at worst fundamentally inferior to their colonial masters. For the African colonies, Mbembe (2001) argues that the continent became constructed as the "radical other" calling into question whether Africa could even be studied through the language of the West. Mignolo (2005: 58) argues that post-independent Latin America was the "sad" idea of "elites celebrating their dreams of becoming modern while they slide deeper and deeper into the logic of coloniality." Particularly with the British colonies, foreign definitions of caste, class, and race complicated local conceptions of the world, introducing new people and ideas (see Goh, 2008). Local and traditional conceptions of self were obliterated, as languages and cultural practices were muddled, lost, or actively destroyed. In many cases, religion was used to "save" the local populations, and the church introduced new practices, behaviors, and ways of thinking (Comaroff and Comaroff, 1991). The transformation of identities and cultures led to cultural backlashes that emphasized sameness and enhanced "local and traditional" conceptions of self, strong nationalist fervor, as well as an antipathy toward anything "Western" (Radics, forthcoming). Although change is not always harmful, the speed and inorganic nature of such changes transformed many Global South societies, leading to serious consequences and responses that can still be felt to this day.

Furthermore, by the 1960s, much of the Global South became independent, and as rights expanded in the Global North, the Global South struggled to find its footing in the postcolonial world. As part of the nation-building process, Global South nations emphasized their unique and "indigenous" cultures, pitting their values against the West, inverting the power relations of the past when Southern cultures were deemed inferior (Mamdani, 2012).[2] Ironically, as Northern nations began to redefine rights of citizenship and personal liberty, many Southern nations retained limitations on civil rights and enhanced codes on "immorality" (Chang, 2014: 320; see Radics chapter in volume). Moreover, such colonial laws were interpreted as part of Southern "indigenous" and local culture, and retained to emphasize that Southern nations were no longer beholden to the political pressures and societal trends of the North (Mignolo, 2005; Gobat, 2013).

"Carnival" of the commons: thematic commonalities across the South

In *Rabelais and His World*, Mikhail Bakhtin (1984 [1934]: 6) argued that carnival activities, and the spectacles and rituals associated with them, "offered a completely different, nonofficial, extraecclesiastical and extrapolitical aspect of the world, of man, and of human relations; they built a second world and a second life outside officialdom." These temporary moments of inversion made it so that people were subject only to the "laws of its own freedom" and that such freedom "has a universal spirit [and] is a special condition of the entire world, of the world's revival and renewal, in which all take part" (ibid. 7). To Bakhtin, such a carnival spirit was utopian in nature, oriented toward the future, and enabled the conceptualization of a new order. Boaventura de Sousa Santos in his "Three Metaphors for a New Conception of Law" (1995) picks up on the power of breaking away from orthodoxy through his use of the metaphor of the "baroque." Using the "baroque" as a cultural metaphor that signifies a form of subjectivity and sociability, according to de Sousa Santos (1995: 576), "the lack of central power endows the baroque with an open-ended and unfinished character that allows for the autonomy and creativity of margins and peripheries." He too sees the power of the carnival, as he goes on to write, "The carnivalization of emancipatory social practice has an important self-reflexive dimension: it makes possible the decanonization and subversion of such practices" adding that "a de-canonizing practice that does not know how to decanonize itself falls easily into orthodox." (de Sousa Santos, 1995: 578). Both scholars draw upon the idea that inverting the existing world order through laughter and play – or what some consider improper, grotesque, exaggerated, eccentric, blasphemous, or subversive – is necessary to envision a new future. Therefore, the previous chapters can be seen not as a post-modern devolution of world order, or a "tragedy of the commons" where individualism and self-interest lead to the downfall of society, but rather as a utopian endeavor to envision a brighter future that includes alternative histories and ways of living, particularly those of Southern nations that are understudied or consistently examined through the lens of the North.

Drawing upon the concept of the carnival, or the metaphor of the baroque, this section will highlight common themes from throughout the South to shed light on how the body, power, and the state, are defined, managed, and controlled. As the themes discussed in this edited volume highlight unique and peculiar phenomena in the South, Bakhtin (1984: 47) reminds us that even if the themes discussed "have a clearly carnival origin, [they still] retain a certain memory of that mighty whole to which they belonged in the distant past." Thus, although different or strange, the themes discussed throughout this volume are still somehow connected to the Global North, the colonial past, or the region they are embedded within. Despite this confusion and ambiguity, several themes can still be identified and will be discussed in turn – from the personal vs. public, alternative manifestations of the justice, to diverse methods of discipline and social control.

a. Public vs. private

One of the deep and long-lasting effects of colonization was its effect on the distinction between public and private behaviors. In *Carnal Knowledge and Imperial Power*, Ann Stoler (2002) discussed how colonial regulation had a profound effect on the intimate lives of Southern societies. From sexual relations, to the rearing of children, subjecting people to the authority of another from a different culture and background led to rules and regulations that transformed even the most private of spaces. From carefully managing racial "degeneration" of the white colonial bureaucrat (Stoler, 1989; Manderson, 1997), to purifying the empire by enforcing a moral code that criminalized "obscene" behaviors or literature that depicted such behaviors as "normal" (Heath, 2010), the colonial state brought to the South new cultural boundaries concerning what was public and private, rigorously regulating both.

In Danish Sheikh's chapter entitled, "Privacy in Public Spaces: The Transformative Potential of *Navtej Johar v. Union of India*," he provides us with a stunning account of the very personal consequences of Section 377 of the Penal Code, a colonial law prohibiting sexual acts "against the order of nature." Unlike the other chapters, his contribution highlights the private, emotional, and creative spaces that are touched and transformed by Section 377 and that took decades to uproot from Indian law. My own chapter entitled, "'First World Problems' in the 'Third World'? LGBT Rights in Singapore" discussed how the same law went a little further in Singapore, specifically targeting gay male sex in Section 377A of the Penal Code. As opposed to focusing on the tension between the public and private upon the individual, my chapter pivots to discuss the social tensions between what society at large believes is appropriate for the individual. Here, we see that the balancing of what "society" identifies as traditional, local, and "Singaporean" can be exclusive and oppressive to those who do not fit society's beliefs of what is acceptable sexual behavior. Lastly, the definitions themselves concerning licit and illicit sexual contact outside a marriage are vividly brought to life in Anisur Rahman's "Criminalizing Adultery in Colonial India." In this chapter, invoking Said (1994) and Stoler (1995), we see a distinctly orientalist lens through which race and power become entrenched in the law concerning adultery. Rahman very astutely then goes on to trace the legacy of such orientalist definitions in modern-day Bangladesh and Pakistan. In all three chapters, the boundaries between public and private become entrenched in the law, leading to the policing of the physical body, limits of sexuality, and even notions of the self.

b. Unexpected manifestations in law and justice

In a special issue that Pablo Ciocchini and I edited in 2018 entitled "Global North Legal Pressures on Global South Societies," we asked "whether or not other individuals from outside of the West can help us understand the meaning of rights in a different way, or what manifold conceptualizations of what constitutes "human rights" outside of the West" (Radics and Ciocchini, 2018: 409). In the same special issue, Jose Manuel Barreto (2018: 486) responded that "the answer is complex and paradoxical – [it is not possible to completely reject the] colonial past and present, or to dismiss them as simply Western." The "North" and the "South" are indelibly entangled. Yet to use purely "Northern" or colonial methods to control Southern societies can lead to unexpected outcomes, or even more oppressive legacies that demand a re-envisioning of notions of justice and fairness. In particular, four chapters in our edited volume discuss some of the limitations and complexities associated with applying Northern or orthodox legal approaches and concepts to Southern societies.

João Araújo Monteiro Neto and Nestor Eduardo Araruna Santiago in "Gambling with Criminal Law: The Legal Paradox of "Jogo do Bicho" (Animal Lottery) Criminalization in Brazil" brilliantly highlight the practice of "jogo do bicho" in the legal shadows of Brazil. Despite numerous attempts to crack down on this popular form of gambling, Neto and Santiago argue that failed attempts to reign in this widespread practice have led to the proliferation of shadow industries and legality. It also highlights the tension between "mafia-like" politics and elite morality – the latter of which exerts the continuous power, while the former facilitates a shadow ecosystem of commercial enterprises and the uncontrolled competition and consumption arising from the game. Elliot Prasse-Freeman in his excellent chapter "Of Punishment, Protest, and Press Conferences" highlights a similar phenomenon of the failure of the state to regulate and control society, breeding alternative forms of protest. Through rich ethnographic data, Prasse-Freeman argues that in Burma, rather than attempting to use the law and the legal system to integrate recalcitrant activists into the rule of law, the authorities have always made their supremacy above the law more or less explicit. In such cases, "rule of law" is for show, and protesters take advantage of this situation to "create new political sites [and] produce conflagrations that expose the state as executing rule *the wrong way*."

On the other hand, the state also serves as the site to continuity (and attempted ruptures) with the "distant past." In Carolina Yoko's "(Cr)Immigration in the Dominican Republic?" she explores the deep history of slavery, racism, and how such legacies manifest in criminal and immigration laws. She traces contemporary (cr)immigration policies to the Trujillo dictatorship over the country in the 1930s, where his fascist and eugenic tendencies were influenced by Nazi Germany. Racist policies over time did not wane, and instead received further inspiration from (cr)immigration policies in the United States, which arguably also supports a policy that makes immigration from light-skinned countries easier and that treats migrants from darker skinned countries as criminals. Continuity between the past and the present can also be found in Argentina. In Julieta Mira's "Cosmologies of Federal Criminal Procedural Reform: Democratizing and Humanizing Criminal Justice in Argentina," she effectively highlights the long and drawn-out process of transitioning the nation from the "inquisitorial" to the "accusatorial" criminal justice system, and discusses the "cosmologies," or ideal representations of the social order according to activists attempting to facilitate this transition. What is striking, however, are the arguments used. From democratization and humanizing the judicial system, to modernizing and reforming that which is "old and obsolete," activist cosmologies in this case interpret past practices as outdated, antiquated, and inhumane, begging the question of what "new" image the ideal Argentine criminal justice system should build itself upon.

c. Judicial mechanisms and due process

Finally, this edited volume explores judicial institutions and how they function across the South. Responding to local conditions, Southern judicial institutions grapple with issues found in the North but are also subject to other factors such as extreme economic disparity, gender inequality, or a rise in crime and criminality. Moreover, Ciocchini (2017: 2) argues that the "authoritarian past of the majority of countries in the Global South, and the consequently weak democratic institutions, have shaped the development of the courts, as well as of the other criminal justice institutions." Engaging a number of influences from the Northern "rule of law" model (Comaroff and Comaroff, 2006), to the post-authoritarian, "transitional justice" movements to atone for the sins of the past (Skaar, 2016; Huneeus, 2010) or the growing "penal populism" found in both the North and South (Pratt, 2007; Müller, 2012), the important institution of the judiciary has the potential to place a check on competing political institutions, uphold the rights of citizens, and transform the lives of individuals caught in a growing web of illegalities.

Exploring the wave of criminal justice reform in Latin America, Wilson Hernández in "Sacrificing Justice for Efficiency? Examining Premature Dismissal Rates in Peruvian Corruption Cases" discusses attempts by the Peruvian government to create a more efficient mechanism to evaluate the most complex corruption cases, as well as to reform the Criminal Procedure Code that replaced the old written and inquisitorial system with an oral and less bureaucratic one based on adversarial models – similar to what was explored in Mira's chapter on Argentina. While these reforms promised greater justice and efficiency in the judicial handling of corruption cases, Hernández's chapter argued that justice was sacrificed for efficiency. Using an innovative research method of quantifying cases in which the new system prematurely dismissed corruption cases, Hernández found incorrectly dismissed cases are due to individual or systemic incentives fostered by the efficiency impetus. Also experiencing a wave of reforms, particularly as a response to attempts to facilitate transitional justice, in Brazil, one area of the law concerning sexual crimes seems to have evaded reform. In Emilio Peluso Neder Meyer and Claudia Paiva Carvalho's chapter entitled "Sexual Crimes and Transitional Justice before Courts in Brazil," they argue that despite efforts to reform the courts, by refusing to admit testimony of a rape victim during the military regime, the Brazilian judicial system fails to recognize sexual crimes for what they are – crimes against humanity. Through applying a conservative interpretation of evidentiary rules to crimes committed under the military dictatorship and viewing such claims as time barred not exempt from the tolling of the statute of limitations available in crimes against humanity cases, not only does the court prohibit sex crimes from being reviewed by the court, but it also exposes the inability of the court to deal with gross human rights violations of the past.

Latin America is not the only region struggling with judicial reform. Southeast Asia also experiences massive problems with managing judicial efficiency and prioritizes punishment overdue process. Pablo Ciocchini's in-depth exploration into extrajudicial killings in the Philippines due to the president's War on Drugs exposes how a massive backlog of cases, in addition to overworked and understaffed prosecutors and police officers exacerbate an already overwhelmed judicial system. Ciocchini argues that a byproduct of this scenario is the rise in plea bargaining with two key consequences: on the one hand, weak cases end up in a conviction, and on the other, judicial actors being able to reinsert a rehabilitation focus in the antidrug campaign. Jayson Lamchek in "Arresting a Due Process Revolution: The Reform of Indonesia's Code of

Criminal Procedure and the Persistence of History" examines a similar phenomenon in Indonesia, except from a historical perspective. In his chapter, Lamchek delves into the background of failed attempts to reform the Indonesian criminal procedure code due to deeply ingrained colonial and authoritarian tendencies that facilitate the preservation of a punitive system over one that protects defendant's rights and due process. At the end of his chapter, Lamchek highlights that such a punitive attitude toward crime in Indonesia can be seen in Latin America as well as in the Philippines.

Theoretical implications and conclusions

Bakhtin (1984: 256) reminds us that "the birth of the new, of the greater and the better, is as indispensable and as inevitable as the death of the old." At the same time, de Sousa Santos (1995: 571) argues, "The paradigm of modernity is undergoing a deep and irreversible crisis. Having exhausted its possibilities of renovation, its continuing prevalence as the dominant paradigm is due to historical inertia." Could a Southern criminology provide the world with a new and novel way to move forward? Carrington et al. (2016: 1) describes Southern criminology as the "development of a more transnational criminology that is inclusive of the experiences and perspectives of the Global South, that adopts methods and concepts that bridge global divides and that embraces the democratization of knowledge production as a political aspiration." Although Moosavi (2019) highlights Southern criminology's limitations such as its focus on a few selective countries and "lack of theoretical interrogation," we believe that this edited volume provides an example of how Southern criminology can be useful. By providing a glimpse into the conditions of nations throughout the Global South – big and small, rich and poor, geopolitically powerful and weak – we find the same pressures and processes as these nations grapple with the imposition of legal and criminological concepts imposed from the Global North. We showcased a diverse range of scholarship produced by those based in the regions they study, or who have spent years deep in the field researching the issues they care about. Finally, we make no pretense to create a new subfield, or a new legal orthodoxy, but rather have provided rich and critical analyses of the complex processes taking place in the context of criminal legalities in the Global South.

Yet how do we "learn from the South" or create "thick" theory when the region itself is vast and plagued with dissimilar and conflicting processes – from a "punitive turn" and a cultural backlash against the "West," to progressive attempts to undo the damage of authoritarian regimes? Beyond exploring the consequences to colonization, deep contextualized studies bound together by thematic commonalities provide us with opportunities to develop new mechanisms and tactics to deal with our increasingly globalized world. Bhabha (1994: 2) reminds us that "the social articulation of difference, from the minority perspective, is a complex, ongoing negotiation that seeks to authorize cultural hybridities . . . that [can] constitute a radical revision in the concept of human community itself." It is undeniable that through migration metropoles in the North have become a fertile ground for the hybridization of cuisine, music, styles, technology, and ideas. Moreover, tragedies outside of the West such as catastrophic environmental pollution in Japan in the 1950s, or genocidal inter-religious violence during the Indian partition, turned nations like Japan into one of the largest exporters environmental activists (Avenell, 2017), or inspired Martin Luther King Jr. and the civil rights movement to take on a similar approach to Gandhi's nonviolent civil disobedience (Chakrabarty, 2013). Through exploring criminal legalities in the Global South, innovative solutions may emerge to invert world order. By seeking commonalities across the Global South, we not only acknowledge the richness of different histories and experiences in our world but also move beyond the fetish of the rule of law to create a legal order that instead of simply aiming to efficiently regulate crime, focuses on effectively guaranteeing human dignity and encouraging mutual respect between and within the Global North and South.

Notes

1 Ironically during the Cold War, as part of its cultural offensive, the United States was a major exporter of the idea that capitalism led to freedom, even if African American children were spat at and prevented from attending newly integrated schools in the South (LaFeber, 2002: 199). The United States was also instrumental in toppling Latin American democracies and propping up military dictatorships in their place (Grandin, 2010).

2 Mamdani (2001: 33) in *When Victims Become Killers* states that "by politicizing indigeneity, the colonial state set in motion a process with the potential of endlessly spawning identities animated by the distinctions in indigenous and non-indigenous, and polarizing them." He further develops this point in *Define and Rule: Native as Political Identity* when he states, "What is believed to be traditional society is not something that has existed in any past. It is essentially what has existed in the colonial and neo-colonial present" (Mamdani, 2012: 96). Thus by reifying "tradition," the colonial state created the indigenous culture that postcolonial elites would then eventually wield as a political tool.

References

Auyero, J. & Sobering, K. (2017) "Violence, the State, and the Poor: A View from the South." *Sociological Forum*. July. DOI: 10.1111/socf.12362.

Avenell, S.A. (2017) *Transnational Japan in the Global Environmental Movement*, University of Hawai'i Press, Honolulu.

Aydin, C. (2007) *The Politics of Anti-Westernism in Asia: Visions of World Order in Pan-Islamic and Pan-Asian Thought*, Columbia University Press, New York.

Bakhtin, M. (1984) *Rabelais and His World*, Indiana University Press, Bloomington.

Barreto, J.M. (2018) "Decolonial Thinking and the Quest for Decolonising Human Rights." *Asian Journal of Social Science*, vol. 46, no. 4/5.

Bhabha, H.K. (1994) *The Location of Culture*, Routledge, New York.

Bello, W. (1990) *Dragons in Distress: Asia's Miracle Economies in Crisis*, Institute for Food and Development Policy, San Francisco.

Bentley, J. (1990) "A New Forum for Global History." *Journal of World History*, vol. 1, no. 1, pp. iii–v.

Carrington, K., Hogg, R. and Sozzo, M. (2016) "Southern Criminology." *British Journal of Criminology*, vol. 56, no. 1, pp. 1–20.

Chakrabarty, B. (2013) *Confluence of Thought: Mahatma Gandhi and Martin Luther King, Jr*, Oxford University Press, Oxford.

Chang, S. (2014) "The Postcolonial Problem for Global Gay Rights." *Boston University International Law Journal*, vol. 32.

Chatterjee, P. (1993) *The Nation and Its Fragments: Colonial and Post-Colonial Histories*, Princeton University Press, Princeton.

Ciocchini, P.L. (2017) "The Relevance of Criminal Courts in the Global South." *Laws*, vol. 6, no. 4.

Comaroff, J. & Comaroff, J.L. (1991) *Of Revelation and Revolution*, University of Chicago Press, Chicago.

Comaroff, J. & Comaroff, J.L. (2006) *Law and Disorder in the Postcolony*, University of Chicago Press, Chicago.

Connell, R. & Dados, N. (2014) "Where in the World Does Neoliberalism Come from? The Market Agenda in Southern Perspective." *Theory and Society*, vol. 43, no. 2, pp. 117–138.

de Sousa Santos, B. (1995) "Three Metaphors for a New Conception of Law: The Frontier, the Baroque, and the South." *Law & Society Review*, vol. 29, no. 4, pp. 569–584.

Foucault, M. (1977) *Discipline and Punish: The Birth of the Prison*, Vintage Books, New York.

Gobat, M. (2013) "The Invention of Latin America: A Transnational History of Anti-Imperialism, Democracy, and Race." *The American Historical Review*, vol. 118, no. 5, pp. 1345–1375.

Goh, D. (2008) "From Colonial Pluralism to Postcolonial Multiculturalism: Race, State Formation and the Question of Cultural Diversity in Malaysia and Singapore." *Sociology Compass*, vol. 2, no. 1, pp. 232–252.

Grandin, G. (2010) *Empire's Workshop: Latin America, the United States, and the Rise of the New Imperialism*. Macmillan, New York.

Guha, R. (1983) *Elementary Aspects of Peasant Insurgency in Colonial India*, Oxford University Press, New Delhi.

Heath, D. (2010) *Purifying Empire: Obscenity and the Politics of Moral Regulation in Britain, India and Australia*, Cambridge University Press, Cambridge.

Hobson, J.A. (1988) *Imperialism: A Study*, third ed., Unwin Hyman, London.

Hollender, R. (2015) "Post-Growth in the Global South: The Emergence of Alternatives to Development in Latin America." *Socialism and Democracy*, vol. 29, no. 1, pp. 73–101.

Huneeus, A. (2010) "Judging from a Guilty Conscience: The Chilean Judiciary's Human Rights Turn." *Law & Social Inquiry*, vol. 35, no. 1, pp. 99–135.

LaFeber, W. (2004) *America, Russia, and the Cold War, 1945–2002*, Ninth ed., McGraw-Hill, Boston.

Langer, M. (2007) "Revolution in Latin American Criminal Procedure: Diffusion of Legal Ideas from the Periphery." *The American Journal of Comparative Law*, vol. 55, no. 4, pp. 617–676.

Lorway, R. (2014) *Namibia's Rainbow Project: Gay Rights in an African Nation*, Indiana University Press, Bloomington.

Mamdani, M. (2001) *When Victims Become Killers: Colonialism, Nativism, and the Genocide in Rwanda*, Princeton University Press, Princeton, NJ.

Mamdani, M. (2012) *Define and Rule: Native as Political Identity*. Harvard University Press, Cambridge, MA.

Manderson, L. (1997) "Colonial Desires: Sexuality, Race, and Gender in Colonial Malaya." *Journal of the History of Sexuality*, vol. 7, no. 3, pp. 372–388.
Mbembe, A. (2001) *On the Post Colony*, University of California Press, Berkeley.
Middell, M. & Naumann, K. (2010) "Global History and the Spatial Turn: From the Impact of Area Studies to the Study of Critical Junctures of Globalization." *Journal of Global History*, vol. 5, pp. 149–170.
Mignolo, W. (2005) *The Idea of Latin America*, Blackwell Publishing, Oxford.
Moosavi, L. (2019) "A Friendly Critique of 'Asian Criminology' and 'Southern Criminology'." *British Journal of Criminology*, vol. 59, no. 2, pp. 257–275.
Müller, M. (2012) "The Rise of the Penal State in Latin America." *Contemporary Justice Review: Issues in Criminal, Social, and Restorative Justice*, vol. 15, no. 1, pp. 57–76.
Nandy, A. (1988) *The Intimate Enemy: Loss and Recovery of Self under Colonialism*, Oxford University Press, New York.
O'Brien, P. (2006) "Historiographical Traditions and Modern Imperatives for the Restoration of Global History." *Journal of Global History*, vol. 1, pp. 3–39.
O'Donnell, G. (1993) "On the State, Democratization and Some Conceptual Problems: A Latin American View with Glances at Some Postcommunist Countries." *World Development*, vol. 21, no. 8, pp. 1355–1369.
Palmer, B. (1994) "Homage to Edward Thompson, Part II." *Labour/Le Travail*, vol. 33, pp. 13–68.
Patalinghug, E.E. (2011) "Crime Rates and Labor Market Opportunities in the Philippines: 1970–2008." *Economics Letters*, vol. 113, no. 2, pp. 160–164.
Pratt, J. (2007) *Penal Populism*, Routledge, London.
Radics, G. (Forthcoming) *Emotions and Politics: Islamic Separatism in America's Colony*. Book manuscript in progress.
Radics, G. & Ciocchini, P. (2018) "Introduction: Continuities and Ruptures in Global North Legal Pressures on Global South Societies." *Asian Journal of Social Science*, vol. 46, pp. 409–419.
Said, E. (1994) *Orientalism*, Penguin, New York.
Sarkar, S. (1997) *Writing Social History*, Oxford University Press, New York and New Delhi.
Skaar, E., García-Godos, J. & Collins, C. (eds.) (2016) *Transitional Justice in Latin America: The Uneven Road from Impunity towards Accountability*, Routledge, Abingdon.
Stoler, A. (1989) "Making Empire Respectable: The Politics of Race and Sexual Morality in 20th-Century Colonial Cultures." *American Ethnologist*, vol. 16, no. 4, pp. 634–660.
Stoler, A.L. (1995) *Race and the Education of Desire: Foucault's History of Sexuality and the Colonial Order of Things*, Duke University Press, Durham.
Stoler, A. (2002) *Carnal Knowledge and Imperial Power: Race and The Intimate in Colonial Rule*, University of California Press, Berkeley.
Thompson, D. (2001) *Essential E.P. Thompson*, New Press, New York.
Thompson, E.P. (1980) *The Making of the English Working Class*, Penguin, Harmondsworth.
Wacquant, L. (2009) *Punishing the Poor: The Neoliberal Government of Social Insecurity*, Duke University Press, Durham.
Whyte, D. (2009) "Naked Labour: Putting Agamben to Work." *Australian Feminist Law Journal*, vol. 31, no. 1, pp. 57–76.

Index

Note: Page numbers in bold indicate a table on the corresponding page.

For Product Safety Concerns and Information please contact our EU
representative GPSR@taylorandfrancis.com
Taylor & Francis Verlag GmbH, Kaufingerstraße 24, 80331 München, Germany

www.ingramcontent.com/pod-product-compliance
Ingram Content Group UK Ltd.
Pitfield, Milton Keynes, MK11 3LW, UK
UKHW021722240926
475702UK00029BA/1793
9780367777470